TENETS *of the* DOCTRINE *of the* SPIRIT-FILLED CHURCH

Volume 2

FRANCIS VLOK

WESTBOW
PRESS®
A DIVISION OF THOMAS NELSON
& ZONDERVAN

WestBow Press books may be ordered through booksellers or by contacting:

WestBow Press
A Division of Thomas Nelson & Zondervan
1663 Liberty Drive
Bloomington, IN 47403
www.westbowpress.com
844-714-3454

Scripture taken from the King James Version of the Bible.

Scripture taken from the New King James Version® Copyright © 1982
by Thomas Nelson. Used by permission. All rights reserved.

ISBN: 978-1-6642-3862-6 (sc)
ISBN: 978-1-6642-3861-9 (e)

Print information available on the last page.

WestBow Press rev. date: 07/07/2021

Contents

PART 4

About the Author

Francis Vlok was born in South Africa in 1947 and educated at Cambridge School, East London. After graduating from high school, he continued his studies attending night classes and graduated from the East London College obtaining an associates banking degree.

It was during 1972 that he was called into the ministry. After being a youth pastor for two years, he continued with his ministerial studies and graduated from the Methodist Church of South Africa in 1977.

While studying for the ministry, he was baptized with the Holy Spirit on January 5, 1975, in his brother's home in Kathu, South Africa. After completing his studies, he and his wife went to Israel in 1977. While visiting the excavations at Qumran, the Lord spoke clearly to him that he was to discontinue everything and complete all unfinished business. The Holy Spirit told him that the Spirit would strip from him all the protestant veneer and spiritually reveal to him the perfect will of God for the church.

He requested a release from his obligations to the Methodist church; and for the next six months, he and his wife, Sandra, sat under the ministry of the Holy Spirit as the Spirit revealed to them the perfect will of God. They set about visiting denominations, asking what their doctrinal tenets were; and after months of searching, they walked into The Christian Fellowship in Retief Street, Pietermaritzburg, South Africa. It was here that he discovered how the fellowship functioned under God's perfect will. They became members in 1978. This denomination, The Christian Fellowship, was established by apostles from the Apostolic Church of Great Britain who were sent by God to South Africa in 1962 to lay the foundation of the perfect will of God in that country.

Francis was called into the ministry in 1979 through the office of two apostles, Reginald Evans and Cyril Wilson, and ordained in 1980. Two years later, God sent him to another city, Port Elizabeth, where the Holy

Spirit led him to start an assembly. This was the fulfillment of his ministry as an apostle. The fellowship in Port Elizabeth grew to maturity; and after seven years, they had several ordained elders and ministers.

During the period from 1979 to 1995, he lectured at the Christian Fellowship's School of Ministry. His continuous studying and teaching of the Word paved the way for him to be the assistant to the president of the fellowship, Apostle Cyril Wilson, in the re-writing of the fellowship's constitution and the establishment of the biblical tenets, beliefs, and principles.

He also wrote the book The Perfect Will of God, which laid down the doctrinal tenets pertaining to the structure and operation of the church as found in the New Testament. This book is still available today.

In 1987, he was appointed Vice President of the Christian Fellowship, South Africa.

The Holy Spirit continued to use Francis to mature the local assembly in Port Elizabeth until 1993 when he was called by the Holy Spirit to relocate to the United States. The call to "go" was clear but without the long-term vision being revealed as to exactly what he would be doing when he arrived in the United States. He moved to Mississippi, U.S., and was asked to preach in various Pentecostal churches. After almost four years of ministering, in 1999, God called him out from the itinerant ministry. The moment he stopped preaching in various churches, a group of believers from two cities, fifty miles apart, simultaneously contacted him in March 1999 asking him to start a Spirit-filled fellowship that stood for the perfect will of God.

The beginnings of the fellowship were almost identical to the church in the book of Acts. The members went from house to house for six months. Thereafter, they searched for a venue that was between the two cities and settled in a rented building in the village of Pachuta, Mississippi. The word "Pachuta" is derived from a Native American language which means "where the pigeons come home to roost." The small fellowship grew slowly but the presence of the Holy Spirit constantly encouraged them to continue steadfastly in the perfect will of God. At the conclusion of a mid-week Bible study, a member of the fellowship approached Francis and said that God had told her to give four acres of land to the fellowship.

Three years later, the fellowship was still a handful of Spirit-filled believers. However, these members inquired when they would construct their own church building. Francis was reluctant to build because he had not received any indication from the Lord about the work other than that it was to start. While he and Sandra were visiting Mildred Rhoden, one of the members, she informed him that there were five ladies in Pachuta who had gathered every week for thirty years asking God to bring to Pachuta a Spirit-filled church that stood for the perfect will of God.

While in prayer for God to reveal His purpose to him, Francis received the revelation from the Holy Spirit that God had brought him and his wife, Sandra, seven thousand miles to Pachuta so that God could fulfill His promise to the five women who prayed for thirty years and establish a Spirit-filled church in the Village of Pachuta. Francis and Sandra Vlok then realized why God had uprooted them from South Africa and brought them to the United States.

Today, the Christian Fellowship has a small assembly in Pachuta that is fulfilling the perfect will of God in accordance with God's promise to five ladies' answered prayers. They have their own land and building; and the ministry has developed today to the point where an evangelist, David Chandler, has been sent to Guyana, South America, several times and the local Pachuta fellowship supports the Guyana ministry. It also supports the ministry in South Africa.

For more than forty years, Francis has been ministering; and during this time, God has instructed him to look after himself and his family and not to receive any remuneration from the church. By the grace of God, he has been able to support them and work in the church. He maintains, that as Apostle Paul stated, that his hands supplied his sustenance while he ministers; and he is no man's debtor.

Francis Vlok has authored a book *The Perfect Will of God* and then fulfilled his longtime mission of writing the *Doctrine of the Spirit-filled Church*.

Part 1

Doctrine of the Word of God: The Bible

a. This tenet is the basis and precept upon which every doctrinal tenet is based.

b. It begins with the Source and method of its contents, Jesus Christ and His privilege and prerogative to dictate the Word to *holy men of God*.

c. It is studied primarily from the aspects of *Revelation* and *Inspiration*.

d. It declares categorically that it is God's word to man and that man was merely an instrument who penned the revealed truths of God's intent and purpose.

e. There is a brief history of the Bible.

f. An account of the "Silent Years" follows

g. The new beginning occurs when the New Testament was written.

h. The compilation of the Canon, both Old and New Testaments.

i. The Bible's message.

Chapter 1

Introduction

*"The Bible is the declaration of who God is and how
He deals with mankind's sin and sins."*

1. Every believer should approach the study of the Word, the sharing thereof, and the reading of the Bible with reverent fear and the utmost respect, first for the Author of the Bible and second for the contents and instruction it contains.

2. Every time the Holy Writ is picked up, read, preached, quoted, or written down, it should be done with humility and with the understanding that, when handling the Word, one is dealing with the divine instrument given through God's love and grace for the benefit of mankind. This is God's domain, and He is the Spokesperson who must be respected and reverenced even as His words declare: *But on this one will I look: on him who is poor and of a contrite spirit, and who trembles at My word* (Isaiah 66:2 NKJV).

3. There have been many educated theologians, great Bible teachers, and ardent students of the Word, whose contributions to explaining the truths contained within the Bible's pages are to be applauded. Some contributors have spent many hours expounding the Bible's message, while others have given insight into the origin and structure of the Word. Their contributions and insights have been studied and considered as this tenet Doctrine of the Bible is expounded.

4. To give this tenet greater clarity, it is set out in the following way:
    a. Source and method God used to convey His Word to mankind
    b. *Holy men of God* called by the Holy Spirit to record the Word

1

    c.   Historic explanation of how the Bible's contents were developed and became the Holy Canon known today as the Bible

    d.   Message contained in the Bible

Source and Method

Revelation and Inspiration of the Word of God.

5.   When considering this holy and divine gift from God, namely, His holy Word, it must never be forgotten who the Author is and for what purpose it is given. Therefore, to fully grasp the sovereignty of the Holy Writ, Spirit-filled believers must accept that the Bible is the revelation of God unveiled through His divine inspiration and penned on the holy pages.

6.   W.A.C. Rowe says, "The Scriptures of truth are pure revelation; they are God's approach to man, not man's approach to God: they bring certainty and brightness about Himself and His purposes. Only God can explain Himself: and only by His Holy Spirit can this be done; *Even so the things of God knoweth no man, but the Spirit of God*" (1 Corinthians 2:11).

7.   There are direct proclamations in the Bible as to its intent and how it is imparted. *Knowing this first, that no prophecy of the Scripture is of any private interpretation. For the prophecy came not in old time by the will of man: but holy men of God spake as they were moved by the Holy Ghost* (2 Peter 1:20-21), and *All Scripture is given by inspiration of God, and is profitable for doctrine, for reproof, for correction, for instruction in righteousness* (2 Timothy 3:16).

8.   To comprehend the depths and riches contained within the Bible's pages, it is of utmost value to grasp the fact that man who is but a mere mortal, granted life for a short season on earth, is given the privilege of receiving from his Creator direct revelation concerning who God is and how He deals with mankind. This is not man writing to man and giving his own ideas to other men; this is the divine, holy, and righteous God speaking to mankind and giving revelation to *holy men* who obediently recorded the *inspired* message from God to mankind.

9.   In one of his sermons, Charles Spurgeon said, "The Bible contains the divine answer to the deepest needs of humanity, sheds unique light

on our path in a dark world, and sets forth the way to our eternal well-being." A grandfather wrote in his granddaughter's Bible that he gave her when she was eleven year's old, "Read it regularly. It holds the solution to all of life's problems." As these anecdotes affirm, the Bible's message reaches across all cultures, nations, tongues, ages, and genders. It is unique in its content, sovereign in its message, and powerful in its application.

10. Lewis Chafer in his book *Systematic Theology* says, "In this Book, God is set forth as Creator and Lord of all. It is the revelation of Himself, the record of what He has done and will do, and, at the same time, the disclosure of the fact that every created thing is subject to Him and discovers its highest advantage and destiny only as it is conformed to His will."

11. Thus said, the understanding that Who it is that is giving this message is not a created being or a man-made institution; it is God Himself revealing who He is to mankind. The Source is who He is. The Source is the Godhead. The Source is the *Word* who was in the beginning (John 1:1). Everything the Bible says is what God says.

12. It is the inspired written Word that exalts the Living Word, Jesus Christ; for He is the *Word made flesh*. Jesus is the revealed Christ, the Son of God and Son of Man who is the Source and Substance of the Word. How magnificent is the revelation that Jesus explains to the two men on the road to Emmaus that the Word references Him; *And beginning at Moses and all the Prophets, He expounded to them in all the Scriptures the things concerning Himself* (Luke 24:27). Only when the two men received the revelation concerning who Jesus was, were their eyes opened to receive the fullness of the message: *Then their eyes were opened and they knew Him; and He vanished from their sight. And they said to one another, "Did not our heart burn within us while He talked with us on the road, and while He opened the Scriptures to us?"* (Luke 24:31-32 NKJV).

Revelation

13. While revelation is a vast subject that encompasses many aspects of a Spirit-filled believer's life, such as the things that have not yet taken place, the revealed wisdom to a believer on a certain subject, and the

unveiling of a truth that is hidden by someone else, this tenet is aligned to revelation from God pertaining to His Word.

14. There is a need to examine the meaning of divine revelation and the reason for it. Millard J. Erickson in his book *Christian Theology* says that revelation is "uncovering what was concealed." There are reasons why human beings are unable to know all things; it is their depravity and sin that separate them from God. Once Jesus Christ is received as Savior, mankind's spirit once again receives revelation from the heart of God. It is, therefore, by revelation that this divine understanding is imparted.

15. Erickson gives the reason why revelation is necessary: "The answer lies in the fact that the humans had lost the relationship of favor which they had with God prior to the fall. It was necessary for them to come to know God in a fuller way if the conditions of fellowship were once again to be met. This knowledge had to go beyond the initial or general revelation . . . for now in addition to the natural revelation of human finiteness, there was also moral limitation of human sinfulness."

16. Flowing from this thought process that revelation from God needed to reach mankind, God speaks forthrightly and in sovereign declarations to man. This revelation is personal and is Spirit to spirit. God now "uncovers" that which was incarcerated in sin and reveals Himself to every born-again human being. His Holy Spirit enters the believer's life and will *guide* [them] *into all truth* (John 16:13).

17. This divine revelation and guidance are given from the mouth of God and recorded in the Holy Writ, the Bible. Such a revealed message must be defined. First, it is from the heart of God. Second, it is from a Source that is beyond man's comprehension. It is from the holy estate of almighty God who decided to give born-again believers the message. Third, it is outside of man's knowledge and wisdom. Servants and handmaidens of God ask, *How can this be?* (Luke 1:34 NKJV).

18. It is not required that believers fully grasp and understand the message when it is revealed. It is out of obedience and with a humble and contrite heart that they receive a hitherto never known or perceived message. Without doubt, they know it is God who has imparted this divine discourse into their hearts because it is encased in His holiness, pureness, and deity.

19. To establish a doctrinal tenet on the supremacy and authority of Scripture, it is important to establish the premise of revelation and inspiration.

20. Revelation is what God reveals to man about subjects and situations about which he has no knowledge or insight. It is God drawing back the veil and showing believers things they never knew or understood. This revelation which is spiritual is from God Himself and not from any particle of man's created structure. It is God revealing to believers, and they are the mere reciprocal.

21. Eugene F. A. Klug explains in the *Encyclopedia of the Bible*, "People have knowledge of God because of God's initiative and activity. God is always the initiator and author of revelation; men are the recipients. God discloses what otherwise would be unknown; He uncovers what would otherwise be hidden" (Deuteronomy 29:29, Galatians 1:12, Ephesians 3:3).

22. Revelation is Spirit-led insight granted to a believer that illuminates his understanding of the Holy Writ's message. The holy sanctuary of the Word is likened to the *secret place of the Most High* (Psalm 91:1). As the believer enters this divine place of solitude, he immerses himself in the presence of the Godhead and waits, meditates, and worships Him. This is the place where a Spirit-filled believer *dwells*. It occurs when he is in the *secret place of the Most High* and under the anointing of the Holy Spirit that the believer receives God's revealed truths. God is constantly waiting for mankind to *enter in* and receive divine revelation from Him.

23. This is not an enhanced human thought about the divine Creator and His handiwork. Even the world sees and receives the truth about creation and who is responsible for it. This is the spiritual imparting from the Holy Spirit to the believer about something contained in the Word and about which he knows very little, or even nothing.

24. Spirit-filled believers have no problem with the concept of revelation as it relates to God's holy Word. They are Spirit-led and therefore, are in tune with the Spirit's message contained in the holy pages. The deep truths imbedded in the Bible are "opened" to the heart and mind of a Spirit-filled believer as they immerse themselves in the message they are reading and believing (1 Corinthians 2:10-14).

25. The message printed in the words on the Bible's pages is not the sum of the message; it is the beginning of the passage along which Spirit-filled believers begins a journey. They receive the Word they are reading and then seek the deeper truths within the written Word. These deeper truths are revealed to the heart that is seeking a deeper knowledge and relationship with Jesus Christ (2 Peter 3:18).

26. Humanistic arguments have always tried to refute the infallibility and inerrancy of the Holy Bible. They maintain it is impossible to accept the sixty-six books in the Bible as a continuous message because it has been recorded by more than forty different writers spanning more than three thousand years. However, these arguments fail to realize that there is only the One Author and He is Jesus Christ, the *Word*. There is nothing *proceeding from the mouth of God* that is unholy or untrue. He is the Holy God; and He is all truth, the Source.

27. Jonathan Black in his book *Apostolic Theology* says, "Because the words of Scripture are God's own words, they are entirely truthful and trustworthy. The words we use for the complete truthfulness of the whole of Scripture are infallibility and inerrancy. To say that the Scriptures are infallible or inerrant means that Scripture is entirely true and trustworthy in everything that it teaches."

28. The Bible is revealed truth. It is revealed through the Holy Spirit into the hearts of holy men. It is the breathed and revealed word that is from God who inspired men to be led by the Holy Spirit and obediently listen to the truth that flows like a river of life from the *mouth of God* (Matthew 4:4 NKJV). Moreover, Scripture affirms, *The God of our fathers has chosen you that you should know His will, and see the Just One, and hear the voice of His mouth* (Acts 22:14 NKJV). It is His word from the depths of His heart which streams forth like rivers of living water into the heart of man. Jonathan Black makes this point more aptly, "The Scriptures are the very words of God, and as such they are authoritative, infallible, inerrant, life-giving, clear, and sufficient."

29. The Source reached down to earth and chose men to receive the divine oracle and to call others to receive the message. This message declared through the mouth of God's prophets spoke volumes to the lost and dying sinners. Even before God sent His only begotten Son, He revealed His purpose to mankind, telling them to prepare the way. This was not a message from a man in authority; this was the message from God Himself.

30. How personal and loving is God's method in revealing His will to mankind, who severed the relationship and burst the bonds of intimate fellowship with God. Yet, it is God who reaches into the miry clay and uses righteous and holy men to relay His love and grace. The revealed Word builds hope in a man's life. They are assured that God has not forgotten them and will not abandon them.

31. God reveals Himself to chosen vessels amongst mankind through whom He sends His word. These are not men of a certain position or education; they are servants of God who are drenched in their task of serving God and who walk in humble obedience to His every command. They are *holy men of God* (2 Peter 1:21).

32. God reveals to them His purpose and will. He entrusts them with the task of disseminating the message to mankind. He anoints them to be worthy vessels of honor who will record the words of God for eternity. The message is so important to God that He seals His written word He gave to holy men with the promise that *the grass withereth, and the flower thereof falleth away: But the word of the Lord endureth for ever* (1 Peter 1:24-25).

33. It is appropriate to quote from the Bible what God has said. In Deuteronomy 18:18, God said to Moses, *I will put my words in his mouth, and he will tell them everything I command him.* King David lay on his deathbed and said, *The Spirit of the LORD spoke through me; his word was on my tongue* (2 Samuel 23:2). Then, there was the prophet of God, Isaiah, who heard the words of the Lord: *my words that I have put in your mouth* (Isaiah 59:21).

34. Perhaps the most significant statement about the revealed word from God to His holy prophets is stated by Prophet Zechariah as he refers to *The words that the LORD Almighty had sent by his Spirit through the earlier prophets* (Zechariah 7:12).

35. Apostle Paul speaks explicitly about the method God has applied when communicating to the church. He says that the words he used were *taught by the Spirit* (1 Corinthians 2:13) and that *God has revealed it to us by his Spirit* (verse 10).

36. Apostle Paul reinforces his writings by making this statement about the Word of God: *I did not receive it from any man, nor was I taught it; rather, I received it by revelation from Jesus Christ* (Galatians 1:12). Just as Apostle Paul, the chosen men of God, *holy men of God,* namely prophets and apostles, were chosen by the Author of the Holy Writ; and they were given its contents to record them from God to mankind.

37. With this in mind, the attitude with which the Holy Word is approached must be unequivocally pronounced, believed, and trusted that it is divinely inspired, totally void of errors, and is for instruction, reproof, and correction. Norman Geisler in his book *Systematic Theology* states, "Jesus said the Bible has indestructibility in that it will never pass away

(Matthew 5:17-18); it is infallible or *cannot be broken* (John 10:35); it has final authority (Matthew 4:4, 7, 10); and it is sufficient for faith practice (Luke 16:31; cf. 2 Timothy 3:16-17)."

38. Spirit-filled believers are emphatic in their belief that there are no errors or omissions in the Word of God. Every word found in the pages of the Holy Writ are pure, holy, and infallible. It is God who chose the men to pen His Word. God separated them and anointed them to be used as instruments to convey God's holy and divine words that reach every human being on earth; for as Jonathan Black discerns, "From the beginning, God has always acted through His Word."

39. The inerrancy of God's Word is based on the fact that the Source, namely God, is all truth and cannot lie. Because he is holy, pure, and righteous, God reveals His Word that gives *hope of eternal life, which God, that cannot lie, promised before the world began* (Titus 1:2). Norman Geisler seals this truth when he says, "It is inclusive of not only what the Bible teaches but what it touches, that is to say, it includes not only what the Bible teaches explicitly but also what it teaches implicitly, covering not only spiritual matters but factual ones as well. The omniscient God cannot be wrong about anything He teaches or implies."

40. Added to this, there is no ulterior motive and hidden agenda within God's Word; it is sovereign and without ambiguity. What God says, He means; and what God means, He says.

41. Because of the inerrancy of the Word, it is infallible. This can be stated because the Source is quick to declare that *all the promises of God in him are yea, and in him Amen, unto the glory of God by us* (2 Corinthians 1:20). The believer's hope and endurance are reinforced by the constant reminder that God is ever faithful, ever present, and ever able to fulfill all His promises. Because God is perfect and without error, His Word is without error.

42. This divine, Holy Writ composed of sixty-six books, can only be accepted and understood when the reader applies his faith in God, towards God, and towards His inspired Word. It is through faith in the deep truths found in this fount of grace and love that man is enriched, saved, and filled with eternal hope of things to come; and therefore, *through faith we understand that the worlds were framed by the word of God, so that things which are seeing were not made of things which do appear* (Hebrews 11:3).

43. This eternal and majestic Word has been written and compiled for every created human being on earth. Its readers include the Jews, the Gentiles, and the Christians. It also has the attention of the angels in heaven. Every living soul is incorporated in the Bible's message which is God's method of touching every heart that has ever lived.

44. Unregenerate man can neither receive nor understand the contents of the Bible until the Holy Spirit draws him to it: *The natural man does not receive the things of the Spirit of God, for they are foolishness to him; nor can he know them, because they are spiritually discerned* (1 Corinthians 2:14 NKJV).

45. Furthermore, the Word contains deep truths that are revealed by the Spirit of God to the righteous believer. It is not revealed to those who walk as babes and carnally before Him as Apostle Paul clarifies, *And I, brethren, could not speak to you as to spiritual people but as to carnal, as to babes in Christ. I fed you with milk and not with solid food; for until now you were not able to receive it, and even now you are still not able; for you are still carnal* (1 Corinthians 3:1-3).

46. History's hallways are covered with events engineered by man, victories achieved by conquering armies, valiant attempts to carve out a social enclave in which people can live in harmony, and tragedies soaked in blood and tears. Within these hallways, there is a record for all to see and read, namely, that God's infinite love reaches past humankind's souls and places them in harmony and peace where the social fabric is of *one mind, one mouth, one Lord, one faith.* This record is none other than the Holy Bible.

Chapter 2

Brief History of the Bible

1. In the Bible's purest form and most authentic languages, Hebrew and Greek, or the progression thereof (namely as expressions and words were enhanced or altered in meaning– for example, YHVH became Yahweh, and then became Jehovah), the message is unbridled by human interference. It is, therefore, of utmost importance that every Spirit-filled believer seeks for the most perfect translation of the original Hebrew and Greek into their language.

2. The deceiver, the devil, has infested too many men whose pecuniary interests have over-shadowed the ultimate purpose of translating the Word by infusing an interpretation, instead of a translation, of the original languages.

3. In spite of these false works and the wayward teachings found in the interpretations of the Holy Word, there are translations that are accurate and convey the true meaning of the Holy Writ. It is here that Spirit-filled believers find themselves engrossed in studying the Word and gleaning from its *God-breathed* message in their own language.

4. God has prevailed throughout mankind's existence and has always presided over His Word. He has preserved His message for all generations; and the Holy Spirit has, throughout these generations, guided men to translate the original languages into the language of the reader in its purest form.

5. At this juncture in studying the Holy Writ, it is expedient that the time frames be considered as to when it was written. Bible students, theologians, and expert archeologists have made many fine studies about the origin of the Bible's manuscripts. They have given detailed

reports on when they believe many of the manuscripts were first received by *holy men* and recorded for mankind's benefit.

6. It is believed, because of the language used and the words framed in the message, that Job was the first book to be written even though the book is not the first book in the Bible.

7. Robert Lee, in his book *The Outlined Bible* makes the following comment about the book of Job: "It is the most ancient book known. It must have been written about the time of Jacob." Since the oldest manuscripts found indicate that the earliest spelling of the word *God* was YWH which is found in the book of Job, most scholars agree that Job was written during the Patriarchal period.

8. The Bible's first book, Genesis, is one of the Bible's first five books known as the Pentateuch. Authorship of these five books is attributed to Moses, the period when they were written is recorded as 1446-1406 B.C.

9. Genesis includes numerous events ranging from the creation of the heavens and the earth; to the creation of the first humans, Adam and Eve; and to events leading to the destruction of human life during Noah's time. These events date to the distant past and then introduce the five Patriarchs.

10. During this Patriarchal period God calls Abram first as the patriarch with whom God establishes a covenant for a people He will choose as His own. The other patriarchs follow, then the enslavement of God's people in Egypt, and then their release from slavery.

11. The remaining four books in the Pentateuch are a record of God's people and His covenant with them, namely the Law of Moses, while they are traveling to the Promised Land. They contain the establishment of the High Priesthood, worship in the tabernacle, strictest rules, the benefits of following them, and the consequences of disobeying them. During this time, the people's commitment to God and His commandments is constantly challenged as they struggle because of their disobedience, in following God's laws.

12. The following twelve books are an account of the history of God's people as they are led by men called of God, Joshua, many Judges, and prophets who were responsible for keeping God's people obedient to His commands. These twelve books record the events from 1300 B.C. until 400 B.C.

13. During this time, the people demand a king as their ruler, thus shunning God's rulership through prophets and judges. God gives them a king, and that begins the rule of the nation by an earthly king.

14. The historical account of the Hebrews is interrupted by the inclusion of five books of poetry, advice, and wisdom for the people. Most of these books were written between 1000 B.C. and 500 B.C.

15. The Old Testament next focuses on God's messages through His ordained prophets, and the ensuing five books were written by "major prophets," given this title because of the length of their prophetical writings. They were in no way superior to the rest of the twelve minor prophets who make up the remainder of the Old Testament.

16. The period of biblical writings closes for almost five hundred years. From 450 B.C. to around 4 B.C. no book written that is included in the Bible. Most of God's people believe His promise that He will send them a King, a Messiah, a supreme ruler and deliverer who will conquer all their enemies. During this time, they wait, for the arrival of their deliverer.

17. It is worthwhile to explore what took place during those four hundred fifty "silent years." Even though no prophecies were recorded or included in the Bible and little appeared to be of value to record after God's people returned to the Promised Land about 500 B.C., important events took place that shaped the spiritual landscape for the arrival of Jesus Christ, the Anointed One.

Silent Years

18. The Old Testament closes a little over four hundred years before Christ (about 425 B.C.) with the Jewish people living in exile in Babylon (Persian Empire) from about 605 B.C. Starting around 538 B.C., small groups of Jews start returning to their homeland.

19. Seven different prophets minister to God's people during this time period. Daniel and Ezekiel, minister to the exiles in Babylon while Haggai, Zechariah, Ezra, Nehemiah, and Malachi ministered to the people who returned to the Promised Land.

20. This four-hundred-year period between the close of the Old Testament and the beginning of the New Testament see a number of significant changes. The people have greatly multiplied and are dwelling in the

Promised Land together with those of other nations who radically influence the Jews.

21. Incredible changes take place—religious, political, cultural, and civil. The Old Testament closes with an exhortation to "remember the Law of Moses" (Malachi 4:4) as well as the promise to *send Elijah to Israel before the day of the Lord.* God would bring about reform in the lives of the people that they might resemble their godly forefathers. If they do not reform, God will visit the land with a curse (Malachi 4:5-6).

22. After God delivers His closing message through the prophet Malachi, He pauses in His communications through men for about four hundred years. However, God's silence is a part of His eternal plan. He has spoken on numerous occasions and through various people; but in the silence that follows, God prepares to speak His greatest and most powerful Word to mankind through His Son, Jesus Christ.

23. Different empires control the known world during these years:
    1. The Persian Era (397-336 B.C.)
    2. The Greek Era (336-323 B.C.)
    3. The Egyptian Era (323-198 B.C.)
    4. The Syrian Era (198-165 B.C.)
    5. The Maccabean Era (165-63 B.C.)
    1. The Roman Era (63-4 B.C.)

24. The political and economic power within these ruling empires dominate the world, including the Holy Land. Every nation under their control is subjected to their political and economic constraints as well as to their religious beliefs. The influences on the subjected nations are so strong that they soon adopt the political habits and pagan religious orders of the ruling empire. Many Jews drift away their Hebraic roots and immerse themselves in the ruling authority's paganism.

25. Two of these ruling empires stand out as having a major world-wide influence that still dominates many nations today. These two are the Greek and Roman Empires.

26. Even though Alexander the Great, king of Greece, Macedonia, and Persia, ruled for only twelve years, he moved at such a horrific pace that the known world is quickly and forcibly thrust into adopting the Greek language.

27. When Alexander storms into Israel and Egypt, he discovers that some religious Israelites have doggedly stood their ground and continued in their faith. During this time, the Jews collate the collection of scrolls

and manuscripts that form the Old Testament. These manuscripts they preserve and hide in Egypt.

28. Upon the discovery of the manuscripts, Alexander, influenced by his advisors, considers the contents, value, and agelessness of these records, and authorizes scribes and Greek scholars to translate the Hebrew scrolls into Greek. Thus, the first-ever translation of the Hebrew Bible consisting of its thirty-nine books was completed by these Greeks around 250 B.C. and it is still referenced by biblical scholars to this day. It became known as "The Septuagint."

29. The Greek language became so entrenched in the known world that it remained the universal language throughout and beyond the silent years. After two hundred years had passed, the Greek language, philosophy, capitalism, and political values remained a prevailing influence, to such an extent that, when the Roman Empire came into power two hundred years later, much of its political, economic, and philosophical practices were still Greek dominated. The Romans even adopted the Greek language and did many international transactions in Greek.

30. The Romans' influence on the various nations was predominantly one of economic growth, improvement, and dominance by their emperor. They are notorious as the empire that ruled Israel during Jesus' earthly ministry and were ultimately responsible for crucifying Him. Their method of ensuring constant growth and development was to extract exorbitant taxes from their subjects.

New Beginning

31. God once again begins speaking to His people. The door opens when the prophet John the Baptist arrives preaching repentance and proclaiming the coming of the Messiah to the Jews in the Judean hills. It is fitting that the Old Testament closes with prophets speaking the oracles of God, and the New Testament begins with another prophet speaking God's message to His people.

32. John's ministry is not willingly accepted even though he proclaims what was written five hundred years earlier by prophets revered by the Jewish religious rulers at the time he proclaims the kingdom of heaven is at hand (Matthew 3:2).

33. Into this turmoil of Roman dominance and a Jewish faith divided between Pharisee and Sadducee, John begins to proclaim that he is the *voice of one crying in the wilderness: "Prepare the way of the Lord; Make His paths straight"* (Mark 1:3 NKJV). John the Baptist, a prophet like the prophets who spoke at the close of the Old Testament, speaks at the opening of this new era proclaiming the arrival of the Messiah.

34. Jesus Christ, the Son of God, walks the earth for thirty-six years during which time He ministers for three years to His people, bringing the good news and announcing His mission to His hometown synagogue members: *"The Spirit of the LORD is upon Me, because He has anointed Me to preach the gospel to the poor; He has sent Me to heal the brokenhearted, to proclaim liberty to the captives and recovery of sight to the blind, to set at liberty those who are oppressed; to proclaim the acceptable year of the LORD." Then He closed the book, and gave it back to the attendant and sat down. And the eyes of all who were in the synagogue were fixed on Him. And He began to say to them, "Today this Scripture is fulfilled in your hearing"* (Luke 4:18-21 NKJV).

New Testament Writers

35. The events that follow Jesus' ministry are faithfully recorded in the compilation of the New Testament. This record of His ministry and the events, teachings, and instructions to the church are as accurate and as inspired as the Old Testament manuscripts. They hold the same anointing, the same infallibility, and are from the same Source, the eternal God.

36. While the Old Testament writings were recorded over a thousand years, the New Testament writings were composed over a period of sixty-five years. The *holy men of God* chosen for the recording of the New Testament message begin with the four men who recorded Jesus' ministry in the four gospels that give details about God's intentions in sending His Son. They further include Jesus' birth, His many miracles, His death and resurrection, and His ascension into heaven. The four gospels are a record of how Jesus' ministry affected first the Jews and then the Gentiles.

37. While they all contain the same message, each gospel directs nations and cultures to understand the gospel's universal message. Matthew

presents Jesus as King, Mark presents Jesus as Servant, and Luke portrays Jesus as Lord and the ideal Man for all. John presents the message through a deep spiritual revelation about who Jesus is and how mankind responds to the eternal Son of God.

38. The first three gospels Matthew, Mark, and Luke, were written in quick succession after Jesus' ascension and the birth of the church. The fourth gospel, John, dating around A.D. 100 was one of the last books to be written in the New Testament. These manuscripts were re-written numerous times and passed to the churches as they mushroomed across the known world, and they became the record to which all believers clung as they heard the testimony of the apostles who had walked and lived with Jesus throughout His ministry.

39. Apostle John speaks to this when he writes his first letter, proclaiming, *That which was from the beginning, which we have heard, which we have seen with our eyes, which we have looked upon, and our hands have handled, concerning the Word of life— the life was manifested, and we have seen, and bear witness, and declare to you that eternal life which was with the Father and was manifested to us- that which we have seen and heard we declare to you, that you also may have fellowship with us; and truly our fellowship is with the Father and with His Son Jesus Christ* (1 John 1:1-3 NKJV).

40. The Lord calls Saul, a Jew, to be the spokesperson to the Gentiles. He is miraculously called when Jesus appears to him on the road to Damascus, changes his name to Paul, and for the next three years reveals to him all the doctrines of Christ.

41. Called and chosen to be the apostle to the Gentiles, Paul immediately starts his ministry amongst the Gentiles. He never forgets to minister to the Jews in the synagogues when he travels from city to city, basically testifying to them that Jesus is the Christ which they never fully accept. Thus, he spends most of his ministry amongst Gentiles throughout the known world.

42. A vital and intricate aspect of an apostle's ministry is the recording of the teachings of Jesus and the doctrine of the church. Hence, it is recorded as the *apostles' doctrine* in Acts 2:42. Apostle Paul was instrumental in teaching the churches the doctrine and principles and beliefs of the church. His teachings were written to the church over a period of thirty years.

43. These epistles, letters, scrolls or manuscripts, and the four gospels were of such value that they were re-written numerous times and passed from city to city where a church had been established. They became the foundational teachings for every member in the first century church. Of these inspired letters, thirteen of Apostle Paul's were accepted into the Canon.

44. The letter to the Hebrews included in the Canon is the only book that does not have an author ascribed to it. In spite of this omission, the book has been included into the canon. Roland K. Harrison in his commentary in the *Bible Encyclopedia Volume B-C* explains the purpose of this anonymous book, "It is an early writing designed, by reasoned exhibition of the superiority of Jesus to Moses and the Levitical priesthood, and of the fulfillment of Old Testament types and institutions in His person and sacrifice, to remove the difficulties of Jewish Christians who clung with natural affection to their temple and divinely appointed ritual."

Compilation of the Canon, Old and New Testament

45. Regarding the Old Testament, scholars have agreed upon no exact date when the thirty-nine books were categorically sealed as the Jewish Bible. One of the only historical records, although somewhat unreliable, is that after the destruction of Jerusalem and its temple in A.D.70 the leading Sanhedrin gathered in Jamnia where they agreed to suspend temple worship and the practice of sacrificing animals, and to set in order the Old Testament Canon.

46. They off-loaded the authority of keeping the Torah and the biblical inspiration of the Jewish Scriptures onto the rabbis who led each synagogue. The custody of the Old Testament Canon that had been sealed by the Sanhedrin then rested fully on the shoulders of the rabbinical priests. To their benefit, rabbis were given the concise and full record of the Old Testament from which they could teach their members.

47. With regard to the books of the New Testament, many scrolls and manuscripts circulated among the churches. However, some churches

did not receive all the writings, and some manuscripts were only partially re-written, situations that created concern among church leaders. They knew a concise "Canon" of New Testament teaching was vital to ensure the unity of the faith and to ensure that the church was in one accord in its beliefs.

48. The earliest collection put together that contained the twenty-seven books of the New Testament is attributed to Athanasius of Alexandria whose influence was crucial in fostering concurrence among believers and church leaders at a conference in Nicea in A.D. 325. Roland Harrison says, "By the commencement of the fourth century unanimity had practically been attained. . . At the Council of Nicea, 'the Holy Scriptures of the Old and New Testament were silently admitted on all sides to have a final authority.'"

49. Then, in A.D. 367 Athanasius made an emphatic statement in a letter that declared the twenty-seven books as the "Canon" of the New Testament. This canon was widely accepted by the early church. Thereafter, the "worldwide" church's leaders met regularly to discuss important issues, one such topic being the compilation of the New Testament Canon. During the Third Council of Carthage in A.D. 397 church leaders agreed that the twenty-seven books widely accepted by most church leaders be the final composition of the New Testament.

50. The church soon accepted that the New Testament Canon be placed alongside the Old Testament Canon and this pairing became the Bible known today. Specific defining principles applied when the twenty-seven books of the New Testament were approved as the "Canon." Henry Thiessen in his book *Introductory lectures in Systematic Theology* gives this definition of the Canon, "It means a reed or rod; then a "measuring-rod" hence a rule and standard. It means an authoritative decision of a Church Council; and that they are those books which have been measured, found satisfactory, and approved as inspired of God."

51. At the outset, the Bible was recorded in written form with no chapters and verses as it has today. While the Old Testament books were, for the most part, an uninterrupted record, some books had divisions that referenced the content. The New Testament was also without chapters and verses. Not until well into the thirteenth century were these changes introduced.

52. Reportedly between 1220 and 1240 the first attempts to add chapters and verses were undertaken. Stephen Langton, the Archbishop of Canterbury in England added chapters to each book of the Bible; and the students of French Cardinal Hugo of St. Cher were responsible for distinguishing verses. The books' current chapters and verses are credited to Robert Stephens, who in 1550 numbered the verses in the Bible as they now appear.

Chapter 3

Bible's Message

1. At the outset, it is appropriate and correct to place the Word of God in its rightful position and preeminent in mankind's existence in the past, present, and future. W. A. C. Rowe expresses this concept best: "The Bible is supreme. This is the Book of God sent to men but is eagerly examined by angels (1 Peter 1:12) and demons (James 2:19 NKJV). It is not only a Book of this world (Psalm 119:103, 105), but of all worlds (Revelation 4:1, 20:15)." This holy communication from God's heart should occupy the loftiest pedestal, the highest position, and command unparalleled respect from every human being. It is even higher than His name, *You have magnified Your word above all Your name* (Psalm 138:2 NKJV).

2. No other book's governance can be compared to the Bible's message and the value it has for mankind. It contains inherent and intrinsic heavenly virtues, and moral, spiritual, and eternal values. Nations, throughout history have clung to its message and teaching. It has been the plumb line of moral virtue, social dignity, and everlasting hope throughout every Christ-centered race, culture, and creed.

3. The Bible is the declaration of who God is and how He deals with mankind's sin and sins. Explaining the Bible's essence more fully, W. A. C. Rowe relates, "Its great subject is the Godhead, revealed in three persons, Father, Son, and Holy Spirit; the redemption of man from eternal misery and blackest hell, and his promotion to glory and the brightest heaven."

4. Not only does the Bible occupy the place of supremacy in Spirit-filled believers', but it also is the authoritative guide to every utterance and decision they make. Every doctrinal tenet, every measurement of good

and evil, all applications of a spiritual relationship, and all standards of conduct are found in the Bible. Its powerful impact is apparent as the psalmist says, *I have restrained my feet from every evil way, that I may keep Your word* (Psalm 119:101 NKJV).

5. In his enlightening explanation on this subject Lewis Sperry Chafer in his book *Systematic Theology* says, "God is set forth as Creator and Lord of all. It is the revelation of Himself, the record of what He has done and will do, and, at the same time, the disclosure of the fact that every created thing is subject to Him and discovers its highest advantage and destiny as it is conformed to His will."

6. Furthermore, the Bible reveals God's spiritual existence and His supernatural ability to reach from His throne in heaven down to mankind and their needs as it calls Him *The LORD, the LORD God, merciful and gracious, longsuffering, and abounding in goodness and truth* (Exodus 34:6 NKJV). It has such an influence on mankind that those who follow Him say with the Psalmist that *the LORD is gracious and full of compassion, slow to anger and great in mercy. The LORD is good to all, and His tender mercies are over all His works. All Your works shall praise You, O LORD, and Your saints shall bless You* (Psalm 145:8-10).

7. While it is important to consider the supremacy and authority of the Bible, it must never be forgotten that this divine *Word* was handed down to man by God. Thus said, it should be in the forefront of a Spirit-filled believer's mind that God's message *came not in old time by the will of man; but holy men of God spake as they were moved by the Holy Ghost* (2 Peter 1:21).

8. It was God's predicted act and willful purpose that certain men be chosen by Him for this holy task of recording the eternal Word. Herein came together the Holy Spirit's seal upon a man anointed by the Holy Spirit to receive revelation from the Godhead. Through the Holy Spirit's leading, the chosen vessel in perfect unity with the Holy Spirit received the [*God-breathed*] revelation of God's intent and purpose.

9. From the Bible's first book to its last, the focus is constantly on Jesus Christ and His works that ultimately save believers. No other book can claim the authority that the Bible has on this subject. Many noted authors have published works that are like *sounding brass, or a tinkling cymbal* (1 Corinthians 13:1) when compared to the Bible, or like a shining moon against the brightness of the sun. Human authors are earthly bound, and so is their message. The Bible, on the other hand, is authored by heaven's Supreme Commander and directly from His throne.

10. This divinely inspired Holy Writ has a message that is interwoven with various frames and spans generations throughout history. Its message is instructional, promising, and filled with admonishment for those who are disobedient.

11. Ultimately, the Bible is the paramount record for every fellowship and individual believer. In every assembling of the saints, the Bible holds supreme place in the gathering. Every eye and ear are focused and tuned to its message in a meeting. Nothing must ever displace the Word's supreme position in a gathering.

12. Likewise, an individual who separates himself from the din of the world should turn to the lamp at his feet and the light on his pathway (Psalm 119:105) and hide in the *shadow of the Almighty* (Psalm 91:1). It is his *shield and buckler* in the time of trouble.

13. It is appropriate that this tenet focus its attention on the most exquisite explanation of the eternal existence of the Word: *In the beginning was the Word, and the Word was with God, and the Word was God* (John 1:1). Biblical scholar Arthur Pink says, "The Scriptures reveal God's mind, express His will, make known His perfections, and lay bare His heart. This is precisely what the Lord Jesus has done for the Father."

14. The *Word has* always been in existence. The holy manifestation of the oracle of God was revealed when *God, who at various times and in various ways spoke in time past to the fathers by the prophets, has in these last days spoken to us by His Son, whom He has appointed heir of all things, through whom also He made the worlds* (Hebrews 1:1-2 NKJV). The incarnate Christ thus manifested the living testimony of God in the flesh. Henceforth, flowed the continuance of the Word through holy men of the New Testament.

15. Christ is the *Word . . . made flesh* (John 1:14). Apostle John categorically states that John the Baptist was the *voice* while Jesus is the *Word* (John 1:1, 23). Man is the "voice" anointed by God while Jesus is the "Word" anointed by God.

Inspiration

16. While establishing a doctrinal tenet on the supremacy and authority of Scripture, it is important to establish the premise of revelation and inspiration. More succinctly, the focus must be on these two subjects

as they pertain to the Word. Henry Thiessen advises that there should be no confusion between inspiration and revelation: "Revelation is the communication of truth that cannot be otherwise discovered; inspiration has to do with the recording of the truth."

17. It also is important to consider the essence of the intrinsic values contained within the written Word. Spirit-filled believers acknowledge that the entire sixty-six books in the Canon are God's revealed utterances given by Him to men to record His thoughts, words, and promises that He wanted recorded and retained for all time. Eugene Klug clarifies, "Revelation and inspiration are necessary companions in God's disclosing of Himself and His will. They may differ in that, while revelation has to do with divine illumination (given by God in various ways) whereby prophets and apostles knew God and the things of God, inspiration is that divine agency employed by God in the recording of His Word. Thus, inspiration's focal point is first the written text; revelation's focal point is the information or disclosure God gives of Himself and His purposes."

18. Some reliable translations have taken the literal meaning of the Greek word *theopneustos* meaning God-breathed, and recorded it as *inspiration* (2 Timothy 3:16 NKJV, NASB). In fact, however, what Apostle Paul is relating to Timothy is deeper than an inspired utterance from God that He wants recorded for all ages.

19. Apostle Paul is laying down a foundational principal that seals the eternal existence of God's Holy Word. The divine, holy words recorded in the Bible are of such importance to God that He personally induced His very *breath* into every syllable He dictated to holy men. Furthermore, the words breathed by the sovereign, eternal God, have no beginning or end in their existence; they are from the eternal God and, therefore, cannot be eradicated, removed, or altered. They are everlasting in their ability, application, and power as they declare the *grass withers, and its flower falls away, but the word of the LORD endures forever* (1 Peter 1:24-25).

20. When Apostle Paul states that God induced His very breath into every syllable, he affirms that the origin of the Bible is direct revelation from the eternal God to man. Benjamin B. Warfield, who is regarded by many as the authority on explaining "inspiration" and the original Greek word meaning "God-breathed," says in his book *The Inspiration and Authority of the Bible*; "What it [the Bible] affirms is that the

Scriptures owe their origin to an activity of God the Holy Ghost and are in the highest and truest sense His creation. It is on this foundation of divine origin that all the highest attributes of Scripture are built. They are from God, God-breathed, God-given, and God-determined."

21. To summarize what God-breathed (inspiration) entails, it in essence means that the Bible is not man's intelligence reduced to writing; but its every word, the Bible is directly from God, totally His purpose, prose, and presentation without any human additives. Norman Geisler gives a thought-provoking statement on the inspired Word: "Inspiration is the supernatural operation of the Holy Spirit, who through the different personalities and literary styles of the chosen human authors invested the very words of the original books of Holy Scripture, alone and in their entirety, as the very Word of God without error in all that they teach or imply (including history and science), and the Bible is thereby the infallible rule and final authority for faith and practice of all believers."

22. The God-breathed eternal Word is the bulwark that buttresses the divisions distinguishing truth from error, right from wrong, and good from evil; and the book of Hebrews adds *For the word of God is quick, and powerful, and sharper than any twoedged sword, piercing even to the dividing asunder of soul and spirit, and of the joints and marrow, and is a discerner of the thoughts and intents of the heart* (4:12).

23. Inspiration and revelation are, therefore, the authoritative and personal words of God declared to *holy men* and recorded for mankind's benefit. *I have also spoken by the prophets, and have multiplied visions; I have given symbols through the witness of the prophets* (Hosea 12:10 NKJV).

24. Spirit-filled believers know and seek the deep truths within these words. They understand that, as humans are tri-part, (body, soul, and spirit), at their rebirth, they are led by their spirit within to commune with God who is Spirit. This division between spirit and soul is the most important focus they have because they know they must stay spirit-to-Spirit connected. Thus, there must come a *division of soul and spirit*. This division comes by the increase in their knowledge of the Holy Writ.

25. Every human thought, emotion, and natural impulse flows from the soul while all spiritual impartation from the Holy Spirit is into the man's spirit. To be *led of the Spirit*, the believer's spirit needs to be filled to overflowing with matters spiritual. Thus, the need to divide the soul

from the spirit. This need calls the believer to be spiritually in harmony with the Word from which the Holy Spirit imparts His teaching and guidance. The psalmist reveals this harmony as he reflects, *Your word I have hidden in my heart, that I might not sin against You. . . . This is my comfort in my affliction, for Your word has given me life* (Psalm 119:11,50 NKJV).

26. There is no more fulfilling benefit for believers than that they are endowed with the fullness of the Word pulsating through their spirit, as they glean the truths from the Bible which says, *You are my hiding place and my shield; I hope in Your word* (Psalm 119:114 NKJV). This is the "routing out" of the emotional and egotistical attitude of their souls' desires as they empty their souls of all the fleshly lusts and desires and immerse themselves in the Word that has separated soul from spirit. That is the pinnacle when the soul magnifies the Lord as it comprehends His greatness, and the spirit rejoices in its Savior who has redeemed it. Luke records Mary's attestation to this transformation in proclaiming, *My soul magnifies the Lord, and my spirit has rejoiced in God my Savior* (Luke 1:46-47 NKJV).

27. To apply this verse even more deeply, in its application, the Holy Writ is *a discerner of the thoughts and intents of the heart.* The believer is led gently, but convincingly, to the fact that whatever egotistical ideals and imaginings he had of himself, they are vanity and useless in God's eyes. David makes this clear when he says, *But I am a worm, and no man; a reproach of men, and despised by the people* (Psalm 22:6 NKJV). Only the Word can expose this to humankind when it says that the *entirety of Your word is truth, and every one of Your righteous judgments endures forever* (Psalm 119:160 NKJV).

28. Arthur W. Pink in his book *An Exposition of Hebrews* says, "He [mankind] discovers what a vile, depraved, and hell-deserving creature he is. Though, in the mercy of God, he may have been preserved from much outward wickedness in his unregenerate days, and so passed among his fellows as an exemplary character, he now perceives that there dwelleth *no good thing* in him, that every thought and intent of his desperately-wicked heart had, all his life, been contrary to the requirements and claims of a holy God."

29. It is the Word that penetrates deep into the spirit and soul of a believer, bringing man to his knees in humble confession, causing him to seek the sanctifying process of the Holy Spirit. It abases self-pride, and

self-recognition, and replaces it with a humble, contrite heart that seeks nothing else but *Jesus Christ and Him crucified.*

30. The Bible can do this for everyone because of its intrinsic values: holiness (Jeremiah 23:9), truth (John 17:17), divine authority (Matthew 4:4), indestructibility (John 10:35) and everlastingness (1 Peter 1:25), and it is the *oracle[s] of God* (Romans 3:2).

31. This magnificent holy Word, if allowed by the believer, will infiltrate the *thoughts and intents of his heart,* and bring about the spiritual reformation of the soul's attitude to the place where it surrenders all personal, human, and selfish desires to the examination of the Word. Thus exposed, the believer humbly attests, *Behold, thou desirest truth in the inward parts: and in the hidden part thy shalt make me to know wisdom* (Psalm 51:6).

32. Spirit-filled believers must *enter the closet* (Matthew 6:6) and be alone with God because that is the place where they glean the deep truths of the intent and will of God. The greatest example in the Bible of this communion occurs when Isaiah receives the vision of God's holy throne. Isaiah was a man who had audiences with royalty, noblemen, and the ordinary rank and file, a sought-after man in his generation.

33. Yet, when he enters the presence of God, he is granted permission to see the holiest place in heaven; and as he takes notice of its holiness, sovereignty, and righteousness, he immediately realizes that everything he was, stood for, declared to others, and thought of himself, was nothing but absolute *off-scouring* (1 Corinthians 4:13), to the point where he declares, *Woe is me! for I am undone* (Isaiah 6:5). He is literally saying, "Everything I have ever thought I was, have accomplished, could possibly do because of my position and qualifications, is torn to shreds, when I am in the presence of the Lord."

34. Every human sentence, phrased in any human language, is nothing but a dry husk when measured against the nourishment and validity contained in the intrinsic ingredients of the Holy Writ. The Spirit-filled believer hungers and thirsts after its contents and basks in its glorious light claiming *Thy Word is a lamp unto my feet, and a light unto my path* (Psalm 119:105).

35. Scripture is compacted with goodness and instruction, ready to direct believers along the path of righteousness. It is laden with the ever-fresh wholesomeness contained in God's immeasurable love that causes them to *live and move and have* [their] our *being in Him* (Acts 17:28).

Even as the threshing floor sorts the chaff from the wheat, so does the Word divide asunder and discern *the thoughts and intents of the heart* (Hebrews 14:12).

36. It is the undeterred and unshakable truth that will emerge on the Day of Judgment when Jesus, the Word, will tread *the winepress of the fierceness and wrath of Almighty God* (Revelation 19:15). The winepress shows no mercy for the fruit; it has no hindrances that prevent it from pulverizing the fruit, and it is ruthless in its escapade. Jesus declares, *The word that I have spoken, the same shall judge him in the last day* (John 12:48).

37. The unshakable, invincible, inerrant, and infallible Holy Bible given to us from God's heart can be summed up in the words of J. Hudson Taylor, founder of the China Inland Mission; "The living God still lives, and the living Word is a living Word, and we may depend upon it; we may hang upon any word God ever spoke, or ever caused, by His Holy Spirit to be written."

38. Authors have come and gone. Man-made influences via the media have sown discord and confusion among generations. Itching ears have gleaned false doctrines from smooth-mouthed talkers. Some have walked away from the Bible's truth confessing that the truth is too hard to uphold, and some have tried to block out the sound of the Word. However, the time-worn sails of the holy, divine, sovereign Word of God have survived these tempests. Those who choose to stay in the ship of life, have their faith rooted in the Bible's message and are ever strong, because the anchor holds (Hebrews 6:19-20).

Part 2

1. DOCTRINE – of God. The introduction of this tenet focuses on the eternal existence of God and the four absolutes pertaining to God.
   a. God is Eternal.
   b. God is Omnipresent.
   c. God is Omnipotent.
   d. God is Omniscient.
2. DOCTRINE – The Godhead. The explanation of the Godhead is a revealed truth that can only be accepted by faith. Their unity of essence and their unilateral affirmation of all they do, is found in the Bible. Within the Godhead dwells the divine characteristics of wisdom, mercy, truth, faithfulness, and glory.
3. DOCTRINE – The Nature of God. God's nature has five attributes:
   a. Love,
   b. Divine,
   c. Holy,
   d. Pure,
   e. Righteous.

Chapter 4

The Doctrine of God

1. God is. It is a doctrinal *fact* that God is the eternal and everlasting existing Spirit that holds all things in His hands: *The eternal God is your refuge, and underneath (are) the everlasting arms* (Deuteronomy 33:27 NKJV).

2. It is not a fact that God exists simply because the Bible says so. The Bible exists because God exists. It is God who *breathed* His word into existence for man's benefit (2 Timothy 3:16). The incorruptible Word is, therefore, eternal as is the One who uttered it into existence is eternal: *Forever, O LORD, Your word is settled in heaven* (Psalm 119:89 NKJV).

3. The very existence of God is not a fantasy; it is a fact. God is *Alpha and Omega* (Revelation 1:8) which literally means "without beginning and without end." Likewise, it is also accepted as meaning "before the beginning and after the ending."

4. God is Spirit. Norman Geisler in his book *Systematic Theology* (Volume Two), quotes declaring, Stephen Charnock's "God is a pure Spirit, He has nothing, of the nature and tincture of a body . . . whoever conceives Him as having a bodily form . . . instead of owning His dignity, detracts from the super-eminent excellency of His nature and blessedness."

5. The Word declares God's *understanding is infinite* (Psalm 147:5). It is immeasurable, endless, and unlimited. Referring to His entirety as being unified in all His essence and nature, it is correct to state that God is One. The Scriptures declare that *The LORD our God, the LORD is one* (Deuteronomy 6:4). Because He is infinite in His understanding, all His absolutes and attributes are, therefore, infinite. They are identical because whatever God possesses, that is what He is. All His absolutes

and attributes refer to the oneness of His essence. Stating this fact declares that, if God is infinite in one absolute and attribute, He must be infinite in all His absolutes and attributes since He is an indivisible Spiritual Being.

6. When focusing on God as a Spiritual Being, there should be a clear understanding that He is an essence and a substance and not a mere idea or a personification of an idea. God is Spirit, and as such He transcends human comprehension known in man's puny mind as only substance. In essence, God's nature is Who He is, and substance is the product of His divine handiwork. Apostle Paul explains the authoritative power God has over all things when he says, *For by Him all things were created that are in heaven and that are on earth, visible and invisible, whether thrones or dominions or principalities or powers. All things were created through Him and for Him* (Colossians 1: 16 NKJV).

7. While the Word declares God is Spirit (John 4:24), He is also a substance, namely a spiritual substance, which is invisible and untouchable. Apostle Paul explains that Jesus is *the image of the invisible God, the firstborn over all creation* (Colossians 1:15). God's ability to show Himself physically and visibly is apparent when He appeared to Moses on Mount Sinai and demonstrated His glory to him (Exodus 33:18-23). Furthermore, Jesus is the physical and bodily representation of the Godhead, for Jesus is *the image of the invisible God* (Colossians 1:15), and *in him dwelleth all the fullness of the Godhead bodily* (Colossians 2:9).

8. Unlike kings and rulers today who inherit their rulership, God is the ruler over all things and has not inherited His kingship and rulership. He has the supreme ownership and rulership of everything He has created because He was before all things He created (John 17:5).

9. To begin this explanation, the Bible is clear that God is "before" "previous" "prior" to all things. Before anything existed, God is (exists). The Psalmist makes this very clear when he says, *Even from everlasting to everlasting, You are God* (Psalm 90:2 NKJV). Jesus prays to the Father stating that He was loved by His Father *before the foundation of the world* (John 17:24). God's announcement that He is *I AM* (Exodus 3:4) expresses the fact that He is always ever present; He is not "I was" or "I will be" but *I AM*.

10. Spirit-filled believers never question God's eternal existence. Neither do they need an explanation as to God's sovereignty and rulership throughout His eternal reign. Their acceptance and spiritual

application of who God is, is rooted in the premise that God the Holy Spirit, who dwells in them, reveals to them all truths pertaining to God as the Scripture says, *he* [the Holy Spirit] *He will guide you into all truth* (John 16:13). This personal witness in their spirits comes from God's revelation to them that He is the great *I AM*.

11. All the attributes pertaining to God are identical. His power, everlasting existence, knowledge, wisdom, and His glory are identical to His Being because whatever God has, that He is (Revelation 5:12). God's servant James states that with God *there is no variation or shadow of turning* (James 1:17 NKJV). Third-century theologian Novatian of Rome (AD 235 250) gives more clarity on this Scripture saying, "God never changes or transforms Himself into other forms, lest by changing He should somehow appear to be mortal. Therefore, there is never any addition of parts or of glory in Him, lest anything should seem to have been wanting to the perfect One in the first place."

12. God Himself declares *For I am the LORD, I change not* (Malachi 3:6). Gregory the Great states that "Because God is unchanging, no shadow can cut off His light." Severus of Antioch summarily declares, "He [God] remains firm and unchanging in His being." All of God's absolutes and attributes are steadfast and are constantly the same; there are no changes in Him from generation to generation. He is eternally the same.

13. The doctrine of God is rooted in the four "absolutes" that encompass God. He is *Eternal, Omnipresent, Omniscient,* and *Omnipotent.* These four absolutes are all orchestrated from their nucleus, *Love,* which is who God is (1 John 4:8).

God is Eternal

14. Too little is understood about the eternal absolute of God. This situation is due in part to the human mind's inability to fully grasp an eternal state because everything that involves human life is measured in "time." God has no "time" measurement. He is outside of this limiting incarceration that is peculiar to man and His earthly creation. In fact, God, spiritually, has no measurement of any kind such as distance, space, and time that can be applied to any one of His absolutes and attributes.

15. God existed before man, and thus existed before the matrix of time was formulated. Apostle John records Jesus' prayer, *Now, O Father, glorify Me together with Yourself, with the glory which I had with You before the world was* (John 17:5 NKJV), asking His Father to manifest this glory which they had together before time existed.

16. God, in His eternal absolute, can purpose the eternal condition of the human soul because He *has called us with a holy calling, not according to our works, but according to His own purpose and grace which was given to us in Christ Jesus before time began* (2 Timothy 1:9 NKJV).

17. W.A.C. Rowe in his book *One Lord One Faith* says, "He is the forever, unchanging God. The eternal One goes on through the ceaseless ages in His greatness, goodness and glory. Nevertheless, all these qualities of absolute deity have been brought to bear upon man in exceeding gentleness and tenderness" (2 Samuel 22:36).

18. God made infallible promises, and one of these is eternal life in Him. Moreover, this was promised by Him even before the world began. Apostle Paul makes the emphatic statement about this when he speaks of the *hope of eternal life which God, that cannot lie, promised before the world began* (Titus 1:2). In *The Expositor's Bible Commentary* D. Edmond Hiebert states that in the book of Titus "God promised this eternal life 'before the beginning of time', before the ages of time, begun at creation.' William Kelly therein concurs, asserting 'It was a promise within the Godhead when neither the world nor man yet existed.' The promise is rooted in the eternal purpose of God for man."

19. God's eternal existence, an existence that is without beginning or ending, dwelled prior to the creation of anything material and physical. Such a defining statement derives from the belief that God has no beginning. Therefore, in His state of eternal existence, God has never been without thought, spiritual activity, and attributes consisting of love, pureness, righteousness, divinity, and holiness. He was, is, and will always be the sovereign, divine deity, and ruler of all things throughout all eternity.

20. The most striking aspect of God's eternal existence is the that He purposed salvation though His Son long before He laid the foundation of the world. Apostle Paul expresses this in the most exquisite way when he says, *Blessed be the God and Father of our Lord Jesus Christ, who has blessed us with every spiritual blessing in the heavenly places in Christ, just as He chose us in Him before the foundation of the world,*

that we should be holy and without blame before Him in love (Ephesians 1:3-4 NKJV).

21. In order for God to fulfill His promise of eternal life in His Son, Jesus Christ, He has always presided over His purpose. He had the ability to give this perfect gift to mankind even long before He created anything physical and material. Thus, salvation is embedded in God's eternal existence. Likewise, the method to secure this eternal salvation for mankind was entrenched in the eternal, intrinsic, and holy state of His eternal blood. Apostle Peter records this fact when he says, *You were not redeemed with corruptible things, like silver or gold, from your aimless conduct received by tradition from your fathers, but with the precious blood of Christ, as of a lamb without blemish and without spot. He indeed was foreordained before the foundation of the world, but was manifest in these last times for you* (1 Peter 1:18-20 NKJV).

22. Salvation though Christ's shed blood, is from God's sovereign heart that flooded mankind's presence with His unending love. He took the eternal blood from His very being, the eternal Spirit, and poured it out on Calvary's Hill. As incomprehensible as it might be to believe and accept, it was God Himself, giving His life for mankind's sin. Jesus, in His love *through the eternal Spirit offered Himself without spot to God, [to] cleanse [mankind's] conscience from dead works to serve the living God* (Hebrews 9:14 NKJV).

23. God applied His eternal absolute, intertwined it with His eternal attribute, love, and sealed it with His eternal blood that produced eternal life for the whosoever believes in Him (John 3:16, 1 John 1:7).

24. In the vast subject of the doctrine of creation pertaining to man, within God's eternal existence, He produced ages, dispensations, and periods involving man on this earth. These are measurements that endeavor to explain God's creation, both physical and spiritual.

25. Furthermore, if God is the Creator of these periods, then He also is the Creator of time. Similarly, to create these things, He had to be before they were created. Therefore, He is before what He created, and is outside of His created measurement of time. These dimensions of time, space, and distance came from the eternal God who launched them from His eternal existence.

26. It is impossible to exact a moment in God's eternal existence when this happened because He is eternally existing and outside of time. What man has tried to fathom is the current age of what God created, but

such determination is impossible because man uses measurements of time, distance, and space which God introduced in His eternal existence that precedes such measurements.

27. It is imperative that Spirit-filled believers understand the spiritual fact that God has never left His eternal status. He has been, is, and always will be eternally in existence. From His eternal existence, He miraculously introduced the created forms. The moment in time when God did this is irrelevant. What is relevant is that God created them.

28. If trying to fathom the time when God created all things is what exhausts men's energies, then they have forgotten to focus instead on the Creator Himself who fashioned the Cosmos, created the flora and fauna on earth, and breathed the breath of His Spirit into a form in the dust and gave it human life in His image and likeness.

29. The warp of time must be excluded from the expression that God is eternal, for eternity does not have a measurement of any sort. It is of perpetual duration.

30. As eternal, God has no commencement and is always in the "now" when mankind relates to His existence. *I AM* (Exodus 3:14) expresses that God is unchangeable and was, is, and always will be the same sovereign, almighty, and holy God. Everything about God is always constant and eternal as the Psalmist says, *Thou art the same, and thy years shall have no end* (Psalm 102:27).

31. God personally declares, *I am the LORD, I do not change* (Malachi 3:6 NKJV). Likewise does the writer in the New Testament say, *Jesus Christ is the same yesterday, today, and forever* (Hebrews 13:8 NKJV). It is, therefore, without confusion and needs no debate that the eternal God is never changing and is constantly in mankind's presence in the exact same way throughout every generation.

32. Everything that can be seen, touched, and experienced will wither, tarnish, wilt, or fade from man's memory. However, God, in His eternal and immutable state will not and cannot change or become irrelevant because He is always in the *now*. Whenever and whatever the born-again believer is about, God is *now* in that event in their life.

33. God's infinite existence has no parts because, if God had various parts, He would not be infinite. Therefore, it is fundamentally true that He who has no parts cannot change. There is nothing about God that wilts, tarnishes, or fades away. He is eternal in His ever-now *I AM* presence, and He is forever the same.

34. In His immense love for His highest creation, mankind, God willingly bestows this glorious absolute of eternal life on him. His word promises *that whoever believes in Him should not perish but have everlasting life* (John 3:15-16; Romans 6:23 NKJV).

35. Spirit-filled believers who operate in the Apostles' Doctrine (Acts 2:42) receive by revelation from the indwelling Holy Spirit the *deep things of God* (1 Corinthians 2:10). God's eternality is so all-encompassing that the Spirit-led believer is immersed in the spiritual endowment of the eternal Holy Spirit. Their ability to function in the anointing of the Holy Spirit is the recognition that an eternal Spirit dwells within their bodies (1 Corinthians 3:16).

36. Spirit-filled believers do not rely on their physical experiences or emotional encounters. The basic premise from which they launch their faith is vested in the knowledge that God whom they serve is eternal and, therefore, can do according to His good pleasure as and when He so chooses (Acts 1:7).

37. Unlike other denominations that align themselves with human intellect and instruction, apostolic believers have no question about the eternal state of God. Like the bastions of old, when the church was born on the Day of Pentecost, Spirit-filled believers today continue to experience the eternal indwelling Spirit flooding their being and without question know that the eternal Spirit resides in them.

38. Apostolic believers not only believe God is eternal but also live and breathe His eternal existence that resides in them; *for in Him* [they] *live, and move, and have* [their] *being* (Acts 17:28).

39. This leads them to have a holy reverence for God because they do not show "lip service" having *a form of godliness but denying the power thereof* (2 Timothy 3:5). In their hearts, they know that He is eternal. As such, apostolic believers move gingerly and with caution towards every deed and command the Holy Spirit infuses in their spirits.

40. In essence, they are in awe of the eternal existence of God and have a reverence for the revealed truth that the Holy Spirit imparts to them.

41. For them, God's eternal existence needs no explanation. There is no discourse to prove God's eternal state; neither do they consider that any rational discussion should be made on this subject that is divine and holy. Spirit-led believers *receive by revelation* the eternal existence of God, and unconditionally accept it (Galatians 1:12).

42. The character trait that inevitably flows from such hearts as theirs is humbleness. Knowing that they have been granted this privilege that the sovereign eternal God chooses to dwell in them, they abase themselves in His presence and *therefore humble* [themselves] *under the mighty hand of God* (1 Peter 5:6 NKJV). Their praise and worship magnify His eternal existence as they proclaim, *Now unto the King eternal, immortal, invisible, the only wise God, be honour and glory for ever and ever* (1 Timothy 1:17).

God is Omnipresent

43. *Am I not a God near at hand, says the LORD, and not a God afar off? Can anyone hide himself in secret places, so I shall not see him? says the LORD. Do I not fill heaven and earth? says the LORD* (Jeremiah 23:23-24 NKJV).

44. By God's own word, He is omnipresent. The ever present and all present God in His fullness is constantly everywhere. This absolute transcends man's thinking. The Bible says in 1 Corinthians 2:14 that *the natural man receiveth not the things of the Spirit of God: for they are foolishness unto him: neither can he know them, because they are spiritually discerned.* God's omnipresence needs spiritual application and discernment to be understood by believers.

45. David petitions God, *Where can I go from Your Spirit? Or where can I flee from Your presence? If I ascend into heaven, You are there: If I make my bed in hell, behold, You are there. If I take the wings of the morning, and dwell in the uttermost parts of the sea, even there Your hand shall lead me, and Your right hand shall hold me. If I say, "surely the darkness shall fall on me," even the night shall be light about me: indeed, the darkness shall not hide from You, but the night shines as the day; the darkness and the light are both alike to You* (Psalm 139: 7-12 NKJV).

46. When considering God's omnipresence, the word that aligns itself with His all-encompassing existence in and everywhere is "immensity" which means "vastness" denoting His omnipresence as immeasurable.

47. Norman Geisler says: "God is not in space nor is He limited by space: He is present at every point in space, but He is not part of space or limited to it, He transcends all space and time."

48. The acceptance of God's omnipresence is both encouraging and frightening. God's always being present in every thought and deed

encourages the believer to follow the Bible's instruction that *whatsoever thy hand findeth to do, do it with thy might* (Ecclesiastes 9:10). Conversely, if the believer does not reverence the presence of God in everything he does, when he sins, the witness of God's presence, no matter where he is, brings him into the reality that God's convicting power of the presence of sin is a frightening thing.

49. Henry Thiessen checks the unbeliever in his efforts to escape the presence of God when he says, "The thought of His presence is subduing and encouraging. To the unbeliever it is a source of warning and restraint. No matter how much he may try, he cannot escape from God. Neither distance nor darkness hide from Him: *Neither is there any creature that is not manifest in his sight: but all things are naked and opened unto the eyes of him with whom we have to do* (Hebrews 4:13). This consciousness often checks the sinner in his evil ways and leads him to seek God."

50. As an indivisible Being, God is not separable; namely, one part of God cannot be separated from Him and be in one place while the rest of Him is elsewhere. He is always in His fullness everywhere all the time.

51. God's immensity defines Him as always being everywhere constantly in His fullness. Even in His immeasurable and divine existence before He created anything, God, who is outside of time, space, and distance, was and is always there.

52. In His omnipresence, the Bible declares, *God, who made the world and everything in it, since He is Lord of heaven and earth, does not dwell in temples made with hands. Nor is He worshipped with men's hands, as though He needed anything, since He gives to all life, breath, and all things* (Acts 17:24-28 NKJV). Furthermore, God gives a glimpse of who He is when the Prophet Isaiah says, *The whole earth is full of His glory* (Isaiah 6:3 NKJV).

53. God's omnipresence is shared with man in measured portions because human mind cannot comprehend its immensity. First, God manifests His glory in the measure that man can spiritually grasp it. His Spirit is the witness to Spirit-filled believers that God, whom they worship and serve, is glorious and holy. Their utter depravity is expressed when they say as Isaiah said, *Look down from heaven, And see from Your habitation, holy and glorious. Where are Your zeal and Your strength, The yearning of Your heart and Your mercies toward me? Are they restrained?* (Isaiah 63:16 NKJV).

54. God is untouchable and so glorious that He cannot be taken for granted. God is to be constantly recognized by the believer as God manifests extracts of His glory to them. In this glimpse of His glory, there is divine revelation that empowers the believer to experience the fullness of God's presence as Apostle Paul says to the church at Colossae, *He is the image of the invisible God, the firstborn over all creation. For by Him all things were created that are in heaven and that are on earth, visible and invisible, whether thrones or dominions or principalities or powers. All things were created through Him and for Him. And He is before all things, and in Him all things consist* (Colossians 1:15-17).

55. Second, God's omnipresence is witnessed when believers look on His creation. They are in awe of His mighty power that flung the stars into the heavens, fashioned the landscapes of earth, and breathed the breath of life into a human body. No human being can do any of these things. It is out of nothing that God spoke into existence all things.

56. In all things, God is always all-present, whether spiritually or materially. God's personal declaration through His prophet says, *Do I not fill heaven and earth?* (Jeremiah 23:24 NKJV). One of the best comments on God's omnipresence is from Augustine (A.D. 354-430) who said, "God so permeates all things as to be not a quality of the world but the very creative substance of the world, ruling the world without labor, sustaining it without effort. Nevertheless, He is not distributed through space in a physical sense so that half of Him should be in half of the world and half in the other half of it. He is wholly present in all of it in such a way as to be wholly in heaven alone and wholly in the earth alone, and wholly in heaven and earth together; not confined to one place, but wholly in Himself everywhere."

57. All the above statements are affirmed by the Spirit-filled believer. In addition, the Spirit-filled believer testifies that the Holy Spirit dwells in his body (1 Corinthians 3:16). This is the promise Jesus gave to His disciples when He said, *But you shall receive power when the Holy Spirit has come upon you* (Acts 1:8 NKJV).

58. The Holy Spirit, who is omnipresent throughout the entirety of God's existence and creation, now resides within the believer. This infilling only takes place when the believer is baptized with the Holy Spirit (Luke 3:16), a concept contrary to other denominations that believe the Holy Spirit is received within the believer when he is born again.

59. The Holy Spirit now resides in the Spirit-filled believer's body, and as such the gifts of the Holy Spirit are manifested in their fullness by the indwelling Holy Spirit through the believer (1 Corinthians 12:1-13).

60. God's omnipresence throughout the world is now more personal to the Spirit-filled believer in that the glorious presence of the Holy Spirit is now not only upon him but also within him.

61. This was the basis of the birth of the church of Jesus Christ on the Day of Pentecost. The born-again believers experienced the Holy Spirit's presence surrounding them, and then by faith they received the Spirit who took up residence within them. Henceforth, the apostolic church functioned under the anointing of the Holy Spirit as He operated through them (Acts 2:1-4).

62. Even though many denominations have strayed from this vital truth and experience, there is still a remnant who follow in the fullness of the apostolic doctrine that was birthed when the omnipresent Holy Spirit took up residence within the human frame, enabling believers to continue *steadfastly in the apostles' doctrine and fellowship, in the breaking of bread, and in prayers* (Acts 2:42 NKJV).

63. It is God Himself who now resides in man, and not merely around and among men.

God is Omnipotent

64. God is all-powerful, all-consuming, and everywhere at the same time. He is never less powerful in one place than another and is never less effective in other parts of His creation than He is in any given part of His creation.

65. Not only is God simultaneously all-powerful in every part of His creation, but God also is self-sufficient and unlimited in every aspect of His Being. He has no need of anyone to instruct Him or support Him with an additional power source.

66. There is nothing God cannot do. Neither is there anything God needs to do. What is impossible in man's thought is possible with God. He has power to do, choose, not do, and refuse to do. He has declared, *Behold, I am the LORD, the God of all flesh. Is there anything too hard for Me?* (Jeremiah 32:27 NKJV).

67. Spirit-filled believers are ever conscious of the almighty power existing in God. In addition to this awareness, they comprehend that this power

and ubiquitous presence never leaves them because within them dwells this power; and they are assured by Apostle Paul, *if the Spirit of Him who raised Jesus from the dead dwells in you, He who raised Christ from the dead will also give life to your mortal bodies through His Spirit who dwells in you* (Romans 8:11 NKJV).

68. Furthermore, Spirit-filled believers cling to God's word that God can, and will, defeat Satan and all the evil he has spewed on mankind. The indwelling power of the Holy Spirit supplies the believers' every need (Philippians 4:19), and reigns victorious in their lives as declared by Apostle Paul, who assures, *I know whom I have believed and am persuaded that He is able to keep what I have committed to Him until that Day* (2 Timothy 1:12 NKJV).

69. The word that is aligned with God's omnipotence is infinite: *Great is our Lord, and of great power; his understanding is infinite* (Psalm 147:5). Thus said, God is unlimited in His power and His understanding of all things. He possesses foreknowledge, and He can direct His power in any direction His infinite knowledge desires. Norman Geisler articulates God's omnipotence well when he says, "God is infinite in His Being. God possesses power, as is indicated by His mighty acts. However, as we have seen, whatever God 'has' that He is, for He is absolutely one. So, whatever applies to him applies to His whole Being rather than just part of it. Hence, if God is infinite and powerful, then He must be infinitely powerful."

70. God's infinite existence allows Him to be limitless in every aspect of every attribute in His nature. He is absolute in all His thoughts and actions. This omnipresence and strength stems from an intrinsic holy manifestation of who He is that demonstrates His glory. God is, in essence, all good. He will defeat evil and rule in righteousness as determined in His time. This consummation will take place because God is omnipotent and never fails to perform His promises *for all the promises of God in Him are Yes, and in Him Amen, to the glory of God through us* (2 Corinthians 1:20 NKJV).

71. God, who raised His Son, Jesus Christ, from the dead, now speaks to believers through His risen Son; and has seated Jesus Christ on the highest seat of honor, power, and authority (Hebrews 1:1-3,13). God did this because He can raise the dead. God did this because He can elevate His Son to the highest seat of honor and power. God has infinite power and uses it for His glory.

72. William Rowe says of God's omnipresence, "He meets every need and every exigency. Man is made a free-will agent; if he falls, then a full salvation is ready. God's ways are not temporary expedients; splendid after thoughts: they are ways of foreknowledge and predestination (Isaiah 46:10). Crowning the sum of all God's qualities and abilities is His perfect and holy will (Romans 12:2). He executes His counsels and judgments and carries out His eternal purpose and *none can stay His hand. God ruleth overall,* planning, controlling and achieving. Truly, He is the *El Shaddai,* the All-Sufficient Lord (Genesis 17:1)."

God is Omniscient

73. God is all-knowing. This quality transcends human comprehension because man can only see and know *in part* (1 Corinthians 13:12) that which is of God. Only God knows Himself and *knows all things* (1 John 3:20).

74. God has full knowledge of all things whether they be in the past, present, or future; and He knows them perfectly in His eternal existence as He declares, *For I am God, and there is no other; I am God, and there is none like Me, declaring the end from the beginning, and from ancient times things that are not yet done, saying, 'My counsel shall stand, And I will do all My pleasure'* (Isaiah 46:9-10). Furthermore, God does not have a thought process in the manner that man thinks. He has instant and immediate full thought concerning everything, both from the past, in the present, and regarding the future. There is no process that He applies. Everything is immediately available to Him without any sequence or process.

75. William Rowe explains God's omniscience: "God knows all the needs of all His creatures (Matthew 6:8). His mind is Infinite, comprehending all things from eternity to eternity. His knowledge and His understanding are limitless (Psalm 147:5)."

76. Millard J. Erickson says, "We are all completely transparent before God. He sees and knows us totally. He knows every truth, even those not yet discovered by humankind, for it is He who built them into the creation."

77. Referencing God, the Father, God the Son, and God the Holy Spirit, the most sublime aspect of their existence is that they know each other

perfectly; and only they have this perfect knowledge of each other. There is one undivided divine nature in the Godhead which exists and manifests itself in three personal subsistences as Matthew explains, *No one knows the Son except the Father. Nor does anyone know the Father except the Son, and the One to whom the Son wills to reveal Him . . .* (Matthew 11:27 NKJV).

78. God's all-knowledge is not the result of His having reasoned things to be; neither does God have this infinite knowledge from experience. Herbert Lockyer gives an all-encompassing statement about God's omniscience when he says, "God has intuitive, simultaneous, infallible perceptions of Himself, and all other beings and events. Past, present, and future are as an open scroll to Him, and His all-knowledge is not the result of reasoning, as with man, but is intuitive, perfect, and eternal. He sees and knows everything."

79. It is outside man's intellect for him to comprehend that everything that has happened in the past is fully known by God. Likewise, everything that is in the present anywhere and all things that are going to be are fully known by the omniscient God. To quote a contemporary apostle, Cyril Wilson, "Nothing escapes God's attention."

80. It is worthy to join in the accolade expressed by the Psalmist: *O LORD, You have searched me and known me. You know my sitting down and my rising up; You understand my thought afar off. You comprehend my path and my lying down, and are acquainted with all my ways. For there is not a word on my tongue, but behold, O LORD, You know it altogether. You have hedged me behind and before and laid Your hand upon me. Such knowledge is too wonderful for me; it is high, I cannot attain it* (Psalm 139:1-6 NKJV).

81. It is appropriate that every Spirit-filled believer echo Apostle Paul's declaration as he exalts God's omniscience, *Oh, the depth of the riches both of the wisdom and knowledge of God! How unsearchable are His judgments and His ways past finding out* (Romans 11:33 NKJV).

LORD GOD...Lord God

82. The word is emphatic in its proclamation that God is Father, Son, and Holy Spirit. The extrapolation of the word "GOD" (all capital letters) which is used numerous times in the Old Testament is the explanation

of the *Godhead*. When used in this way, "GOD," it refers to God in His most holy, almighty, sovereign, and divine nature.

83. Furthermore, GOD is the definitive explanation in Hebrew as JEHOVAH. When translated into all capitals it embraces the full extent of God as "creator" and "revealer." The first description of this is found in Genesis 2:4 when the writer uses "LORD God" to explain God as both "revealer" and "creator." The Hebrew word for God as "creator" is "Elohim". The Hebrew word for "revealer" is "Jehovah" which is translated as LORD (all capital letters).

84. It is used this way (LORD God) in Genesis 2:4 to explain that the entire Godhead in His most holy, eternal, almighty, sovereign, and divine nature is the one who reveals His creation to man.

85. Henceforth, whenever the translation renders all capitals for GOD and LORD it is declaring that the full capacity of the eternal Godhead is involved.

86. The rendering of these two words in all capitals, LORD GOD, is the translation of the word "Jehovah" that contains every provision for man. It is the sum of the seven compound names wrapped up in Jehovah:

87. Jehovah-Jireh means "provider" (Genesis 22:13-14). Jehovah-Rapha means "healer" (Exodus 15:26). Jehovah-Nissi means "banner" (Exodus 17:15). Jehovah-Shalom means "peace" (Judges 6:23-24). Jehovah-Raah means "shepherd" (Psalm 23:1). Jehovah-Tsidkenu means "righteousness" (Jeremiah 23:6). Jehovah-Shammah means "present" (Ezekiel 48:35).

Chapter 5

The Godhead

1. Herbert Lockyer says: "The Godhead is composed of three Persons coeternal, co-equal; and the same in substance but distinct in subsistence permeates the Bible. This sacred doctrine is above reason."

2. The entire explanation of the Godhead is a revealed truth that can only be accepted by faith. Their unity of essence and their unilateral affirmation of all they are and do, are found in the holy pages of the Bible.

3. The Godhead is Who God is. This One God is unique in all His qualities and power. The power source that flows from the divine nature and deity within the Godhead possesses the same qualities and has the same abilities when used by the Father, or the Son, or the Holy Spirit. Each member of the Godhead does not have its own unique qualities, deity, or measure of power distinct from the other; they all function and operate from within the same source.

4. However, each Member of the Godhead, the Father, the Son, and the Holy Spirit has a unique application of these qualities and power. Therefore, the source is the same yet with a different application by each Member of the Godhead.

5. The words "Trinity" or "Triune" God are not entirely biblical in their definition of God; neither are they found in the Holy Writ. While expressing the Godhead's nature and divinity in one accord, these word-definitions could be interpreted as separating the power and operating abilities of each Member of the Godhead. It does, at times, incorrectly portray the emphasis that each Member of the Godhead has its own independent power and methodology.

6. The "oneness" of the Godhead is a fundamental teaching of the Holy Writ. Anyone who opposes this vital teaching violates God's emphatic statement in His opening of the Ten Commandments, *I am the LORD your God* (Exodus 20:2).

7. Thus said, the Hebrew declaration, *Hear, O Israel, the LORD our God, the LORD is one* (Deuteronomy 6:4 NKJV), is the truthful statement that God is Creator and revealer. It further supports the statement, *Let Us make man in Our image* (Genesis 1:26 NKJV). *Then the LORD God formed man of the dust of the ground* (Genesis 2:7 NKJV)

8. This confirms that God is the One who reveals Himself and creates all things. The One who creates is the Son of God, *the Son of His love* (Colossians 1:13). *All things were made through Him* (John1:3 NKJV). Again, the Bible says, *for by Him all things were created that are in heaven and that are on earth, visible and invisible* (Colossians 1:16 NKJV).

9. The opening salvo of the Holy Writ that welcomes man's eyes in Genesis 1:1, *In the beginning God created the heavens and the earth* announces for the first time the word "God." The Hebrew word used in this context is "Elohim." The full translation for Elohim is "Eternal One Who Created." This rendering makes an emphatic declaration of the eternal existence of the Godhead. The Father, the Son, and the Holy Spirit have always been together in existence and will always be one.

10. Wayne Grudem in his book *Systematic Theology,* gives an interesting explanation regarding a more apt rendering of the completeness of the Godhead which enables man to comprehend the equality and full measure of the Godhead. He says, "The Father is 'fully' God. The Son is 'fully' God, and the Holy Spirit is 'fully' God."

11. God is One LORD, explained in the New Testament as the Godhead, namely Father, Son, and Holy Spirit, and has eternal existence, as Apostle Paul references, *His eternal power and Godhead* (Romans 1:20), and in whom is fullness of the Godhead bodily; *For in [Jesus Christ] dwelleth all the fulness of the Godhead bodily* (Colossians 2:9). The Spirit-filled church emphatically believes in one eternal God and heralds the anthem, *Now to the King eternal, immortal, invisible, to God who alone is wise, be honor and glory forever and ever. Amen* (1 Timothy 1:17 NKJV).

12. The fullest understanding of the Godhead is beyond mankind's comprehension and can only be given to him by revelation from

the Holy Spirit. Herbert Lockyer says, "The sacred mystery of the trinity [Godhead] is one which the light within man could never have discovered."

13. The Word reveals God as being eternal in unity as three Persons (1 Peter 1:2). These three Persons, who are one in substance and essence, have entity in the most perfect unity of thought and purpose (1 John 5:7); and they are equal in glory, majesty, and power.

14. Their inseparable and indivisible nature of One causes the presence and action of One to implicate the presence and action of the Others. The Bible says, *But when the Helper comes, whom I shall send to you from the Father, the Spirit of truth who proceeds from the Father, He will testify of Me* (John 15:26 NKJV).

15. Stephen D. Renn, author of *The Expository Dictionary of Bible Words*, describes the definition of God when termed *YHWH* occurring one hundred eighty times in Genesis in the Old Testament: "God has appeared to Abraham and his descendants by the name 'God Almighty', but has not made Himself known to them as 'LORD'. The uniqueness of God's revelation to Moses lay not in the mere knowledge or articulation of the name *YHWH*, but rather in the divinely given insight that *YHWH* is the ever-present, all-powerful God, the redeemer of His people, and the One who keeps His solemn promises pledged under the oath of the covenant. Such a revelation had not been imparted to the patriarchal predecessors of Moses–they only had the promise."

16. God's progressive revelation of Who He is continues through the New Testament, and culminates in the decree that Jesus Christ, the Son of God, was exalted by the Father, for *it pleased the Father that in Him all the fullness should dwell* (Colossians 1:19 NKJV). In addition, the highest honor that can be bestowed on Jesus is that *in him dwelleth all the fulness of the Godhead bodily* (Colossians 2:9).

17. Matthew Henry gives a clearer illustration of this when he says, "Under the law, the presence of God dwelt between the cherubim, in a cloud which covered the mercy-seat; but now it dwells in the person of our Redeemer, who partakes of our nature, and is bone of our bone and flesh of our flesh, and has more clearly declared the Father to us. The fullness of the Godhead dwells in Christ really, and not figuratively; for He is both God and man."

18. Consequently, all the Godhead's power and authority now reside in Jesus Christ who has been given the highest elevation by the Father

who seated Him at His own right hand and sealed Jesus' office of authority and power with the scepter of righteousness (Hebrews 1:8-13). The Lord Jesus Christ personally stated that *all power* (authority) *is given unto me in heaven and in earth* (Matthew 28:18).

19. It is vital that Spirit-filled and Holy-Spirit-led believers understand that within the Godhead there is perfect equality of all things pertaining to their deity. The intrinsic divine nature within the Godhead is equal in all three Persons. The Bible is emphatic and saturates the pages of the Holy Writ with the fact that the operation of the Godhead composed of the three Persons who are co-eternal and co-equal, and even being the same in substance, yet distinct in subsistence, always functions this way.

20. The operation of the entire Godhead is inevitably present when God's divine purposes are in operation. This is no more apparent than at Jesus' baptism when *Jesus came up immediately from the water; and behold, the heavens were opened to Him, and He saw the Spirit of God descending like a dove and alighting upon Him. And suddenly a voice came from heaven, saying, "This is My beloved Son, in whom I am well pleased"* (Matthew 3:16-17).

21. William Rowe says, "While each Person is verily God, each Person is not God apart from the other two Persons; they are inseparable. They are not three Gods, but One."

22. The prominent manifestation of the Godhead's equal and distinct operational abilities is evidenced at the birth of the church in Jerusalem on the Day of Pentecost. It was Jesus Christ, the Holy Son, who said, *Behold I send the Promise of My Father upon you; but tarry in the city of Jerusalem until you are endued with power from on high* (Luke 24:49 NKJV). The *power from on high* was explained by Jesus who said, *You shall receive power when the Holy Spirit has come upon you* (Acts 1:8), thus explaining the involvement of the entire Godhead.

23. The Father purposes salvation for mankind and *sends forth His Son* (Galatians 4:4 NKJV). The Son was always with the Father who sent Him at the appointed time into the world, giving Him a name that is above every other name, JESUS. Jesus affirms He is the embodiment of God in the flesh when He states, *I and my Father are one* (John 10:30).

24. The Son fulfilled the Father's will and created all that is apparent to mankind. Then *in these last days* (Hebrews 1:2 NKJV) and *when the fullness of the time had come, God sent forth His Son* (Galatians

4:4 NKJV). Jesus Christ is the fulfillment of the Father's predestined will. Henceforth, believers proclaim *Blessed be the God and Father of our Lord Jesus Christ, who has blessed us with every spiritual blessing in the heavenly places in Christ, just as He chose us in Him before the foundation of the world having predestined us to adoption as sons* (Ephesians 1:3-5 NKJV).

25. The Holy Spirit is commissioned by the Father and the Son to reveal the intent and purposes of God the Father to mankind. He is also the comforter and teacher of all things pertaining to God. The Holy Spirit's anointing that is in every Spirit-filled believer reveals (teaches) to him all truth because as Apostle John explains, *The anointing which you have received from Him abides in you, and you do not need that anyone teach you; but as the same anointing teaches you concerning all things* (1 John 2:27).

26. It is, therefore, correct to state that all things are from the Father through the Son because as Apostle Paul states, *For us there is one God, the Father, of whom are all things, and we for Him; and one Lord Jesus Christ, through whom are all things, and through whom we live* (1 Corinthians 8:6 NKJV); and they are revealed to mankind by the Holy Spirit (Ephesians 3:5 NKJV).

27. This subject is so vital to Spirit-filled believers that they approach it with reverence and humility because they know they are entering the presence and very essence and nucleus of Who God is.

28. These believers know that their most intimate discourse with God occurs when they *enter into thy closet, and when thou hast shut thy door* [in prayer] (Matthew 6:6), that they reverently approach the Father in the name of Jesus and worship Him in spirit and in truth as the Holy Spirit gives them utterance. Herein is the blending of man's spirit with Holy God in the entirety of the Godhead.

29. Spirit-filled believers know they have reached the place of the reconciliation that was broken in the Garden of Eden, and they discern God's promise that He would restore the relationship through His Son's death on Calvary and His resurrection when they enter God's holy presence this way. This is once again the fellowship with the Father and the gentle leading of the Holy Spirit who takes believers into the truth about spiritual things because *the natural man does not receive the things of the Spirit of God, for they are foolishness to him; nor can he know them, because they are spiritually discerned* (1 Corinthians 2:14 NKJV).

30. This intimacy, closeness, and spiritual communion with the Godhead is what every believer's prayer should embrace. God's heart desires this blending of the human spirit with His Spirit in the most holy and pure communication (prayer). This is *the effective, fervent prayer of a righteous man* that *avails much* (James 5:16 NKJV).

31. The scriptural word for "the Three-in-one," "Trinity," or "Triune" God is the "Godhead"; and as such, the doctrine of the Spirit-filled church applies this biblical word.

Characteristics Applicable to the Godhead

32. *Wisdom*. God's wisdom is outside of human conception. He is the very embodiment of wisdom which encompasses every thought and action emanating from Him, *in whom are hidden all the treasures of wisdom* (Colossians 2:3 NKJV). An early father of Christianity, Chrysostom (AD 349-407), says about this profound declaration by Apostle Paul that "Christ knows all things. 'Hid,' for don't think that you truly and already have all things. These are hidden also even from angels, not from you only; so that you ought to ask all things from Him. He Himself gives wisdom and knowledge. Now by saying 'treasures,' he shows their magnificence by saying 'all' that He is ignorant of nothing, by 'hid,' that He alone knows."

33. When Apostle Paul says *in whom are hidden all the treasures of wisdom,* he is not implying that wisdom is never available to mankind. It is a "treasure" that can be found by those who seek it from God. It is a personal attribute of God that man cannot reach out in unrighteousness and grab for their own benefit. This "treasure" is hidden in the heart of God. The believer who seeks the Lord with his whole heart and asks God to reveal to him this secret treasure (wisdom) he will receive bountifully from God's heart: *If any of you lack **wisdom**, let him ask of God, that giveth to all men liberally, and upbraideth not; and it shall be given him* (James 1:5).

34. The length, breadth, and depth of God's wisdom is impossible to fully comprehend; for the Holy Writ says, *Oh, the depth of the riches both of the wisdom and knowledge of God! How unsearchable are His judgments and His ways past finding out* (Romans 11:33 NKJV).

35. *For the Lord gives wisdom; and from His mouth come knowledge and understanding* (Proverbs 2.6 NKJV). All actions and words from God are wise. In essence, He is the source of all true wisdom; and, therefore, everyone else that has wisdom has received it from God.

36. God's wise and knowledgeable applications are always correct because He knows which means are the most effective to achieve a perfect end. God's omniscience enables Him to be wise.

37. Wisdom is the application of knowledge. It is also using knowledge perfectly and in the correct manner. God never makes a mistake or gives the wrong instruction. He is the personification of perfect wisdom which is expressed by James when he says *but the wisdom that is from above is first pure, then peaceable, gentle, willing to yield, full of mercy and good fruits, without partiality and without hypocrisy* (James 3:17 NKJV).

38. *Goodness.* God is ready to deal with man kindly, gently and in goodness. More appropriately, God always deals with man in this manner. He is unchanging in His goodness towards mankind, and He was, is, and will always be this way, as He has said, *for I am the Lord, I change not* (Malachi 3:6 NKJV), and the Word attests to His eternal goodness, *the goodness of God endureth continually* (Psalm 52:1). Moreover, God abounds *in goodness and truth* (Exodus 34:6 NKJV).

39. There is no place on earth where mankind dwells that is void of God's goodness; *the earth is full of the goodness of the LORD* (Psalm 33:5 NKJV). Conversely, that which is not filled with goodness is from an evil and sinful heart and unacceptable to God.

40. God's goodness is like a healing balm and food for the soul that hungers after God. The Psalmist says, *Oh, that men would give thanks to the LORD for His goodness, and for His wonderful works to the children of men* (Psalm 107:15 NKJV).

41. The person who is shown God's goodness is drawn by the Holy Spirit to see and accept the Originator of goodness and in so doing know *that the goodness of God leadeth* [him] *thee to repentance* (Romans 2:4).

42. The evidence of the enduring goodness is demonstrated by those who are led by the Holy Spirit's indwelling fruit (Galatians 5:22). The stabilizer of men's feet on the righteous path is having the ability to walk in God's goodness, helping him *keep to the paths of righteousness* (Proverbs 2:20 NKJV).

43. *Mercy.* God's mercy is poured out on those who are guilty of sinning against Him. Mankind in his inherent sin is utterly guilty of transgressing God's righteousness and holiness. He is, therefore, at the mercy of God to be forgiven. God alone has this power to forgive sin.

44. Mercy can only be shown to the guilty; those who are not guilty do not need mercy because they have not transgressed anyone. Mankind is guilty from the creation of Adam and Eve who perpetrated the original sin that is inherently in all born on earth after them as the Bible says, *for all have sinned and fall short of the glory of God* (Romans 3:23). This guilt is against the holy and pure God in whom there is no sin.

45. God's mercy is the fruit of His inherent love. It is because He loves mankind that He enacts His mercy forgiving a repentant heart. The quality of God's mercy is unparalleled and always apportioned in the same measure to every repentant heart. Its quality contains the fullness and ability to forgive man's inherent sin; He shows no partiality (Ephesians 6:9) and never compromises His uprightness as He declares, *for the LORD your God is God of gods and Lord of lords, the great God, mighty and awesome, who shows no partiality nor takes a bribe* (Deuteronomy 10:17 NKJV).

46. From the throne of God in heaven, namely the highest seat of authority, God has the mercy seat upon which the sacrificed blood of His only Son was placed as the sufficient offering that invokes God's mercy to all who approach Him by faith; and *the blood of Jesus Christ His Son cleanses us from all sin. He is faithful and just to forgive us* (1 John 1:7,9 NKJV).

47. *Faithful.* God is the only true faithful companion man can fully trust. He has promised those who walk in His steps that He *will never leave* [them] *nor forsake* [them] (Hebrews 13:5). He is completely reliable and steadfastly constant, always fulfilling His promises as the Psalmist says of God, *Your faithfulness endures to all generations* (Psalm 119:90 NKJV).

48. God's faithfulness is greater than that of a friend even though He is a friend (John 15:15). His faithfulness is greater than that of a Father even though He is a Father (John 20:7). His faithfulness is greater than any rule or decree even though He is the One who sets rules and decrees in order (Matthew 28:18).

49. God is so faithful that what He says He will do, He does. His strong right hand holds believers as they walk in righteousness as He declares,

Fear thou not; for I am with thee: be not dismayed; for I am thy God: I will strengthen thee; yea, I will help thee; yea, I will uphold thee with the right hand of my righteousness (Isaiah 41:10). Believers cling to His promises and declare unequivocally *great is thy faithfulness* (Lamentations 3:23).

50. God is faithful because He is unchanging and will always show the same faithfulness to every generation. *Therefore know that the LORD your God, He is God, the faithful God who keeps covenant and mercy for a thousand generations with those who Love Him and keep His commandments* (Deuteronomy 7:9 NKJV).

51. Let this be the seal and final proclamation from all believers regarding God's faithfulness as they quote God Himself when He declares *nevertheless My lovingkindness I will not utterly take from him, nor allow My faithfulness to fail* (Psalm 89:33 NKJV).

52. *Truth.* The Scriptures declare that He is *the only true God* (John 17:3). John says *that we may know Him that is true* (1 John 5:20 NKJV). This translation into the English language of "true" is the same meaning attached to "genuine" and "real." For God in Jesus Christ is truthfully "real and genuinely" *God manifested in the flesh.*

53. Jesus makes the personal declaration, *I am the truth* (John 14:6), and He has testified and witnessed to the truth. God is, in essence, truth personified in Jesus Christ.

54. There are numerous responses from God in His word about falseness, lying, and deceitfulness. God states He cannot lie (Titus 1:2). He also abhors lying or false witness to the extent that He commands Israel never to lie (Exodus 20:16).

55. While the origin of truthfulness is from the heart of God, the root of lying is from the devil's deception that casts doubt on the truth and causes people to compromise their values and character and ultimately be drawn into bearing false witness. Apostle Paul speaks to church members and tells them *not lie to one another* (Colossians 3:9 NKJV).

56. As Scripture declares that God is the only true God, it automatically positions all other gods as false. God is the *only true God* and, as such, the only One to whom mankind can go to receive truth about anything. Consequently, whatever is in the mind of God, there is no taint of an ulterior motive that is contrary to His actions or thoughts. His motives equal His actions and vice versa.

57. Among the vicarious works of the Holy Spirit in repentant people's hearts that includes the exposition of God's immense love, His gracious

offer of forgiveness, and His impartation of righteousness in believers' hearts, the most significant revelation to those repenting of their sin, is that they are faced with the realization that the One to whom they are confessing their sin is genuine (true) as they spiritually experience their sins being washed in the shed blood of Jesus Christ. This born-again moment in their lives is filled with the seal of the Holy Spirit as it reveals God's truthfulness that He will forgive and justify them in His presence.

58. The genuineness of the repentant sinner who truly believes that God cannot lie is engulfed in the promise that his sin is forgiven. From this truth, he steps into the world by faith as a new creation (2 Corinthians 5:17 NKJV) who believes that what he has done is accepted by the *only true God* and is sufficient to now be called a *son of God* (Romans 8:14).

59. Until Constantine became the ruler of Rome (A.D. 313), Christians were punished and martyred for their belief in Jesus Christ. In those fledgling years of the early church, the bulwark that fortressed their conviction was their constant faith that was embedded in the fact that, when they departed from the sinful path that they were walking (idolatry and ungodliness), they believed that what God promised was from His truthfulness and that He could not lie. They believed that, if they confessed their sin and believed in their heart that Jesus is the Christ and that He was raised from the dead, God, who is true, would forgive their sin and give them everlasting life. It was so entrenched in their souls that they were prepared to die because they believed God would not lie to them.

60. It is through this intrinsic characteristic that God, who is true, exists in truthfulness in every aspect of His thoughts and actions. His love produces this precious characteristic of truthfulness in all His ways.

61. *Glory.* The overriding characteristic that is unique to God is His glory. No one anywhere and nothing ever created can claim the majesty and the magnificence of His glory (Psalm 145:5). Everything else is counterfeit. *The brightness of His glory* (Hebrews 1:3), Jesus, the Christ (anointed One), and the holy presence of the Holy Spirit cause believers to fall prostrate before Him.

62. God's glory is the manifestation of His presence. It is spiritually discerned. It shines in the spirit of the Spirit-filled believer's spirit and witnesses to him that God, the Holy Spirit, is present.

63. His glory is the evidence of His impeccable reputation and requires the utmost honor and reverence from believers.

64. It is expedient to focus on the explanation the Word gives about the risen Savior, Jesus Christ. All the highest honors and promotions the Father bestows on Jesus are shadowed by the *brightness of His glory.* The writer in the letter to Hebrews says, *God, who at various times and in various ways spoke in time past to the fathers by the prophets, has in these last days spoken to us by His Son, whom He has appointed heir of all things, through whom also He made the worlds* (Hebrews 1:1-2 NKJV). Arthur W. Pink in his book *An Exposition of Hebrews* says, "The prophets, the angels, Moses, Joshua, the Levitical priesthood, the Old Testament men of faith, each come into view; each is compared with Christ, and each, in turn, fades away before His greater glory."

65. Jesus is highly exalted by the Father and is given the seat at the Father's right hand. In the exaltation of the Son, the writer expresses the words, *who being in the brightness of His glory* (verse 3), adorning Jesus with the unique and sovereign manifestation that exists within the Godhead, namely, their glory.

66. And, here Jesus is exalted as the *brightness,* meaning He is the light that shines forth from the Godhead's glory. Arthur Pink continues, "Just as far as the personal glory of the Son excels that of the prophets, so is the revelation God made through Christ more sublime and exalted than that which He made under Judaism. In the one He was made known as *Light*–the requirements, claims, demands of His holiness. In the other, He is manifested as *love*–the affections of His heart are displayed."

67. Furthermore, it is appropriate that the words of Jesus be studied regarding the Godhead's glory. It is in the gospel of John, chapter seventeen, that Jesus allows His faithful eleven disciples to look beyond the veil and witness the divine interlude between the Son and His Father. It is here that the Christian's *Apostle and High Priest* makes the most solemn and personal intercession. It is apt that in Jesus' prayer He references the glory He had with His Father: *Father, the hour has come. Glorify Your Son, that Your Son also may glorify You* (John 17:1).

68. With all His attributes securely held intact, Jesus prays to His Father asking, *Glorify Me together with Yourself, with the glory which I had with You before the world was* (John 17:5 NKJV). In all the miracles and

words Jesus spoke, He and the hearers glorified God every time. Jesus never once sought the glory that belonged to the Father. However, this was the time when, if He were glorified by the Father, the world would see and know God, *the only true God, and Jesus Christ whom* [He had] *sent* (John 17:3 NKJV).

69. Arthur Pink in his exhaustive work *Exposition of the Gospel of John* says, "Observe what Christ sought: to be glorified by the Father–not to be enriched by men, not to be honored by the world. Christ [also] prayed for this glory in order that He might glorify the Father."

70. God's glory fills the expanse of His creation, manifesting itself in every crevice, mountain top, and valley. Furthermore, the *Shekinah* glory impregnates the spirit of the Spirit-filled believer who radiates the Holy Spirit's presence.

71. God's glory manifests to believers that He is present. The glory of His presence produces spiritual light that enlightens believers' path enabling them to walk in His righteousness. Wayne Grudem says, "It is very appropriate that God's revelation of Himself should be accompanied by such splendor and brightness, for this glory of God is the visible manifestation of the excellence of God's character."

72. Unbelievers shun God's glory while believers run towards the *Light of the world* (John 8:12).

God the Father

73. Fatherhood is the most inspiring role the Godhead can deliver. God the Father denotes the custodianship of men who accept His offering as their provider, protector, and supplier of their every need.

74. Fatherhood is rooted in the very nature of God. Spirit-filled believers confess that *there is one God, the Father, of whom are all things, and we for Him* (1 Corinthians 8:6 NKJV).

75. God the Father is the eternal *Elohim* and source of all life. In Him all things are purposed and brought about. It is the securest expression of *agape* and is the fulfillment of the Father's unique function as the "parent" over His children, namely His sons and daughters.

76. Wayne Grudem explains the fatherhood role as the Father in the Godhead as follows: "What then are the differences between Father, Son, and Holy Spirit? There is no difference in attributes at all. The

only difference between them is the way they relate to each other and to the creation. The unique quality of the Father is the way He *relates as Father* to the Son and the Holy Spirit."

77. God is Father to all mankind and operates with equality to all. He is impartial and apportions equal measure when dealing with man. According to the prophet Malachi, God is Father to everyone; *have we not all one Father? Has not one God created us?* (Malachi 2:10 NKJV).

78. Consequently, God the Father relates to mankind as the Father who is personal to mankind. He is not remote and a "step-father" who looks from a distance with no responsibility over His children. He watches closely and with all diligence as the Psalmist declares, *Thou art my father, my God, and the rock of my salvation* (Psalm 89:26).

79. God's Fatherhood relationship is "one-on-one" with all mankind. His caring and provisions are unlimited and impartial. Matthew concurs by assuring, *For your heavenly Father knows that you need all these things* (Matthew 6:32 NKJV); and Apostle Paul affirms, *My God shall supply all your need according to His riches in glory by Christ Jesus* (Philippians 4:19 NKJV).

80. Creation, including mankind, is entirely at the discretion of the Father's will. He orchestrates all actions and predestines their beginning and end through His omniscient and omnipresent foreknowledge. The Word declares, *Are not two sparrows sold for a copper coin? And not one of them falls to the ground apart from your Father's will. But the very hairs of your head are numbered. Do not fear therefore; you are of more value than many sparrows* (Matthew 10:29-31, 18:14 NKJV).

81. Therefore, all things pertaining to creation and mankind are at the discretion of the Father's will. This is the overriding attribute of the Father's function, namely, that He wills (His intention and purpose) all things into existence and always knows all things.

82. In this divine will that the Father has, He is abundant in mercy (2 Corinthians 1:3). God, who is love, shows mercy pardoning the repentant sinner and forgives him. Because of His great mercy, He shows him grace. Likewise, to those who reject His love and offer of mercy, judgment and condemnation must be metered out to the lost sinner.

83. It is expedient that the Father's role in the Godhead be studied. The Father is the presiding head to whom both the Son and the Holy Spirit

submit. The Father sent the Son. The Father commissioned the Holy Spirit. Jesus demonstrates this when He calls on His Father in the Garden of Gethsemane: *Father, if thou be willing, remove this cup from me, nevertheless not my will, but thine be done* (Luke 22:42). Another reference of Jesus' submission to His Father occurs when He says, *But now I go away to Him who sent Me* (John 16:5 NKJV).

84. In the Godhead that is co-eternal, co-equal, and co-existent, Jesus knows His place and acknowledges that Fatherhood within the Godhead is equal in power, operating in unity with the Son and the Holy Spirit. Yet, authoritatively, as to the role of Father, Jesus says, *I am going to the Father, for My Father is greater than I* (John 16:28 NKJV).

85. Jesus confirms the Holy Spirit's submission to the Father when He mentions *the Helper, the Holy Spirit, whom the Father will send in My name* (John 16:26 NKJV). Apostle Peter also speaks of *those who have preached the gospel to you by the Holy Spirit sent from heaven—things which angels desire to look into* (1 Peter 1:12 NKJV).

86. Clearly, the Holy Spirit is "promised" and "sent" by the Father into the world and to empower believers. Luke records this when he writes, *And being assembled together with them, He commanded them not to depart from Jerusalem, but to wait for the Promise of the Father, "which," He said, "you have heard from Me."* (Acts 1:4 NKJV). The confirmation of the Holy Spirit's submission to the Father is vouched when Apostle Peter says, *Having received from the Father the promise of the Holy Spirit, He poured out this which you now see and hear* (Acts 2:33 NKJV).

87. To clarify the role of Father, the Godhead always works in unity of purpose. Within this unity of purpose, it is the Father who has the authoritative position which can be compared to His being the "source" of all things. The Son is the "sacrifice" that opened the way to salvation, and the Holy Spirit is the "supplier" of the power to convict sinners and empower Spirit-filled believers. They always work in one accord, co-equal, co-existent, and co-eternal.

88. Fatherhood is bound together in the indivisible chord of the Father's unconditional love. It is from His heart that He expresses Himself, *agape*, to the world (John 3:16) and towards believers as He commissions the Holy Spirit to empower them to be *more than conquerors through Him who loved* [them] (Romans 8:37).

God the Son

89. Pertaining to the Godhead, the Son is first expressed as *the Word. In the beginning was the Word, and the Word was with God, and the Word was God* (John 1:1).

90. The Son, *the Word,* has always been of the Godhead, and in fulfilling the will of the Father *the Word became flesh and dwelt among us* (John 1:14 NKJV). Thus, the eternal existence of the Son is expressed prior to His human Sonship as *the Word.*

91. The opening verses of Apostle John's gospel account causes the believer to look past the physical and material aspects of Jesus that pertain to His life on earth. It invites the believer to seek the intrinsic, holy, and pure existence of the Godhead, as well as the Godhead's underlying omniscience, omnipresence, and omnipotence. This is expressed in human terms as Deity manifested in the flesh.

92. Arthur Pink in his *Exposition of the Gospel of John* explains the opening verse of Apostle John's gospel: "*In the beginning was the Word,* and we are equally unable to grasp the final meaning of this. A 'word' is an expression: by words we articulate our speech. The Word of God, then, is Deity expressing itself in audible terms. *And the Word was with God,* and this intimates His separate personality, and shows His relation to the other Persons of the blessed [Godhead] Trinity. *And the Word was God.* Not only was Christ the Revealer of God, but He always was, and ever remains, none other than God Himself. Not only was our Savior the One through whom, and by whom, the Deity expressed itself in audible terms, but He was Himself co-equal with the Father and the Spirit."

93. To verify the eternal existence of Jesus Christ, Apostle John gives an undisputable reference that Jesus is in the eternal Godhead and has always been there. He declares, *In the beginning was the Word.* He does not say that "from the beginning the Word, Jesus, was there," but that Jesus Christ was *in the beginning with God.* Whatever the Godhead was about, Deity within the spoken word was announced through Jesus Christ.

94. Arthur Pink asserts, "Christ is the final spokesman of God. Closely connected with this is the Savior's title found in Revelation 1:8, *I am Alpha and Omega,* which intimates that He is God's alphabet, the One who spells out Deity, the One who utters all God has to say."

95. The writer of the New Testament letter to the Hebrews makes the prolific announcement about how God spoke in the last days: *God, who at various times and in various ways spoke in time past to the fathers by the prophets, has in these last days spoken to us by His Son, whom He has appointed heir of all things, through whom also He made the worlds; who being the brightness of His glory and the express image of His person, and upholding all things by the word of His power, when He had by Himself purged our sins, sat down at the right hand of the Majesty on high* (Hebrews 1:1-3 NKJV).

96. Apostle John seals the eternal existence of Jesus Christ when he says, *All things were made through Him, and without Him nothing was made that was made* (John 1:3 NKJV). The emphasis is on the statement that *without Him nothing was made that was made* which concludes that Jesus was Deity co-existent, co-equal, and co-eternal within the Godhead.

97. From the outset *the Word* was the creator of all things; *all things were created through Him and for Him* (Colossians 1:16 NKJV), *one Lord Jesus Christ, through whom are all things, and through whom we live* (1 Corinthians 8:6 NKJV). Matthew Henry gives a conclusive statement on this subject when he says, "God made the world by the word (Psalm 33:6) and Christ was the Word. By Him, not as a subordinate instrument, but as a co-ordinate agent, God made the world (Hebrews 1:2)."

98. Jesus the Christ, the Son of God, fully God, and co-equal in all aspects of the Godhead, is Deity personified, declaring (speaking), and bearing witness and testimony to mankind.

99. To fulfill the eternal purposes of God, the Father sent forth His Son (*the Word*) into the world *to make all see what is the fellowship of the mystery, which from the beginning of the ages has been hidden in God who created all things through Jesus Christ; to the intent that now the manifold wisdom of God might be made known by the church to the principalities and powers in the heavenly places, according to the eternal purpose which He accomplished in Christ Jesus our Lord* (Ephesians 3:9-11 NKJV).

100. Jesus Christ, the only begotten Son of the Father was *for this purpose* [. . .] *manifested, that he might destroy the works of the devil* (1 John 3:8). Jesus, the Son did this when He offered Himself as the sacrifice for sin.

101. Spirit-filled believers confess that the Lord Jesus Christ is the Son of God (Romans 1:4) who is both Lord and Christ (Acts 2:36). Furthermore,

the word of Eternal God emphatically teaches that Jesus Christ is the only begotten Son of God and He is unequivocally God (John 10:30).

102. Spirit-filled believers believe in Jesus Christ's incarnation and virgin birth (Matthew 1:20). Jesus Christ lived a sinless life on earth, fulfilled all the will of His Father in performing miracles, was love (*agape*) expressed in human form, and was crucified and raised from the dead.

103. Having accomplished the Father's purpose, the Son is endowed with Kingship over the Kingdom of God. Further, He is declared Lord of the church and baptizes believers with the Holy Spirit into the church which is His body. He has ascended into heaven where the Father exalted Him and gave Him the seat of honor and authority, saying, *Sit at My right hand, till I make your enemies your footstool* (Hebrews 1:13 NKJV).

104. Henceforth, the Son is the *Apostle and the High Priest* (Hebrews 3:1), *advocate* (1 John 2:1), and intercessor for the saints (Romans 8:34).

God the Holy Spirit

105. The Person of the Holy Spirit is of absolute equality with the Father and the Son and is equal to them as the source of all power and blessing (John 14:16-17, 26).

106. The omnipresence of the Holy Spirit has always been with mankind with His working upon them. From the birth of the church on the Day of Pentecost, the Holy Spirit has been and is now resident in believers who experience through faith the baptism with the Holy Spirit. The evidence of His indwelling is manifested by the initial physical sign of speaking with other tongues as the Holy Spirit gives them utterance (Acts 2:4).

107. The Holy Spirit's omnipresence will continue eternally throughout all generations of man.

108. The Holy Spirit possesses all the attributes of Deity. He is the Spirit of life (Romans 8:2), He is truth (John 16:13), is holiness (Ephesians 4:30), is eternal (Hebrews 9:14), and is omnipotent, omniscient, and omnipresent (Psalm 139:7).

109. Possessing these attributes of Deity, the Holy Spirit performs those acts and revelations that pertain to God. No human being can do what God

can. Man can make, but God creates. Creation was the prerogative of the divine Deity and implemented by the Spirit at creation (Genesis 1:1).

110. The Holy Spirit is sent by the Father and the Son to reveal to believers the deep spiritual message of God (1 Corinthians 2:10-11). He convicts the sinner and comforts the believer (John 16: 7-14).

Chapter 6

The Nature of God

1. The Word declares, *For My thoughts are not your thoughts, nor are your ways My ways, says the LORD. For as the heavens are higher than the earth, so are My ways higher than your ways, and My thoughts than your thoughts* (Isaiah 55:8-9 NKJV).

2. The essence of God's nature, His thought process, and the actions resulting from His nature, are completely opposite to man's nature. Man's nature stems from the stained "sin nature" inherited from Adam and Eve's fall into sin and death in the Garden of Eden. God's nature is unblemished.

3. The original nature that was given to Adam when God created him was perfect. However, Adam's nature had to be proved (tested) to qualify its righteous and pure condition. Until Adam's nature had gone through the test, it was "innocent." This innocence kept his nature in a perfect state, namely, without sin.

4. The test God laid on Adam's heart and soul hinged on one attribute: be obedient to God's command that *of the tree of the knowledge of good and evil you shall not eat* (Genesis 2:17 NKJV).

5. Adam disobeyed God's command and ate of the tree of knowledge of good and evil. This resulted in the contamination of Adam's nature, and the sin of disobedience permeated his natural abilities. The result of his disobedience was the enactment of God's proviso: *For in the day that you eat of it you shall surely die* (Genesis 2:17 NKJV).

6. Thus, Adam exchanged his "innocent" nature for one that acquired knowledge of good and evil. His nature had to be tested to prove that

it was worthy of its innocent state. He failed by disobeying God's one command.

7. Since then, now residing in man is the sin-stained nature that is contrary to God's nature.

8. God purposed through His Son, Jesus Christ, a reconciliation of the relationship with mankind. Jesus took upon Himself the sin of mankind and was condemned to hell to pay the punishment of a sinner and, more so, the sin-stained nature of mankind.

9. Jesus perfected the process, and man can now be reinstated to his original state with God. This state is returned to him when he decides to accept Jesus Christ as Savior. Once this is done, God in Jesus Christ and God the Holy Spirit once again dwells within a man's spirit. Essentially, it is the indwelling nature of God that now resides within man's spirit.

10. What follows is the application of God's indwelling nature within man. This implementation of God's nature by man in his daily life is what ultimately draws him to have a closer relationship with Jesus Christ.

11. What then are the contents of God's nature that man must pay the closest attention to as he *draws nigh unto God?* (James 4:8). There are five intrinsic and fundamental attributes (or elements) in the distinctive nature of God as revealed in the Bible. These attributes require a gracious response of the people to His grace as they become molded into His likeness. These attributes are the following:

Love
Divine
Holy
Pure
Righteous

12. To express each attribute in the fullest extent, it is important to understand them and be considered from God's perspective and not analyzed by man's intellect. God's ways are higher than man's ways and His thoughts are above man's thoughts. Therefore, God's nature must be examined from His Word. Therein is hidden the foundation of every attribute and the effect it must have on mankind.

13. At the outset, let it be known that God is indivisible and completely One. When considering His attributes, the intention is not to dissect God into various parts, but merely establish His total uniqueness and unity within all that He is.

14. The Apostle Paul exhorts the brethren to *look not at the things which are seen, but at the things which are not seen* (2 Corinthians 4:18 NKJV). Here he relates the trials and struggles the believers endure in the physical and visible ("seen") aspects of life to the indwelling Holy Spirit's conquering power. His focus is not fixed on the sufferings or victories of the flesh, but rather on the unseen attributes of God's nature within him. His relationship with Jesus Christ is more valuable to him than any "seen" accomplishment or struggle.

15. The application of God's nature in a believer's life is the most effective testimony he can have. Hence, the Word declares *for in Him we live, and move, and have our being* (Acts 17:28).

16. When the five attributes are mentioned in the Bible, it is vital that they are measured against the four "absolutes" that constitute the infinity of God.

17. Man has no vocabulary to express the eternal "existence" of God. Man's finite mind cannot fully comprehend the infinite God.

18. God is outside of "measurement". God is beyond man's capability of categorization. Nothing is measurable against God's actuality as an infinite Being.

19. The four "absolutes" pertaining to God, in human terms, are that He is:

Eternal

Omnipotent

Omnipresent

Omniscient

20. These absolutes encircle God's nature. They are a binding cord that holds the eternal state of God's nature intact. They surround the five attributes like a fortress wall that shields God's infinite nature.

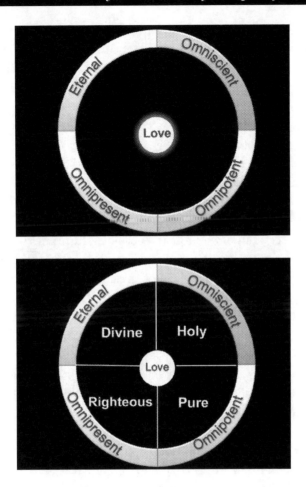

God is Love

21. Within the circle of God's four absolutes, resides the center of who He is–love. God is not a God of love; He is love (1 John 4:8). The remaining attributes contained in His nature are intrinsically wrapped in love. Hence, love is the center of all that God is. Love is, therefore, *a wheel in the middle of a wheel* (Ezekiel 1:16 NKJV).

22. If there has ever been an attack on the Godhead, then it is the deceit and confusion Satan sows in people's minds regarding who God is. The divine, holy presence of God flows from the very Being of who God is. *God is Love*; He is not the God who loves, He is entirely Love.

23. The Greek concept of the word "love" loosely translated into the English language dilutes the very essence of who God is. Flesh to flesh, the word is "eros" in Greek, but translated as "love." This is directed at the feelings between a man and a woman. Brotherly love is "phileo" which is also translated as "love," is the expression for the feeling between people, kinship, and is charitable in its application. Finally, the love that is God is "agape," yet translated as "love."

24. At the outset, let it be known and believed that there is no fruit or by-product of God that is "agape." God's eternal Spiritual existence, omniscience, omnipotent, and omnipresence is altogether Agape.

25. The awesome, unexplainable ever-present presence and involvement in every aspect of all of creation and act of God is immersed in this one revelation: *God is Love*. Every human being has a constant demonstration of Agape when they view God's creation. Every minute detail of the magnificent creation leaves believers aghast as they absorb the manifestation of the love that divinely formed the habitat and cosmos.

26. Yet, the personal experience every person has when he encounters Agape as the Holy Spirit reveals who God is and immerses them in unending love. Love/Agape opens the door to man's spirit to expose God to him. This is the relevance Jesus referenced when He told Nicodemus, *you must be born again*. It is because *God so loved the world* that the Holy Spirit reveals Agape–God. This Agape bursts forth into the heart/spirit of the person. Apostle Paul speaks of *Christ in you, the hope of glory* (Colossians 1:27). Love/agape takes up residence in the born-again believer's spirit, and he becomes a *new creation* (2 Corinthians 5:17).

27. *God is Spirit* (John 4:24), and the intrinsic attribute that constitutes God is entirely agape. To illustrate the explanation further, water constitutes both the elements of hydrogen and oxygen, which are two atoms that form a liquid substance of water when combined. Conversely, God is entirely agape, and He contains only one element, namely, love/agape.

28. The nature of God must, therefore, be anchored in who God is. It is because God is love/agape that the spiritual attributes of righteousness, holiness, pureness, and His divine presence flow from His heart to mankind. His absolutes of eternality, omnipresence, omnipotence, and omniscience are the effects of the composition of who He is. The entire Godhead, Father, the Word (Son), and Holy Spirit, are entirely love.

29. Every activity the Godhead undertakes is propelled by their unconditional love that always has a desire to replenish, build, mature, and improve a believer's life.

30. To adequately describe the qualities of this love, man must forgo his human and carnal aspiration of love. God is Spirit, and His agape can only be *spiritually discerned* (1 Corinthians 2:14).

31. When a Spirit-filled believer gets a glimpse of this immense agape, it raises him up on eagles' wings (Isaiah 40:31). Such revelation exposes him to the deepest intentions of God's divine purposes for him.

32. God – Agape – desires a spiritual personal relationship with mankind whom He created. He desires a righteous, sanctified, and holy spirit/ heart to be intricately fused in His love. His ultimate desire is not for wealth, health, or pleasures forever more for His children. (He has the windows of heaven wide open, and they are already being poured out (Malachi 3:10)). What He desires is a spiritual relationship with a holy saint.

33. The entrance into His presence brings spiritual light (Psalm 27:1), and this light brings the Spirit-filled believer into a place where he abandons everything he desires for himself and pours out his being (everything he is) so that God can work through him to perform His will. The source of love is God; and from the pinnacle of this source, a river begins to flow through the Spirit-filled believer's life touching others *for Christ's sake* (2 Corinthians 12:10). The Spirit-filled believer has no idea, or even concern, for God's intentions in using him as a river of life. His only focus remains on the source, agape/love, that flows through him.

34. When Spirit-filled believers reach this height in their relationship with Agape, then they know the measure of their insignificance compared to God's all-in-all love. Agape breaks through the barriers of self-will, self-righteousness and selfishness. It bursts asunder the hindrances of "I can't," "I'm not worthy," and "My past is too corroded by sin" as it gushes forth like a river of living water nourishing all who cross his path. In the Bible Jesus declares, *He who believes in Me, as the Scripture has said, out of his heart will flow rivers of living water. But this He spoke concerning the Spirit, whom those believing in Him would receive; for the Holy Spirit was not yet given because Jesus was not yet glorified* (John 7:38-39 NKJV).

35. Spiritual Agape knows no boundaries. It is most active, expressing its truest intentions when the Holy Spirit exposes this love to a person kneeling at the Cross. Furthermore, Agape, demonstrates its deepest intentions when a believer confesses his sins, and the crimson flow of the Blood of the Cross cleanses him from all sin (1 John 1:7). Even more so, Agape fulfills its fullest intentions when He casts a repentant heart's sin into the sea of forgetfulness and remembers them no more.

36. Apostle John exalts God and who He is, Agape, to the loftiest pedestal and crowns biblical teaching by focusing on love. Love is the foundation of everything God intended *for God so loved the world* (John 3:16, 17:23, 1 John 3:16).

37. Apostle John continues his declaration on love by embracing God's Agape that is continually being demonstrated towards mankind; and consequently, that same agape flows through believers towards brothers and sisters in Christ, *in this the love of God was manifested toward us, that God has sent His only begotten Son into the world, that we might live through Him. In this is love, not that we loved God, but that He loved us and sent His Son to be the propitiation for our sins. Beloved, if God so loved us, we ought also to love one another* (1 John 4:9-11 NKJV).

38. The human mind cannot fully comprehend or express the contents of the statement *God is love.* Agape lovingly recognizes, reveals, and redeems the sinner's condition. God removes every hindrance which sin encapsulates in a repentant man's heart. It is a lightning strike on the repentant heart immediately removing the impediment of inherent sin, and a gentle rain of blessed assurance, comfort, and caring for His beloved that culminates in the promise of eternal life to everyone who believes. Consequently, to them who shun this precious gift, they are left to the peril of their unrepentant condition, and subsequently, must face His wrath and judgment because *He who believes in the Son has everlasting life; and he who does not believe the Son shall not see life, but the wrath of God abides on him* (John 3:36 NKJV).

39. Extending from this inner circle of love and surrounded by the four absolutes, reside the remaining attributes of God's nature.

Chapter 7

God's nature is Divine.

1. Continuing the doctrine of God's nature, God's holy word declares that His nature is *divine*. Apostle Peter refers to God's nature *as His divine power* [that] *has given to us all things that pertain to life and godliness, through the knowledge of Him who called us by glory and virtue, by which have been given to us exceedingly great and precious promises, that through these* [we] *may be partakers of the divine nature, having escaped the corruption that is in the world through lust* (2 Peter 1:3-4 NKJV).

2. Ancient translators have used the Greek word *theios* to mean "Godhead." The more accurate translation is "divine nature" and is used only twice in the Bible. It signifies the "totality" of the deity of the Godhead. "Divinity" *(theios)* is the expression emphasized in the Greek as One who is above all things without beginning and end and is entirely sovereign, sacred, and unique. There is only One God; and it is the divine God, Creator of all things. When extending the word *theios* to *theotes*, this all-encompassing declaration is also understood to mean the "Godhead" in the New Testament, namely "all of God."

3. Thus the Bible correctly records that God's nature is divine, meaning it is rightly emphasizing that God is totally sovereign and sacred; and there is none other like Him.

4. The only One to whom this adjective can be applied is God. Nothing else ever created, and nothing else sculptured from man's hands out of the most precious of commodities can ever be declared divine. Let the Holy Writ express God's divinity: *God, who made the world and everything in it, since He is Lord of heaven and earth, does not*

dwell in temples made with hands. Nor is He worshiped with men's hands, as though He needed anything, since He gives to all life, breath, and all things. And He has made from one blood every nation of men to dwell on all the face of the earth, and has determined their preappointed times and the boundaries of their dwellings, so that they should seek the Lord, in the hope that they might grope for Him and find Him, though He is not far from each one of us; for in Him we live and move and have our being, as also some of your own poets have said, 'For we are also His offspring.' Therefore, since we are the offspring of God, we ought not to think that the Divine Nature is like gold or silver or stone, something shaped by art and man's devising (Acts 17:24-29 NKJV).

5.   It is, therefore, correct to declare that God's nature is divine, encompassing every aspect of Him, reaffirming that each attribute in His nature is divine. Divinity can only be ascribed to God, the eternal, the omniscient, omnipotent, and omnipresent One. He alone as Creator of all things is the Supreme Being and who is divine.

6.   Delving a little more deeply into God's divine nature reveals the first description worthy of consideration is the expression the "deity" of God. When applied to God, it expresses the uniqueness of God as the Supreme Being, Creator, and Eternal One. Human comprehension of God's eternal existence cannot be fully explained, and thus "deity" is used to denote His fullness in all things.

7.   *The International Standard Bible Encyclopedia, Volume D-E* gives the following explanation of "deity": "Deity is the term that defines the essence of God and the quality of the Divine. It is a character trait that makes God who He is and sets Him apart as worthy of worship."

8.   Furthermore, God's divine nature is *sovereign*. There is nothing that is not under His control or ever happens without His knowledge. He alone is the Supreme Commander who orchestrates His universe, His earthly creatures, and their habitat. He alone has the supreme authority to control everything He has made.

9.   Sovereignty is God's ability to control and govern over all things. He is the ruler over all reality. Because God is divine and He is responsible for all things created, He has dominion over all things. His words and actions are final, and He needs no one and nothing to tell Him what to do. His declarations, decisions, and instructions are without

questioning. No one can ever question God's judgments and His rulership, and ask, *If He takes away, who can hinder Him? Who can say to Him, what are You doing?* (Job 9:12 NKJV). *As for the Almighty, we cannot find Him: He is excellent in power, in judgment and abundant justice* (Job 37:23 NKJV).

10. In His sovereignty, God encompasses all wisdom and is the Source of it. Embodied in this immeasurable wisdom, God executes His sovereignty for the benefit of mankind.

11. In His perfect sovereignty, God is revered, honored, and worshiped by everyone. His wisdom, power, strength, and glory are the description of Who He is because His divine nature is sovereign.

12. God's sovereignty is best described in His holy Word by the heavenly host who said, *I heard the voice of many angels around the throne, the living creatures, and the elders; and the number of them was ten thousand times ten thousand, and thousands of thousands, saying with a loud voice: 'Worthy is the Lamb who was slain to receive power and riches and wisdom and strength and honor and glory and blessing!" And every creature which is in heaven and on the earth and under the earth and such as are in the sea, and all that are in them, I heard saying: "blessing and honor and glory and power be to Him who sits on the throne, and to the Lamb, forever and ever!"* (Revelation 5:11-13 NKJV).

13. To expand the explanation further, God's divine nature is *sacred*. It is eternally divine and, thus, eternally sacred. It is inherently blameless and without blemishes. From His throne, His divine utterances are sacred and, therefore, sacrosanct and without question.

14. By contrast to the worldly decrees that are termed "sacred" and are declared from earthly kings, and stem from a sin-stained heart, the sacred decrees from God's throne are from a pure, wise, and holy King and Lord. The subjects ruled by an earthly king question the decrees from their king. On the other hand, the decrees from God are never questioned by believers.

15. God's instructions are sacred and followed by believers because every utterance from the holy throne is saturated in God's divine holiness, wisdom, glory, and power.

16. So sacred are His words that He is present in them: *In the beginning was the Word, and the Word was with God, and the Word was God. And the Word became flesh* (John 1:1; 14 NKJV).

God's nature is Holy.

17. The most sublime attribute of God's nature is the fact that He is holy.
18. To fully define this holy state is impossible. However, the following explanation declares God's holiness best as Dr. Herbert Lockyer says, "As the absolute holy One God is free from evil and hates and abhors sin (Leviticus 19:2). He is 'glorious in holiness.' (Exodus 15:11). As the sun cannot darken, so God cannot act unrighteously, 'He is the Holy One' (Job 6:10). Holiness is His inward character–not merely a trait of His Being, but His very essence–not one of a list of virtues but the sum of all excellencies rather than an excellence."
19. When God's holiness begins to be understood in man's finite mind, holiness provokes a holy reverence (fear) within the human soul and spirit. God's holiness is His Spiritual covering, His indwelling dynamo, the instigator of His thought process, and the reason for His actions.
20. It is not merely the understanding on the part of man to declare that God is a holy God. God, Himself, declares, *For I the LORD am holy* (Leviticus 20:26). Again, God declares, *For I am God and not man, the Holy One in your midst* (Hosea 11:9 NKJV).
21. God's most emphatic intrinsic attribute that separates Him from mankind is His holiness. It is the essence of who He is, and holiness can never be abandoned nor ignored in everything God is and does.
22. Jesus Christ, the holy One (Luke 1:35), declares that His Father is holy. He prays, *Holy Father* (John 17:11). The Son of Man is not slack concerning the reference to His Father's holy nature. He addresses God the Father by acknowledging the Father's highest attribute, namely His holiness. Furthermore, when teaching the Jews to pray, Jesus directs them to proclaim that their heavenly Father's name is incomparable and unique; *hallowed be thy name* (Matthew 6:9).
23. In an attempt to acknowledge God in His unique and most significant attribute, the seraphim that are charged with the custody of the holy throne of God circle the throne; and the only accolade they voice in His presence is *holy, holy, holy is the LORD of hosts; the whole earth is full of His glory* (Isaiah 6:3 NKJV).
24. The seraphim do not address God's unlimited power, His omnipotence, omniscience, omnipresence, or His eternal state. They are engulfed in God's holy estate.

25. God's holiness is above man's finite intellect. His unlimited holiness knows no boundaries, and it is far deeper and higher than the human mind can comprehend. In an attempt to explain God's holiness, it is best to divide God's holiness into three categories: spiritual, sacred, and separate.

26. *God is Spirit* (John 4:24) and the Godhead, Father, Son, and Holy Spirit are holy. God is the source of holiness. He has been and will always be holy. The intrinsic measure of God's spiritual existence is His holiness.

27. God does not have to do anything to prove He is holy. He does not have to explain how He is holy because God is infinitely above human comprehension and, therefore, His perfect holiness is outside man's intellect. It is man's acceptance, by faith, that God, whom man serves, is beyond the grasp of the human definition of perfect holiness.

28. God is viewed in the human spirit as the matchless and incorruptible source of spiritual edification. The command, *Be ye holy, for I am holy* (1 Peter 1:16), resounds in the human spirit, knowing that the source of the holiness that God is exacting from His children is Himself.

29. Holiness, and any reference to it, is intrinsically blended into who God is. Man cannot mention God without referencing the fact that He is holy. This attribute is the spiritual presentation of the entire constitution of God. As Spirit, there is not one aspect of Almighty God that is not holy; *No one is holy like the LORD* (1 Samuel 2:2 NKJV).

30. God's Spirit permeates every corner of His creation with His holiness. There is never a place He has created that can hide from His presence. In the vast expanse of His creation in the heavens, the cosmos, or within the human frame, God's Spirit is presented as holy.

31. Man's response to God and His holiness is first the acceptance that wherever God is spiritually evidenced, there His holiness is. The exquisite spiritual presence is discerned in the human spirit when man realizes the corruptible sinful state he is in as opposed to the holy spiritual attribute within the Holy God's presence.

32. The acknowledgement and acceptance that God's holy presence is everywhere is the reason why mortals bow down and worship God and say like the Psalmist, *Exalt the LORD our God, and worship at His footstool–He is holy* (Psalm 99:5). Mankind's acknowledgment of God's holiness reaches into man's spirit and demands attention. This results in the second step believers take: they either reject or accept God's holiness. Believers receive the holy presence of God and surrender to the Holy Spirit and worship God *in spirit and in truth* (John 4:24).

33. Man's spirit is the receptacle and place that responds to God's holiness. Because God is Spirit, He interacts with believers' spirits to direct their decisions and activity. This spiritual interaction is confirmed by Apostle Paul who says man *is joined to the Lord is one spirit with Him* (1 Corinthians 6:17 NKJV). The Gospel of Luke records, *My spirit has rejoiced in God my Savior* (Luke 1:47 NKJV). Apostle Paul states that it is from his spirit that he serves the Lord, whom he asserts, *I serve with my spirit* (Romans 1:9 NKJV).

34. Not only is the holy attribute spiritual, but it is also sacred.

35. There is no comparison or measurement the human mind can conjure up to match the sacred holiness of God. It is sacred because it is unique to God. His very being is entirely holy, making it sacred, which is without measurement. God's sacredness is inimitable to Him, and it has no equivalent.

36. It is so sacred that those who attempt to mimic God's sacred holiness or even consider declaring that they are as sacred are nothing but self-righteous and become self-indulgent.

37. Every "sacred" edifice created by human hands, every utterance declared by the human tongue proclaiming that they are as sacred as God are a mere shell by comparison to the intrinsic sacredness attributed to God's holy nature.

38. In this declaration that God's holy nature is sacred, every created being must show respect and honor to God. It is not merely fitting that believers show the highest level of respect; God's sacred holiness demands it.

39. It is, therefore, without contradiction, that He who is holy speaks words that are holy. God's words are for the believers who understand that His words flow through their spirits, and that they have been uttered from their sacred God who is incomparable and unique.

40. The ultimate definition of God's sacred holiness is best expressed when declared "incomparable" and "unique." Its being divine, unblemished, and sacred can only be attributed to God's holiness. Unlike everything man strives to accomplish and "be" that requires him to experience a spiritual rebirth, have his sin blotted out, be sanctified in the washing of the holy Word, and put off the ways of the flesh to become a worthy cleansed child of God, there is nothing God had to do, has to do, or still needs to accomplish His sacred holiness.

41. God's sacredness is inherent in His very nature that needs no additional development or adjustments. God's sacred holiness is sovereign to Him. Thus, sacredness occupies the loftiest pedestal in heaven's throne room as it presents God's holiness to those who love Him.

42. This holy attribute is not only spiritual and sacred, but it is also entirely separate.

43. There is nothing and no one who can claim his holy existence as emanating from his own doing. God alone is holy, and His very Alpha and Omega existence (without beginning and without end) is holy. God's holiness is unique to Him and separates Him from everything else.

44. *Come out from among them and be separate, says the Lord* (2 Corinthians 6:17 NKJV) is the command God gives to His children. This separation is necessary for the believer to *be holy, for I am holy* (1 Peter 1:16 NKJV). He instructs His children to separate themselves like this because He is separate from all sin and uncleanness.

45. God's separateness is unique to Him because it is impossible for Him to be contaminated. He is the Author of His distinguishable trait of holiness which separates Him for everything else. God did not have to create holiness; He is holy. Neither did God have to acquire holiness; He is inherently holy. God did not have to sacrifice any other attribute so that His holiness could be separated from all else; He is holy and, therefore, separated from all frailty and sin.

46. Consequently, on the Day of the Lord and at the Great White Throne Judgment, Holy God, represented by His eternal holy Son, Jesus Christ, will take His place as the holy God and judge according to His holiness. Apostle John says, *Who shall not fear You, O Lord, and glorify Your name? For You alone are holy . . . for Your judgments have been manifested* (Revelation 15:4 NKJV).

47. Such then is God's holiness. It is immeasurable, all encompassing, and intrinsically existing in every aspect of His nature.

Chapter 8

God's nature is Righteous.

1. The dominant reflection cast from every word in the Bible, relates to the absolute righteousness of God and the utter depravity of the human soul. Apostle Paul is emphatic when he declares, *There is none righteous, no, not one* (Romans 3:10 NKJV). He continues by affirming *the righteousness of God, through faith in Jesus Christ, to all and on all who believe. For there is no difference; for all have sinned and fall short of the glory of God* (Romans 3:22-23 NKJV).

2. God's righteousness has no comparison, and no creature has this inherent attribute. Only God is inherently righteous as the Psalmist proclaims, *Righteous are You, O LORD, and upright are Your judgments* (Psalm 119:137 NKJV). The very foundation of God's dealing with man from His heavenly spiritual throne contain the attributes of *righteousness and justice* [that] *are the foundation of* [His] *throne* (Psalm 89:14 NKJV).

3. Chrysostom (A.D. 349-407) gives insight to the everlasting, inherent righteousness of God when he says, "Paul does not say that the righteousness of God has been 'given' but that it has been 'manifested,' [revealed] thus destroying the accusation that it is something new. For what is 'manifested' is old but previously concealed. He reinforces this point by going on to mention that the Law and the Prophets had foretold it."

4. Unlike man, God's righteous nature did not need a sacrifice to make Him righteous; neither did God need to repent of anything to make Him righteous. He is righteous, and the basis of the relationship and the fellowship man has with God is founded upon man's repenting of

his inherent sin (unrighteous state), exercising his faith in the finished work of Calvary, accepting Jesus Christ as Lord, and doing so that he *might be made the righteousness of God in him* (2 Corinthians 5:21).

5. Because God is righteous, which is the essence of His being, He can, therefore, never be unrighteous. It is the intrinsic attribute within His nature that prevents God from being unrighteous.

6. Righteousness is behavior reflecting what is just and right. It is the "rightness" exercised in every thought and action. In this definition, God is always just and right because *the just LORD is in the midst thereof; he will not do iniquity: every morning doth he bring his judgment to light, he faileth not* (Zephaniah 3:5).

7. Being righteous indicates that God's righteous nature permanently operates justly; hence, He always does what is right. While God's holy nature explains His intrinsic attribute of who He is, righteousness is the attribute that explains God's nature in His dealings with mankind. God measures everything mankind does or says against His righteousness.

8. Furthermore, God is righteous because of His mercy and justice. The Old Covenant was the basis of God's mercy towards His people affording them the privilege of learning righteousness. Now in Christ Jesus our Lord, the Better Covenant extends God's mercy to all humanity when He sent Jesus as the sacrifice for the "whosoever will" (John 3:16).

9. Because of the declaration of man's faith in Christ's finished work on Calvary *so also by one Man's obedience* [Jesus obediently giving His life on the Cross] *many will be made righteous* (Romans 5:19 NKJV). Ambrosiaster (A.D. 366) made this profound statement hundreds of years ago about God's righteousness: "What else comes through faith in Jesus Christ except the righteousness of God which is the revelation of Christ? For it is by faith in the revelation of Jesus Christ that the gift long ago promised by God is acknowledged and received."

10. The Law exposed man's unrighteous state, deeds, and thoughts. The governing measurement that exposed people's sin while under the Law was the fact that their actions and thoughts transgressed God's righteousness. The prophets during this time revealed this transgression against God's righteousness when they compared the actions of the people against the standards imposed in the Law.

11. The Law did not reveal God's righteousness, it merely exposed man's unrighteousness that was against God's laws. No one could escape the

punishment for transgressing the Law. People had to do something (sacrifice a spotless lamb) to have their sins covered. The arrival of Jesus Christ on earth was the manifestation (revelation) of God's righteousness in their midst.

12. Apostle Paul reinforces this doctrine when he says, *But now the righteousness of God apart from the law is revealed* [manifested], *being witnessed by the Law and the Prophets* (Romans 3:21 NKJV).

13. It must be understood that while the Law governed mankind's actions and thoughts, they were held accountable for their wrongdoing which was measured against the standards within the Law. The prophets and the Law referenced the fact that the Law originated from a righteous God. However, it was the transgression of the Law and not necessarily against the righteousness of God that posed the punishment, but it was against the Law that they transgressed.

14. The New Covenant is a *better covenant* (Hebrews 7:22) because now into the midst of mankind, righteousness is revealed through Jesus Christ, and it is appropriated to those who repent and receive Him as Lord, *even the righteousness of God, through faith in Jesus Christ, to all and on all who believe* (Romans 3:22 NKJV).

15. Because righteousness is manifested through Jesus Christ, man is blessed by God to have Him appropriate righteousness in his spirit because of what Jesus did and because *of Him you are in Christ Jesus, who became for us wisdom from God—and righteousness and sanctification and redemption.* This is possible only because of what Jesus did on Calvary as Apostle Paul states, *For He made Him who knew no sin to be sin for us, that we might become the righteousness of God in Him* (2 Corinthians 5:21 NKJV).

16. God declares in His word that He alone is the only One who deals justly with mankind; and as He says through Isaiah, *There is no other God besides Me, a just God and a Savior: There is none beside Me* (Isaiah 45:21 NKJV).

17. This emphatic statement by God regarding His uniqueness relates to the fulfillment of His promise that *If we confess our sins, He is faithful and just to forgive us our sins and to cleanse us from all unrighteousness* (1 John 1:9 NKJV).

18. Conversely, if God is to deal justly with a repentant heart, He will meter the same just judgment on the unrepentant heart: *Oh, let the wickedness of the wicked come to an end, but establish the just: for the*

righteous God tests the hearts and minds. My defense is of God, who saves the upright in heart. God is a just judge, and God is angry with the wicked every day (Psalm 7:9-11 NKJV).

19. This "anger" God shows towards the wicked is manifested during the Great Tribulation when God deals justly with the wickedness of the sinner *since it is a righteous thing with God to repay with tribulation those who trouble you* (2 Thessalonians 1:6 NKJV). Furthermore, *You are righteous, O Lord, the One who is and who was and who is to be, because You have judged these things. For* [the wicked] *they have shed the blood of saints and the prophets, and You have given them blood to drink. For it is their just due* (Revelation 16: 5-6 NKJV).

20. God does not have to prove to anyone that He is righteous. His "right" dealing with mankind's sin, the fulfillment of every promise He has made, and the ever-present witness of the Holy Spirit proclaim His righteous nature.

21. With the intrinsic righteousness God's nature possesses and because of it, He is enabled always to be right in everything He does or says. All His judgments are right, and all His promises are *yea and amen* (2 Corinthians 1:20), and *His righteousness endures forever* (2 Corinthians 9:9 NKJV).

22. God does not only always do the right things; He always does things right.

23. His righteous nature produces mercy that is shown to all mankind. This *mercy* produces *grace* that is shed abroad in every repentant sinner's heart. Because of the grace that is shown, God's *forgiveness* gushes forth into the repentant sinner's spirit and soul as the blood of Jesus Christ cleanses him from all sin. Without hesitation, because of the righteous nature of God, He blots out the iniquity within the repentant heart; and the repentant sinner is *justified* and declared *righteous* in God's eyes (Titus 3:4-7). Consequently, God's righteous nature that produces mercy reaches into the miry clay and plucks the sin-stained soul from the devil's clutches and places it in the palm of His hand. *But God who is rich in mercy because of His great love with which He loved us, even when we were dead in trespasses, made us alive together with Christ (by grace you have been saved), and raised us up together and made us sit in the heavenly places in Christ Jesus* (Ephesians 2:4-6 NKJV).

24. God shows mercy because He deals justly and rightly with every repentant sinner's heart. The Psalmist says, *Have mercy upon me, O God, according to Your loving-kindness; according to the multitude of Your tender mercies, blot out my transgressions* (Psalm 51:1 NKJV).

25. Mercy can only be shown to the guilty. The innocent do not need mercy. The just God deals justly and with loving-kindness fulfills His promise that, *if we confess our sins, He is faithful and just to cleanse us* (1 John 1:9 NKJV). God honors His Word, and continually shows mercy towards the guilty heart that repents *for His mercy endures forever* (Psalm 118:1 NKJV).

26. It is because God's nature is righteous that He shows mercy that produces this immeasurable pardon towards the repentant heart. The moment the individual repents, confesses his sin, and seeks God's forgiveness, the Father spiritually applies the blood of Jesus that blots out the iniquity within the heart; *the blood of Jesus Christ his Son cleanseth us from all sin* (1 John 1:7).

27. The righteous God demands that the believer be righteous; for without the righteousness of God residing in the believer's heart, there can be no relationship and fellowship between God and man. Created man has no righteousness of his own. It is imputed to him by God; and as such, man is wholly dependent on God's grace *that* [he] *might become the righteousness of God in Him* (2 Corinthians 5:21 NKJV).

God's nature is Pure.

28. The intellectual and worldly dictionary expresses *pure* as something or someone being *flawless, perfect, genuine, and virtuous.* Taking these interpretations of *pure* to their logical conclusion, the Holy Writ must surely reference these adjectives; and it does.

29. God's *pure* nature is flawless, without spot or blemish. The Word declares, *the words of the LORD are pure words, like silver tried in a furnace of earth, purified seven times* (Psalm 12:6 NKJV). God's *words* are pure. They can only come from a pure heart, a pure state of being, and a pure motive.

30. Every utterance and every action emanating from God's heart is flawless in its intent and application. It is never contaminated by impure intentions or motives. God's motives and intentions with mankind are

pure, exacting His righteous and just promises. There is *no variation or shadow of turning* (James 1:17 NKJV); and what God has done, is doing, and will continue to do forever is always pure because it emanates from His pure heart.

31. The eternal existence of God makes the declaration that God's purity is flawless a unique statement. God has been and always will be flawless. This truth is what supports the definition of His being pure. God's nature is, therefore, unstained. It is no wonder that Apostle John says, *His countenance was like the sun shining in its strength* (Revelation 1:16 NKJV). His *countenance* displays the *brightness of His glory* (Hebrews 1:3 NKJV) which is none other than His sovereignty, holiness, righteousness, and pureness which is flawless, perfect, and genuine.

32. God is forever without spot or blemish. God's nature is untarnished and stainless. The very presence of Jesus on earth manifested (revealed) the purity of the Godhead because Jesus is the One *who knew no sin* (2 Corinthians 5:21 NKJV) and was the only One who can be acclaimed as such because the Holy Writ declares, *For such a High Priest was fitting for us, who is holy, harmless, undefiled* [pure and flawless], *separate from sinners, and has become higher than the heavens* (Hebrews 7:26 NKJV).

33. God is apart from sin. Sin has no ability to tarnish His existence. Sin cannot enter the realm of God's pureness because unlike mankind, His nature is pure and without any flaws through which sin can enter. Hence, God's pure attribute is termed flawless.

34. Satan constantly seeks for the flaw in mankind's nature. He searches their actions to determine their intentions. Once he has established the kink (flaw) in man's armor, he enters through the flaw and sows his evil intentions that provoke sinfulness. God has no kink (flaw) in His nature. Satan can never find a foothold in God's pure nature. God is above every reproach and approach from Satan. And, Satan knows this fact.

35. Inasmuch as God's nature is flawless, so is it perfect as declared in Jesus' own words, *your Father which is in heaven is perfect* (Matthew 5:48). Perfection is outside of measurement. There are no degrees of perfection. Hence, God's pureness is unblemished and never contaminated by the slightest taint of imperfection.

36. Because God's nature is pure, thus perfect, all His ways are, therefore, perfect. The Bible declares, *As for God, His way is perfect* (Psalm 18:30;

2 Samuel 22:31 NKJV). There is never any imperfect, guile infested motive aligned in God's ways. Every way intended and implemented by God is perfect from its inception.

37. It is a foregone conclusion that, if God's ways are perfect, then His works are perfect: *He is the Rock, His work is perfect* (Deuteronomy 32:4 NKJV). Flowing from God's pure heart that has perfect intentions, His perfect works emanate.

38. This state of perfection is constantly applied in all of God's intentions and works. He is beyond variance in His nature and character: *Every good gift and every perfect gift is from above, and comes down from the Father of lights, in whom there is no variation or shadow of turning* (James 1:17 NKJV).

39. God's pure nature has yet another explanation: it is genuine. In God's pureness, the flawless, perfect pureness is instigated from God's heart. This is not a copied or adapted pureness; it is genuine (real) pureness. It is not a front for a different intention; it is genuine in its existence and has no ulterior motive contrary to God's pure intention and purpose.

40. Flowing from His nature, every commandment God produces is from a genuine heart that desires ultimate blessings for His people. The *commandment of the LORD is* [genuine] *pure, enlightening the eyes* (Psalm 19:8 NKJV). The Psalmist continues in his praise saying, *Your word is very pure* (Psalm 119:140 NKJV), emphasizing that it is more than refined; it is genuine.

41. From every vantage point, God establishes a pure motive; and His observation and evaluation of each circumstance are from a genuine heart. *You are of* [free from defect or filth, i.e., genuine] *purer eyes than to behold evil, and cannot look on wickedness* (Habakkuk 1:13 NKJV). God does not even consider nor perform acts of wickedness. He is repulsed by evil and wickedness.

42. God never considers any compromise of His pureness because His genuine pureness does not contain elements that permit an imitated and inferior pureness to match or influence His genuine pureness.

43. Because God's nature is pure, it is unquestionably virtuous. The moral soundness of every aspect of God reflects His pure nature. The character traits that are produced from His excellent uprightness declare His virtuous intentions. God acts with unsurpassed wisdom. *The wisdom that is from above is first pure, then peaceable, gentle,*

willing to yield, full of mercy and good fruits, without partiality and without hypocrisy (James 3:17 NKJV).

44. God's infinite virtue, which never varies, has always been in existence, and will continue forever. It is in this pure attribute that He can perform His miraculous perfect will in and through believers. It appears inconceivable that God, who is pure, desires and does the unthinkable and imparts into man His righteousness through Jesus Christ. From His holy, undefiled, and pure heart, God receives the repentant heart's confession that Jesus Christ is Lord of his life. Then, into the sin-stained heart, the blemished soul scarred by evil intentions and impure thoughts, God forgives him, blots out his iniquity and floods his heart (spirit) with His pure nature.

45. The ultimate result of God's virtue is found in His pure desire to always do good things for mankind. Evil intentions do not have the slightest probability of invading God's pureness.

46. In conclusion, God's nature is pure. This attribute contains biblical evidence that illustrates God's pureness as flawless, perfect, genuine, and virtuous. What then is the impact that His pure nature has on believers who *follow his steps?* (1 Peter 2:21).

The Impact of God's Nature on a Believer's Walk in Christ

47. Residing in every born-again believer, God's nature must flow through every word and deed performed. When His nature is evidenced, it is the manifestation of His indwelling existence within the believer's heart as the Bible says, *but if the Spirit of Him who raised Jesus from the dead dwells in you, He who raised Christ from the dead will also give life to your mortal bodies through His Spirit who dwells in you* (Romans 8:11 NKJV).

48. The definition of "pure" in the human spirit, soul, and body means it is "free from any contamination." It is not intermingled with any other substance contained in the original carnal nature but is purely God's nature operating within the born-again spirit.

49. The old nature or carnal nature that is now subjected to God's nature must no longer exhibit its immoral, blemished, corrupt, and defiled

conduct. The indwelling Holy Spirit, who has impregnated God's divine, holy, righteous, and pure nature in the believer's spirit, gives life to the believer in its purest form.

50. The foundation of a believer's faith becomes immovable when the declaration is made that *it is God who arms me with strength and makes my way perfect* (Psalm 18:32 NKJV). The initial step of recognizing that in himself the believer has no ability to bring the carnal nature to perfection opens the pathway for God's nature to begin reforming his ways.

51. Once he recognizes that it is God who now dwells within him, *the steps of a good man are ordered by the LORD* (Psalm 37:23 NKJV).

52. The sanctification of man's soul begins as the purifying process of God's nature starts to refine the believer's walk. The immoral state of the carnal nature is imprisoned, and God's pureness becomes the moral compass that directs *the steps of* the *good man*. The result of walking in Christ's steps and being led by the Holy Spirit compels the believer to *behave wisely in a perfect way . . . to walk within my house with a perfect heart* (Psalm 101:2 NKJV).

53. This moral cleansing requires that saints *keep* [themselves] *pure* (1 Timothy 5:22). This moral purifying process occurs when the believer casts *down arguments and every high thing that exalts itself against the knowledge of God, bringing every thought into captivity to the obedience of Christ* (2 Corinthians 10:5 NKJV).

54. This purifying process God's nature brings about in believers' lives causes immoral thoughts and actions to be shunned. *Now to the pure all things are pure, but to those who are defiled and unbelieving nothing is pure; but even their mind and conscience are defiled* (Titus 1:15 NKJV). When believers commit to this process, the Holy Spirit begins to sow righteousness into their spirit, and the sanctifying process exposes those things that are contrary to God's holiness and pureness.

55. Because the soul is made pure, the thoughts and deeds should align with God's flawless pureness, causing the thoughts and deeds to be blameless. Now the pivotal compass point which the believer follows is God's command: *I am Almighty God, walk before Me and be blameless* (Genesis 17:1 NKJV).

56. With this divine leading of the Holy Spirit, Spirit-filled believers commit to their walk and presents *their bodies a living sacrifice, holy, and acceptable to God*. In this new *way* (John 14:6) that they strive to

uphold, they are assured of God's promise that says, *Behold, God will not cast away the blameless* (Job 8:20 NKJV).

57. Flowing through the believer's spirit, God's pure nature eradicates guilt. God's forgiveness is without partiality to the one who repents and confesses his sin. There is no stain of guilt that lingers; neither is any condemnation laid at the repentant heart's door, for *If we confess our sins, He is faithful and just to forgive us our sins and to cleanse us from all unrighteousness* (1 John 1:9 NKJV). This promise is supported by the statement that *there is therefore now no condemnation to those who are in Christ Jesus* (Romans 8:1 NKJV).

58. The pure attribute of God's nature should be so interwoven in the believer's soul and spirit that no corrupt thought or deed is produced. It will remain in an incorruptible state so long as the believer declares, *I will set nothing wicked before my eyes; I hate the work of those who fall away; it shall not cling to me. A perverse heart shall depart from me; I will not know wickedness* (Psalm 101:3-4 NKJV).

59. The result of the sanctified moral state, the blameless conduct, the guilt-free conscience, and the cleansed soul and spirit enables the believer and makes him capable of walking undefiled before God. Ultimately, man is to be holy. Oswald Chambers in his daily reading book, *My Utmost for His Highest,* states, "We must remind ourselves of the purpose of life. We are not destined to happiness, nor to health, but to holiness. At all costs, a person must have a right relationship with God. God has only one intended destiny for mankind–holiness. His only goal is to produce saints."

60. It is Jesus Christ who through the shedding of His blood enabled repentant souls to become pure undefiled believers because He *gave Himself for us that He might redeem us from every lawless deed and purify for Himself His own special people, zealous for good works* (Titus 2:14 NKJV).

61. When the heart is undefiled and pure in all its motives and is sanctified by the Holy Spirit, then this scripture becomes a reality in the believer's life: *Blessed are the pure in heart,* [undefiled] *for they shall see God* (Matthew 5:8).

Part 3

Doctrine of Jesus Christ

9. DOCTRINE – The Divine Person, the Son
    a. Jesus is God manifest in the flesh. Jesus is the only begotten Son of God. His deity is declared and found in the Bible when in the opening salvo of his majestic account of Jesus Apostle John declares the Divine Person: *In the beginning was the Word and the Word was with God, and the Word was God.*
    b. The Divine Person, the LORD Jesus Christ
    Believers know and seek a relationship with Jesus who is their Lord and Savior. He is the anointed Lord Who is the head of the church. The Word made Flesh: The miraculous conception and perfect salvation plan is invested in Jesus Christ. There will never be any explanation as to how this took place, and yet it stands as the pillar of the Christian faith, that Jesus was made flesh.
10. DOCTRINE – The Divine Person: Jesus Christ's Two Natures
    a. The Divine Nature
    b. The Human Nature
11. DOCTRINE – The Lord Jesus Christ's Eternal Work
12. DOCTRINE – Jesus died for mankind.
13. DOCTRINE – The Precious Blood of Jesus
14. DOCTRINE – Jesus' Spirit and Soul descended into the place of the dead.
15. DOCTRINE – The Resurrection of Jesus Christ
    There is no greater or more outstanding proclamation than the fact that Jesus was raised from the dead by the glory of the Father. It is the most significant and ultimate expression of God's power and love that

is presented to mankind who accepts by faith the conclusive fact that Jesus was raised from the dead.

16. DOCTRINE – Jesus Christ's Ascension and Present Work

This chapter expounds the place to which Jesus ascended, His exaltation to the highest seat of honor, and His current position of Apostle and High Priest. His prophetical, priestly, and kingly offices are also discussed to help understand the significance of the eternal spiritual office He occupies, His spiritual office of advocate and His intercessory role.

Chapter 9

Doctrine of Jesus Christ

The Divine Person, the Son

1. *Thou art the Christ, the Son of the living God* (Matthew 16:16). Without hesitation and disbelief, Spirit-filled believers echo this statement about Jesus. The entire relevance of the gospel message is based on this declaration by faith that Jesus is the only begotten Son of the living God.

2. *Concerning his Son Jesus Christ our Lord* (Romans 1:3), there can be no salvation unless the Lord Jesus Christ is received, accepted, and believed to be the Person He is declared to be in the Holy Writ. This is the vital confession all believers make because they know that neither *is there salvation in any other, for there is no other name under heaven given among men by which we must be saved* (Acts 4:12). Believers know that they are called to *believe on the Lord Jesus Christ, and* [they] *will be saved* (Acts 16:31 NKJV).

3. Jesus is neither a myth nor a figment of imagination; He is a fact, a living Being, and a Person who has influenced every nation on earth. There has never been, and never will be anyone who has accomplished what Jesus has. Everything Jesus did is saturated with the very essence of His nature and deity, namely love. He has changed and still does change innumerable lives, turns hatred into love, channels His presence into believers' hearts, and turns man's despair into hope.

4. History records the beginning of change as it hangs on the hinges of a stable door in Bethlehem. A few years later through the holy One who was born in a stable, the greatest act of love was expressed on a cruel

cross outside the walls of Jerusalem, the city of peace. It was here that the miraculous resurrection event occurred, and death was conquered, and eternal life was freely offered to "whosoever" accept Him, Jesus Christ, by faith.

5. John Richter says it the best; "His pierced hands lifted empires off their hinges, turned the stream of centuries out of its channel, and He still governs today.

6. "Countless figures who attempted to shape history through their dictatorial force and unnecessary slaughtering of human flesh on the battlefield, have never amounted to anything as huge as Jesus Christ achieved through His love. One such ruler, Napoleon, as carnal as he was declared, 'I founded a great empire, but upon what did I depend? Upon force. Jesus founded His empire upon love, and to this very day millions will die for Him. Jesus Christ was more than man.'"

7. Now comes this statement that surpasses every attempt by man's puny mind to express the magnitude of Jesus' existence. The Holy Writ proclaims with resounding ecstasy that is echoed through every generation that Jesus Christ is *declared to be the Son of God with power according to the Spirit of holiness, by the resurrection from the dead* (Romans 1:4 NKJV).

8. It is fitting that consideration of this vast subject begins with its focus on the glorious Person of the Lord Jesus Christ. Throughout the entire Word of God there is a golden thread that pertains to Jesus Christ. The Old Testament declares Him to be the exalted divine Person whose *name shall be called Wonderful, Counselor, The Mighty God, The Everlasting Father, The Prince of Peace* (Isaiah 9:6).

9. Flowing through the Word, countless prophetical references are made about Jesus the Person. One such exaltation is declared through the mouth of a prophet who said, *Behold the virgin shall conceive and bear a Son, and shall call His name* [God with us] *Immanuel* (Isaiah 7:14 NKJV). The highest accolade that could be given to Jesus came from His own Father: *This is my beloved Son, in whom I am well pleased* (Matthew 3:17).

10. The affirmation of Jesus Christ's deity does not culminate in the Old Testament. Apostle John boldly unsheathes the *two-edged sword* (Hebrews 4:12) as he announces in the opening salvo of his Holy Spirit inspired gospel record who Jesus is: *In the beginning was the Word . . .*

and the Word was God . . . and the Word became flesh and dwelt among us (John 1:1,14 NKJV).

11. Apostle Paul takes it further by stating that Jesus *who, being in the form of God, thought it not robbery to be equal with God* (Philippians 2:6), confirming Apostle John's explanation that Jesus is the *Word* Who is *God*. Then, with full confidence, Apostle Paul says, in Christ *dwells all the fullness of the Godhead bodily* (Colossians 2:9).

12. These words expressed by the two apostles affirm the unquestionable deity of the Lord Jesus Christ. To seal Christ's deity, the deepest proof of this is declared by Jesus Himself when He says, *I and My Father are one* (John 10:30), *before Abraham was I am* (John 8:58).

13. Myer Pearlman in his book *Knowing the Doctrines of the Bible* states, "Jesus was conscious of two things: a special relationship to God whom He describes as His Father; second, a special mission on earth—His 'Father's business.'

15. "He put Himself side by side with the Divine activity... *My Father worketh hitherto, and I work* (John 5:17). *I came forth from the Father* (John 16:28). *My Father hath sent me* (John 20:21). He claimed a Divine knowledge and fellowship (Matthew 11:27; John 17:25). He claimed to unveil the Father's being in Himself (John 14:9-11). He assumed Divine prerogatives: omnipresence (Matthew 18:20); power to forgive sins (Mark 2:5-10); power to raise the dead (John 6:39, 40, 54; 11:25; 10:17, 18); He proclaimed Himself Judge and Arbiter of man's destiny (John 5:22; Matthew 25:31-46).

16. "Christ is that Word, because through Him God has revealed His activity, will, and purpose, and because by Him God contacts the world."

17. The writer in the letter to the Hebrews starts with the announcement, *God has in these last days spoken to us by His Son, whom He has appointed heir of all things, through whom also He made the worlds; who being the brightness of His glory and the express image of His person, and upholding all things by the word of His power, when He had by Himself purged our sins, sat down on the right hand of the Majesty on high* (Hebrews 1:1-3 NKJV).

18. Myer Pearlman says, "Christ is the Word of God because He not only brings God's message – He is God's message."

19. Spirit-filled believers have no hesitation in testifying about the Person of Jesus Christ because by faith they confess that Jesus Christ is *the*

Word made flesh. Jesus took upon Himself human nature and was born of a virgin so that He could reveal the eternal God through a human personality.

20. The Person, the Lord Jesus Christ, can only be worshipped as God because He is from God, and is the one true God. He is the Person born of a woman yet conceived by the Holy Spirit; and He carried the eternal, holy, and incorruptible blood from His Father, the Almighty Ancient of Days.

21. Dr. James Orr seals this aspect of the Person of Jesus Christ when he says, "Doctrinally it must be repeated that the belief in the virgin birth of Christ is of the highest value for the right apprehension of Christ's unique and sinless personality. Here is One, as Paul brings out in Romans 5:12, who, free from sin Himself, and not involved in the Adamic liabilities of the race, reverses the curse of sin and death brought in by the first Adam, and establishes the reign of righteousness and life. Had Christ been naturally born, not one of these things could be affirmed of Him. As one of Adam's race, not an entrant from higher sphere, He would have shared in Adam's corruption and doom, and would Himself have required to be redeemed.

22. "Through God's infinite mercy, He came from above, inherited no guilt, needed no regeneration or sanctification, but became Himself the Redeemer, Regenerator, Sanctifier for all who receive Him."

23. Jesus was not making a flattering statement of Himself when He prayed to the Father, *And now, O Father, glorify Me together with Yourself, with the glory which I had with You before the world was* (John 17:5 NKJV). His eternal existence was before the world began, yet He *being in the form of God, did not consider it robbery to be equal with God, but made Himself of no reputation, taking the form of a bondservant, and coming in the likeness of man* (Philippians 2:6-7 NKJV).

24. His glorious Person is *God manifest in the flesh* (1 Timothy 3:16), and Jesus is the only One who can share in the Father's glory (John 17:1,5). God will never give His glory to anyone (Isaiah 42:8). Thus, Jesus is God; and He manifests the glory of God in the flesh on earth.

25. The record in John 5:16-30 is the fitting exaltation by Jesus of Himself, when He astounds His hearers with the greatest explanation of His coequality with His Father. Herein He asserts His deity that He is shown all things the Father does, that He should be honored, and that He is given the authority to execute judgment.

26. To bring the belief that Jesus is the living Son of God into the twentieth century, the glorious Person of Jesus Christ is never more aptly expounded than when Dr. James Allan Francis wrote in 1926, "Nineteen centuries have come and gone and today Jesus is the central figure of the human race and the leader of mankind's progress.... All the kings that have ever reigned put together have not affected the life of mankind on earth as powerfully as has that one solitary life."

27. The glorious Person of Jesus Christ is heralded throughout the world by Spirit-filled saints who worship and praise Him as Lord, Savior, High Priest, and the Son of the living God.

The Divine Person, the LORD Jesus Christ

28. Apostle Peter, standing on the steps of the upper room in Jerusalem, preaches the first message of the church to an inquiring group of people; and he reveals to them their despicable act and the Father's exaltation of His Son when he proclaims, *God has made this Jesus, whom you crucified, both Lord and Christ* (Acts 2:36 NKJV). Spirit-filled believers have no doubt neither do they bear any shame in declaring, alongside the first Holy-Spirit-anointed message ever preached from a church pulpit, that Jesus Christ is Lord.

29. Spirit-filled believers have their faith rooted and grounded in this truth that they are constantly *looking unto Jesus, the author and finisher of* [their] *faith* (Hebrews 12:2 NKJV). Their spirit-man seeks an intimate personal relationship with Jesus Christ. He is always exalted as Lord. French Arrington in his book, *Christian Doctrine*, states that the Lord Jesus "is the object of faith, the subject of preaching and teaching, and the hope of everlasting life."

30. From the earliest time, Christian saints reverenced Jesus as Lord of their lives and *the Christ* is anointed by God to occupy the highest seat of authority at the Father's right hand. The most exquisite statement about Jesus came from the one who doubted Him. Upon recognizing Jesus after His resurrection, Thomas states, *My Lord and my God* (John 20:28). In the vernacular, Thomas spoke only two words: *Adonai* (my Lord) and *Elohim* (my God).

31. Thomas's words are echoed by Spirit-filled believers throughout the world who unashamedly proclaim with the same emphasis that Jesus is their Lord personally. Jesus is their *Adonai*–"my" Lord. This personal and reverent acknowledgment affirms that the risen Savior, the Lord Jesus Christ is not a distant image or instrument carved from an earthly substance by human hands, but the intimate and personal Savior sent from the eternal God to impart His peace to everyone who believes (John 16:33). Christ's deity is never more acknowledged and expressed than when believers declare Him to be their *Adonai* ("my Lord") and their *Elohim* ("my God").

32. *Reach your finger here, and look at My hands; and reach your hand here, and put it into My side. Do not be unbelieving, but believing* (John 20:27 NKJV)–How gracious our Lord is with Thomas. He gives Thomas a greater opportunity than the other disciples to prove that the Lord is the risen Christ. To the other disciples, Jesus only showed His hands and His side (verse20). However, Thomas is invited to reach his hand and *put it into* [the Lord's] *side.*

33. Thomas does nothing physical towards the Lord. In his spirit, he realizes that Jesus, the all-knowing omniscient Lord, knows even what is said though He is not there physically. Thomas realizes that Jesus understands his doubt, and "hears" his statement in the Spirit. Jesus approaches Thomas with love and compassion and offers him more than the rest of the disciples were offered.

34. Thomas needed no physical proof as he supposed would be necessary. The glorious presence of the risen Lord Jesus Christ (the same witness Thomas had about who Jesus was before the crucifixion) is revealed to Thomas the moment he looked upon the Lord. *Thomas answered and said to Him Adonai.* A "look" was all he needed. As with the writer's statement to believers today to be constantly *looking unto Jesus* (Hebrews 12:2), the focus is on the Lord, *the author and finisher* of one's faith.

35. Absolute capitulation of every self-indulgence, self-satisfaction, and personal desire is the condition Spirit-filled believers find themselves in when they confess Jesus as Lord.

36. They declare Jesus as the vicarious Lord who is their Savior, Hope, and Source of perfect peace.

37. W.A.C. Rowe gives an exquisite rendering of the lordship of Jesus Christ, "Christ's Lordship is essentially based upon His own nature.

He is divine, nay, we will use the stronger word, about which there can be no shade of misunderstanding, He is deity.

38. "Jesus Christ is God (1 John 5:20). The outstanding distinction of the Christian faith is that Jesus Christ is God and that *God was in Christ, reconciling the world unto Himself* (2 Corinthians 5:19).

39. "Lordship of Christ is also founded upon His mighty and overwhelming victories. He came into the world to defeat Satan and, through death, to destroy the destroyer's power. Christ was expressly manifested to destroy the works of the devil, and to deliver the sin-bound sons of men (Colossians 2:15).

40. "Amid the splendor of the clustered jewels of glorious angels and ministering spirits and redeemed men God has set Christ, the Eternal and Lustrous One, in the highest, central place, around Whom all other orders but take their subordinate setting. By nature, by conquest, by appointment, our Savior is Lord of all.

41. "Over every kind of life, every crook and cranny of all God's vast, eternal universe the throne of the Lord Jesus Christ holds its massive dominion. The great Millennium's dawn will soon break when the Coming Lord will reign triumphantly as King over all the nations of the world (John 20:28)."

42. The title, Lord, vested upon Jesus Christ is the most befitting one because He is Lord of all, and He has, is, and will always be the divine sovereign God of all flesh and creation. Jesus Himself declared, *All authority has been given to Me in heaven and on earth* (Matthew 28:18 NKJV). There is no one else qualified to take up the judge's seat at the two forthcoming judgments. The Lord, holy and divine, has the credentials to be the sovereign, just, and fair judge of man. He is God and came in the form of man, remained sinless, and conquered death, thus elevating Him to the highest office of the *Lord Jesus Christ* (Philippians 2:11; 2 Thessalonians 1:12).

The Word made Flesh

43. It is fitting that the Holy Bible contains detailed accounts of *God manifested in the flesh*. Likewise, it is satisfying that the world has not forgotten the celebration of Jesus' coming in Bethlehem's manger. While the "Christmas story" told to children reverently proclaims the

birth of the Savior, Spirit-filled believers hunger for deeper revelation that surrounds this historic event.

44. This unique happening should start with the visitation by the angel Gabriel to Mary. The place was neither a kingly palace, nor was the handmaid of the Lord a princess. It was a humble home in which a family who upheld spiritual values lived. There was nothing particular about the city that made it a special landmark for the world trader. The city was small and populated with humble folk who tilled the soil, did handcrafted work, and were labeled as inferior by the so-called educated upper class in the rest of Israel. This is evidenced by the question, *can anything good come out Nazareth?* (John 1:46 NKJV).

45. Into this precious place, Gabriel, the messenger of the Lord God, arrived and had a discourse with the Virgin Mary.

46. This was by far the most important message Gabriel ever delivered. God chose the time and the place, and He chose His worthy angel to bring the news to Mary that she was *highly favored* by God (Luke 1:28). No ordinary messenger and no ordinary woman were they.

47. The angel did not hesitate in announcing that the eternal God was about to perform a miracle that had never happened before. And everything about this miracle was God-ordained and Spiritual. Gabriel calmed her troubled spirit with his *fear not,* and then announced that she will *conceive in her womb* the Holy Son of God.

48. Mary's response was truthful and with good reason: she had never been with a man. This gave Gabriel the opportunity to explain the spiritual intervention in Mary's life. This was not an immaculate conception; it was a miraculous conception. This was Almighty God performing a miracle within His handmaiden by Himself. Gabriel was only the messenger; Mary was the recipient of the miracle.

49. The event purposed by God from the foundation of the world was announced. *The Lamb of God slain from the foundation of the world* (Revelation 13:8) was to be conceived in human flesh. The need to purge mankind of the sin perpetrated by Adam had to be avenged. Only God could do this, and He had to do it as a human. His highest created being, mankind, had destroyed the perfect union between God and man; and only God could restore it.

50. *That holy thing* (Luke 1:35) needed the Godhead's action to bring it to life, and the Holy Spirit impregnated Mary's womb with the *seed.* The

seed was none other than the *word*. Mary proclaims, *Be it unto me according to your word* (Luke 1:38).

51. Mary realized that Gabriel was sent by God and that the words he spoke were from the throne of Almighty God. Herein is the miracle; only God can create something from nothing. God's spoken word exploded the universe into existence. He said, *Let there be* and life sprang forth on the frozen planet, Earth. This same awesome God overshadows Mary, and she miraculously becomes pregnant. There is no physical explanation anyone at any time can render as to how God did it.

52. Gabriel brought the message that was weighed and measured in the scales of God's eternal purposes. The words he uttered that day were Spirit-breathed and Holy Spirit anointed, inspired, and instructed. The sinless seed, the Word, was revealed to Mary; and she was told that her conception would be God-ordained and God-performed (Luke 1:35).

53. Mary received the *word* as she accepted her mission by faith when she utters, *According to your word*. The word accepted and the word appropriated in Mary's womb infused by the Holy Spirit united the Son of God with human nature; *the Word was God . . . the Word became flesh* (John 1:1,14).

54. This is the *seed* spoken of by God to the serpent when He tells him, *And I will put enmity between thee and the woman, and between thy seed and her seed; it* [the seed, the Word, the Son of God] *shall bruise thy head, and thou shalt bruise his heel* (Genesis 3:15).

55. Martin J. Scott gives the following rendition of the incarnation: "The incarnation means that God (that is, the Son of God) became man. This does not mean that God was turned into man, nor does it mean that God ceased to be God and began to be a man; but that, remaining God, He assumed or took on a new nature, namely, human. The Incarnation, therefore, means that the Son of God, true God from all eternity, in the course of time became true man also, in one Person, Jesus Christ, consisting of two natures, the human and the Divine."

56. Apostle Peter gives a superb interpretation of the holy seed that was conceived in Mary's womb which became flesh: *You were not redeemed with corruptible things . . . but with the precious blood of Christ, as a lamb without blemish and without spot. He indeed was foreordained before the foundation of the world, but was manifest in these last times for you . . . having been born again, not of corruptible seed, but*

incorruptible, through the word of God which lives and abides forever (1 Peter 1:18-23 NKJV).

57. This seed, which is the *Word*, is from the eternal God: and it is incorruptible, pure, holy, divine, and became sinless blood. The *lamb slain* was not contaminated with the sin-stained blood of mankind. The Holy Child's veins were infused with the blood that proceeded from the incorruptible *Word* (seed) that impregnated Mary's womb.

58. Apostle Paul says it best: *And without controversy great is the mystery of godliness, God was manifested in the flesh* (1 Timothy 3:16 NKJV).

59. Jesus is absolutely *the Christ, the Son of the living God* (Matthew 16:16).

Chapter 10

The Divine Person: Jesus Christ's Two Natures

1. The church's rapid growth in the first century reached across cultural, racial, and ethnic differences. The glorious message *Jesus Christ and Him crucified* catapulted thousands of human lives from all walks of life *in all Judea, and in Samaria, and unto the uttermost part of the earth* (Acts 1:8), converting them to *the faith* that embodied the forgiveness of sin, and hope in the promise of eternal life, peace, and faith that moved mountains.

2. It was first revealed and preached to humble folk who in their poverty believed that God was the supplier of their every need. However, as church membership grew, countless well-educated and philosophical men also accepted Jesus Christ as Lord of their lives.

3. While there were many educated saints who believed in their hearts that Jesus is the Son of God, some were still struggling to relinquish their head-knowledge and exchange it for Holy Spirit-led faith. Added to this, those who opposed Christianity also presented arguments to support their endeavors to disprove the existence of Jesus Christ as the Son of God. Thus, followed questions that were hitherto never asked, let alone considered. One of the very first questions asked in the first century was this: "Did Jesus Christ have two natures?" Put another way, agnostics challenged, "Prove to us that Jesus Christ had two natures."

4. Throughout the centuries that have followed, this question constantly has reared its head; and many astute theologians have given elaborate explanations on this subject. However, while having no argument with anyone as to the deity and nature of Jesus Christ, the Spirit-filled

believers' unwavering faith in Jesus Christ, as the only begotten Son of God remains the anchor for their souls.

5. This vast subject that flows from the heart of the Father to His Son is of such magnitude that the intrinsic truths of Christ's two natures are hidden in the *secret place of the Most High* and revealed to those who are *seeking the Lord* with a hunger and a yearning to know the *secret things of God.* It is when Spirit-filled believers climb out of the safety of their ship of life and dive into the depths of the Holy Writ that they discover the *deep* [that] *calls unto deep* (Psalm 42:7).

6. When they are delving into the depth of God's treasure trove that contains His secrets that which, He willingly shares with those who are seeking them, God unveils the *mystery of Godliness* and reveals the union of Christ's divine nature with His human nature.

7. Within the divine Christ, who is an equal member of the Godhead, His divine nature took up residence in the Son of Man alongside His human nature. Lewis Sperry Chafer says, "This unique Person [Jesus Christ] with two natures, being at once the revelation of God to men and the manifestation of ideal and perfect humanity, properly holds the central place in all reverent human thinking."

8. This subject cannot be glossed over and made to be nothing more than a "matter-of-fact" observation. This is the holy God sending forth His Son as a human being and at the same time, retaining His deity, holiness, and sovereignty as the God-man. Chafer continues, "Evidence demonstrates the truth that Christ is not only an equal member of the Godhead before His incarnation, but that He retained that reality in the *days of His flesh* (Hebrews 5:7)." The abiding oneness of the Godhead remained perfect after Jesus was born and in the same union that was before the incarnation. It is Jesus who confirms this statement when He said, *Do you not believe that I am in the Father, and the Father in Me? The words that I speak to you I do not speak on My own authority; but the Father who dwells in Me does the works. Believe Me that I am in the Father and the Father in Me, or else believe Me for the sake of the works themselves* (John 14:9-11).

9. The Lord Jesus Christ, the Son of God, and a divine part of the Godhead became flesh and lived a perfect sin-free life making Him pure and holy which brought the deity of Christ into human form and His divine nature alongside His human nature.

The Divine Nature

10. The holy, divine Son of God was born of a virgin, lived a virgin life (sinless life), and died for the sin of the world. He is deity Personified in the flesh, and the divine nature that exists in the Godhead permeated every area of His human frame.

11. W. A. C. Rowe gives the most eloquent explanation of Christ's natures when he says, "God sent His own Son in the 'Likeness of sinful flesh, and for sin, condemned sin in the flesh.' As a new-born babe, He was *That holy thing . . . The Son of God*. He commenced His human life what He always was; what He always maintained in His experience; and what He is, and always will be in glory—absolutely holy.

12. "The Savior of the world was crystal pure in thought, word and action as flowing from a perfect nature whiter than light. There was no spot or blemish in Him (1 Peter 1:19).

13. "Rather was it the fierce and glowing whiteness of the holy fire of deity (Hebrews 12:29). Christ far outstripped the nature and experience of perfect innocence."

14. Christ's divine nature was the criterion by which He did His Father's will while He was on earth.

15. W. A. C. Rowe continues, "The whole nature and attitude of the Master was one of sublime perfection: both in the spiritual and practical. Though He moved in this dark world and amongst the sinful multitude doing good (Acts 10:38), He continued living in the heights of pure and intimate fellowship with His holy Father (Matthew 14:23). He *was in all points tempted like as we are, yet without sin*. Being free from sin and utterly holy, Christ manifested the scintillating radiance of the divine and the human (Matthew 17:2; 2 Corinthians 4:6)."

16. It is impossible for man to save himself from the penalty caused by his sin-stained blood neither will the sin-stained blood of another man be good enough to save the whole human race (Romans 3:23). To satisfy the requirements of God's divine ordinance, God needed a sinless person born of human flesh who carried no sin impediment. God's only Son had the qualifications to fulfill the task.

17. Man needed a Savior, and Jesus Christ is the *Savior of the world* (John 4:42).

18. To meet the exact demands of the eternal Holy God's redemption plan and to execute the shedding of pure, unstained blood, the Savior had

to embody the essentials of deity and humanity that were embodied in His divine holiness. Jesus Christ's divine nature measured up to every standard needed for a perfect salvation.

19. The essential examination of the two natures of Jesus Christ must focus on the eternal purpose of His coming in the form of man. God understood the dilemma of the human race. He was acutely aware of their need to be exonerated from their inherent sin, and God required sinless blood to achieve perfect salvation.

20. How magnificent is the Holy Writ's explanation of this glorious truth as it explains Christ's perfect work. It gushes forth like a torrential river cascading through the canyons of the human soul and spirit when it proclaims, *Inasmuch then as the children have partaken of flesh and blood, He Himself likewise shared in the same, that through death He might destroy him who had the power of death, that is, the devil, and release those who through fear of death were all their lifetime subject to bondage. Therefore, in all things He had to be made like His brethren, that He might be a merciful and faithful High Priest in things pertaining to God, to make propitiation for the sins of the people. For in that He Himself has suffered, being tempted, He is able to aid those who are tempted* (Hebrews 2:14-18 NKJV).

21. God seals His purpose for sending His only begotten Son as He brings down the gavel on any argument about Christ's mission with a thundering declaration that ricochets throughout the world: *For this purpose the Son of God was manifested, that He might destroy the works of the devil* (1 John 3:8 NKJV).

22. Sheer divinity, sheer deity, and sheer holiness embodied the Son of God as He *became flesh.*

The Human Nature

23. Without blurring the fact that the holy divine nature of God entered a human life, consideration must now be given to the human nature within everyone born of woman.

24. To clarify, W. A. C. Rowe states, "As Christ is truly God, so He is truly man. There is a broad, deep stream of sacred instruction concerning the true humanity of our Lord. Our Savior was no mere phantom in human form, with only a show of solidarity before men; He was *bone of*

our bone and flesh of our flesh. Yes, Christ took on real human nature (Hebrews 2:17) and lived a real human life (Acts 10:38).

25. "Elements, supernatural and natural, supreme and simple, stand side by side in amazing combination. The star on behalf of the mighty universe royally salutes the wondrous new-born Child.

26. *"The Son of Man* was one of His most outstanding appellations; Christ used it of Himself in a supreme and unique sense; the name carrying an utterly comprehensive and inclusive meaning. He was never 'a' Son of man, but always 'the' Son of man. Truly, *Jesus Christ is come in the flesh* (1 John 4:2)."

27. Let it be engrained and sealed within every fiber of the human frame and be unequivocally proclaimed that He is *the Son of Man* because His Father is God and He is like no other human born of a woman.

28. Just as Jesus Christ is very God, so is He very man. This does not mean that there are two Persons joined as one. The Son of God is one Person that has two natures, and both these natures in Him are complete and unscathed. They are joined in the glorious Person, the Lord Jesus Christ. Apostle Cyril D. Wilson, an apostle set in the body of Christ refers to "Jesus Christ, begotten of the Father, born of a virgin, human in nature, but absolutely sinless. Christ in Humanity was *a Child Born.* Christ in His Divinity was *a Son Given."*

29. Henry Thiessen in his book, *Introductory Lectures in Systematic Theology,* states, "The Deity of Christ, Christ was conscious of being God incarnate and represented Himself as being such. The constant scriptural representations of the infinite value of Christ's atonement and of the union of the human race with God which has been secured in Him, are intelligible only when Christ is regarded, not as a man of God, but as the God-man."

30. Jesus Christ's holy, pure, righteous, and divine nature took up its abode in the human frame of Jesus of Nazareth and led every thought and action He said and did as a human. Needless to say, Christ's human nature was also pure and sin-free, for *He knew no sin* (2 Corinthians 5:21).

31. Thiessen continues, "Christ had an infinite intelligence and will and a finite intelligence and will; He had a divine consciousness and a human consciousness. His divine intelligence was infinite; His human intelligence increased. His divine will was omnipotent; His human will (was limited)" (Mark 13:32).

32. The Bible is filled with the examples of the Lord's human nature. He expressed all the human characteristics of weariness, hunger, and thirstiness. He also labored like all men do and was also tempted in every way all human beings are, yet without succumbing to any sin.

33. The question that needs to be asked is, "What drove the Lord Jesus to abstain from all appearances of sin and never once entertain the presence of Satan?" Unequivocally, it was His obedience to His heavenly Father's will. He never lost the vision, He never took His eye off the purpose of His coming in the flesh, and He never veered away from any commission His Father demanded of Him, ever faithful to *not My will, but Thine, be done* (Luke 22:42).

34. His constant obedience to the Father's will propelled Him to the point of abandonment of everything He desired for Himself. He cast aside every thought and purpose that meandered through His mind that was contrary to His Father's purpose. Jesus cut off every personal ambition by surrendering every area of His life to His Father; and He confessed, *I can of Myself do nothing. As I hear, I judge; and My judgment is righteous, because I do not seek My own will but the will of the Father who sent Me* (John 5:30 NKJV).

35. It is again emphasized by Jesus when He faces the crowd and said, *For I have come down from heaven, not to do My own will, but the will of Him who sent me* (John 6:38 NKJV).

36. Furthermore, when looking at the answer to the question whether Jesus had two natures, the viewpoint should never be from man's perspective, but rather from God's. This compels one's attention to return to the first created human, Adam. Consideration must be given to Adam's nature that was breathed into him by the Spirit; it was sin-free and perfect in its innocence.

37. Adam knew no sin, and he never sinned while he was obedient to God. However, unrighteousness entered Adam's nature when he sinned by disobeying God's command when he ate the fruit from the tree of knowledge of good and evil. Adam's sin-stained nature is passed on to every human thereafter. The same sin-stained "seed" (blood) flows through every human being *for all have sinned and come short of the glory of the Lord* (Romans 3:23).

38. Focusing on this subject from God's perspective, it is now clear that Jesus had the same sin-free blood Adam had before Adam sinned because Christ's blood was from the Father and infused by the Holy

Spirit. It had the same source Adam's blood had before he sinned. It was/is sin-free. Throughout His earthly ministry, Jesus' blood remained sin-free because Jesus never succumbed to any temptation nor did He disobey His Father's will which is what Adam did.

39. When comparing the two Adams, let the Scriptures speak: *And so it is written, the first man, Adam became a living being. The last Adam became a life-giving spirit. However, the spiritual is not first, but the natural, and afterward the spiritual. The first man was of the earth, made of dust; the second Man is the Lord from heaven. And as we have borne the image of the man of dust, we shall also bear the image of the heavenly Man* (1 Corinthians 15:45-49 NKJV).

40. Millard Erickson says of Christ, "His was a personality that in addition to the characteristics of divine nature [He] had all the qualities or attributes of a perfect, sinless human nature as well."

41. Herbert Lockyer explains, "What He divested Himself of was the constant, outward and visible manifestation of His Godhead. Christ did not surrender deity-He gained humanity.

42. "In His Incarnation He became the possessor of a true humanity in union with His eternal deity. As God, He did not enter a human body or join Himself to man. He became Man, that is, He belonged to the stock of humanity when as the Word, He *became flesh* (John 1:14)."

43. To prevent confusion, it must be clearly understood that Christ's divine nature did not engulf His human nature thus canceling out its existence. They were not fused together to become a different nature; they remained in their distinctive capacities.

44. Millard Erickson continues, "As the image of God, the human is already the creature most like God. The fact that a human did not ascend to divinity, nor did God elevate a human to divinity, but, rather, God condescended to take on humanity, facilitates our ability to conceive the incarnation."

45. The Lord Jesus Christ was tempted in every way all humans are, yet He never fell into Satan's deceitful trap. He *set His face like a flint* towards His purpose of His coming in the flesh.

46. He brought His human nature into subjection to His divine nature and walked in obedience to His Father's will. Even while suffering on the cross, He never lost the purpose of His earthly visitation. He condemned none for what they did to Him; rather He cried to the Father to forgive them (Luke 23:34). As He suffers the worst agony, He

speaks words of life to the repentant thief, *Today you will be with Me in Paradise* (Luke 23:43 NKJV).

47. He was *faithful to Him who appointed Him* (Hebrews 3:2 NKJV); and knowing the consequences of disobedience, He never once gave in to it; but instead, the Lord Jesus faithfully obeyed His Father *and being found in fashion as a man, he humbled himself, and became obedient unto death, even the death of the cross* (Philippians 2:8).

48. In conclusion, it is important to know that the deity of Christ, as immaculate as it is, could not be applied to the redemption of man's sin-stained soul. Neither could Christ's sinless life on earth be sufficient to redeem mankind. There had to be a combination of the divine and human nature being sacrificed on Calvary's Hill.

49. In its entirety, the Lord Jesus Christ had to offer Himself as God and Man for the redemption of lost souls. The schism that existed between God and man was caused by Adam. The redemption and reconciliation were accomplished by God through His Son. And, into this act of love and total redemption of man's lost soul, the Holy Christ with His divine nature was accompanied by His human form with its human nature taking Him to the Cross, not for Himself, but for mankind.

Chapter 11

The Lord Jesus Christ's Eternal Work

1. It is appropriate to consider the exact details of the magnificent subject of the eternal work Jesus Christ did, is doing, and will still do. It is not only appropriate but also vital to consider Christ's works in this way because the Bible declares that the *unsearchable riches of Christ* have been revealed *to make all see what is the fellowship of the mystery, which from the beginning of the ages has been hidden in God who created all things through Christ; to the intent that now the manifold wisdom of God might be made known by the church to the principalities and powers in the heavenly places, according to the eternal purpose which He accomplished in Christ Jesus our Lord* (Ephesians 3:8-11 NKJV).

2. This subject is divided onto four parts: Christ's work before He became the Son of Man; His work while on earth; His present work since He ascended into heaven; and, finally, His future work.

3. To keep the subject in its best format, the work of Christ before He became the Son of Man is discussed in detail under the Doctrine of Creation, and His future work is covered under the chapters of the end times. The remaining two categories will be covered in this section.

Jesus' Words and Work While on Earth

4. The four gospels are the evidence of Christ's work while He walked this earth. In many cases, they contain not only the works but also the

reason for the works. Christ's many works manifested signs, wonders, and miracles, all of which gave the people the evidence that He was sent from God. The Bible says that a ruler of the Jews, Nicodemus, came to Jesus during the night and admitted to Him, *Rabbi, we know that You are a teacher come from God; for no one can do these signs that You do unless God is with Him* (John 3:2 NKJV).

5.   Then, on another occasion, one of the greatest testimonies that Jesus was sent from God is found when Jesus tells a paralytic that his sins are forgiven him, and the onlookers accuse Jesus of blasphemy (Matthew 9:1-8 NKJV). Jesus knows their thoughts, and He knows that they blasphemed Him from their evil hearts. He says to them, *"But that you may know that the Son of Man has power on earth to forgive sins"—then He said to the paralytic, "Arise, take up your bed, and go to your house." And he arose and departed to his house* (verses 6-7).

6.   Jesus' personal statement that He was the Son of Man, as well as the fact that He could heal the paralytic, stunned the people and *when the multitudes saw it, they marveled and glorified God, who had given such power to men* (verse 8).

7.   Jesus constantly manifested the works of the Father. The reason for doing this was to give the people His witness and His testimony of God's fulfillment of His promise to send them the Messiah, and to demonstrate His love.

8.   The most profound witness Jesus brought of the presence of the eternal God was that He shone in this dark world as the *light of the world* (John 1:4). Jesus more than spoke the words of love; He demonstrated love. Likewise, He more than showed pity on the lost; He saved the lost through His sacrificial suffering and death on Calvary's Hill (Romans 5:8).

9.   In all His teaching, He spoke *the words of eternal life* (John 6:68). Never before had the hearers heard such truth uttered from anyone. It sliced through their darkened souls, and His words ploughed deep furrows into their heart ultimately culminating in a life-changing experience.

10.   His words, at times, offended hearers (Matthew 13:57) even though they were the truth. Without doubt, Spirit-filled believers are assured that every word uttered by Jesus Christ was fore-ordained by the Father. His words were life. His words are still life (Ephesians 1:13). His written word is everlasting (1 Peter 1:23). And His God-breathed word will never lose its power (2 Corinthians 6:7; Hebrews 4:12; 1 Peter 1:25).

11. Jesus never spoke with evil intent, nor did He blaspheme the Godhead. Many thought He did, yet they were proved wrong every time.

12. Christ's words were so powerful that they had the divine ability to turn men from their daily tasks after they heard Him call them, saying, *Follow me* (Matthew 4:18-22). They cast aside their occupation and followed Jesus. His words were so divinely inspired and anointed by the Holy Spirit that *immediately they left the boat and their father, and followed Him* (Matthew 4:22 NKJV).

13. The Holy Spirit's anointing is never more divinely expressed than when Jesus said in the synagogue in Nazareth, *The Spirit of the LORD is upon Me, because He has anointed Me to preach the gospel to the poor; He has sent Me to heal the brokenhearted, to proclaim liberty to the captives and recovery of sight to the blind, to set at liberty those who are oppressed; to proclaim the acceptable year of the LORD* (Luke 4:18 NKJV).

14. The indwelling holiness, deity, and divinity in every word Jesus spoke is beautifully expressed by the two men traveling on the road to Emmaus when they say, *Did not our heart burn within us while He talked with us on the road, and while He opened the Scriptures to us?* (Luke 24:32 NKJV). Such an influence from a Human voice will never be equaled, expressed as it was through words that emanated from the holy heart of God's risen Son.

15. The most prolific evidence that Christ's words are life-giving was witnessed when He spoke to Lazarus' dead body as He stood before the tomb and cried, *Lazarus, come forth!* (John 11:43 NKJV). Today, amongst the trillions of words being uttered, Christ's words rise above the din of man's vociferous babbling as fresh, wholesome life that beams into man's soul as a refreshing symphony to calm the troubled heart and guide it into all truth.

16. Not only were His words life-changing and life-giving, but also, they are eternal. They were spoken almost two thousand years ago, and they are still changing lives to this day. Truly, Christ's words have eternal value and influence on people's lives. His own testimony of the origin of His words still resounds in the Spirit-filled believer's spirit: *Do you not believe that I am in the Father, and the Father in Me? The words that I speak to you I do not speak on My own authority; but the Father who dwells in Me does the works* (John 14:10 NKJV).

17. His message not only brought life and hope to the hearer but also contained reconciling utterances that paved the way for the purpose

of His coming to be fulfilled, namely, saving mankind from their sin (Matthew 18:11). Most assuredly, Jesus Christ spoke words that rebuilt the relationship between God and man, and He is *the Repairer of the Breach* (Isaiah 58:12 NKJV).

18. Millard J. Erickson says, "It is important to retain the truths that Jesus reveals God to humanity, reconciles God and humanity to one another, and rules and will rule over the whole of the creation, including humanity." Christ is the Revealer of God, the Ruler both now and to come, and the ever-present Reconciler.

19. Millard Erickson continues, "His pre-existence with the Father was a major factor in His ability to reveal the Father, for He had been with Him . . . *No one has seen God at any one time. The only begotten Son, who is in the bosom of the Father, He has declared Him* . . . (John 1:18 NKJV). He told Nicodemus, *No one has ascended to heaven but He who came down from heaven, that is, the Son of Man who is in heaven*" (John 3:13 NKJV).

20. Jesus not only spoke the words of His Father but also did the works of His Father. His works while words were part of the work, were always holy and pure. They were accompanied by signs, wonders, and miracles that revealed God to those who believed: *Jesus answered them, I told you, and you do not believe. The works that I do in My Father's name, they bear witness of Me* (John 10:25 NKJV).

21. The most revealing acclamation that no one can refute about Jesus' works is this: *Men of Israel, hear these words: Jesus of Nazareth, a Man attested by God to you by miracles, wonders, and signs which God did through Him in your midst, as you yourselves also know* (Acts 2:22 NKJV).

22. Jesus Christ's presence was like summer's bright morning sun bursting onto earth's surface after a period of darkness. He spoke life-giving encouragement and touched lives with His pure works. Everywhere He went, He left evidence that he had been there. No place was too good, too bad, too rich, or too poor for Him to enter. Without controversy and in God's eternal love, *God anointed Jesus of Nazareth with the Holy Spirit and with power, who went about doing good and healing all who were oppressed by the devil, for God was with Him* (Acts 10:38 NKJV).

23. So drastic was the contrast between the works of darkness and Christ's works of life and light that the people were stirred and in awe of His actions. The application of the Law had imprisoned their viewpoint,

shrouded their common sense, and darkened their days. They were shackled by the "do's and don'ts" inflicted on them by the rigid application of the Law that was drummed into them from the ruling Sanhedrin, causing them to follow the Law in fear.

24. Added to this, the dictatorial Roman rulership enhanced the Jews' daily fear as they tried to conform to the Law and simultaneously keep in step with Rome's demands.

25. What they needed was Someone who could show them the way through all this, and God sent His only begotten Son into the world to liberate them. However, He did not obliterate the enemy that enforced its dominance over the people; neither did He bring the peace the people thought the Messiah would. Instead, Jesus Christ intensified many of the Torah's teachings. When He addressed the crowd in the Sermon on the Mount, He said, *You have heard that it was said, you shall love your neighbor and hate your enemy. But I say to you, love your enemies, bless those who curse you, do good to those who hate you, and pray for those who spitefully use you and persecute you* (Matthew 5:43-44 NKJV).

26. Christ's brief ministry on earth was punctuated with miraculous events that have echoed through the ages. His ability to apprehend any sickness, disease, demonic attack, and even the grave, reinforced His deity and inherent power. His soft gentle touch on blind eyes (Matthew 9:29), His pure hands that were placed on the leper (Matthew 8:3), and His grasp of the dead girl's hand (Matthew 9:23-25) were all anointed with His healing touch.

27. Flowing from the Son of God, the anointing of the Holy Spirit streamed forth like a shining light that flooded the body of the sick and the lame (Matthew 15:31). Christ broke the bondage of disease with the touch of His hand, and miracles were performed as He did the works of His Father. The Son of God never looked for accolades; He wanted nothing more than to do His Father's will. On every occasion, as Jesus ministered, lives were drawn to the Father; and the people *glorified God* (Matthew 9:8; Mark 2:12; Luke 7:16).

28. Every miracle proved Christ's deity. Every miracle was a sign given to the people that He was the Holy One. How often the people demanded a sign, and Jesus gave them many. However, many still did not believe in Him. The Lord Jesus Christ's miracles and signs inspired the people to believe in Him. However, Jesus saw many who still did not believe; and He asked, *Why do ye not believe me?* (John 8:45-46).

29. While it is important to be knowledgeable of the miracles Jesus wrought, Spirit-filled believers focus on the deeper truths contained in the purpose for which the Father allowed His Son to perform them. While on earth, it is apparent that Jesus fulfilled the office of a *Prophet;* and after His ascension, He became the *Apostle and High Priest* (Hebrews 3:1) and *King of kings and Lord of lords* (Revelation 19:16).

30. Spoken about from the earliest of times, the Son of God was declared as the Prophet who would speak nothing but the words of His Father: *I will raise up for them a Prophet like you from among their brethren, and will put My words in His mouth, and He shall speak to them all that I command Him* (Deuteronomy 18:18 NKJV).

31. Prophecy is filled with spiritual intentions, and the prophetical words Jesus spoke were from His Father who is Spirit. The depth of meaning to which He took the hearers birthed new life in them: *Blessed are the pure in heart, for they shall see God* (Matthew 5:8). Jesus spoke prophetical truth as he uttered these words. There were some who heard Him and believed, some who accepted Him and saw Him as God (John 20:28), and some who acknowledged Him to be *the Christ, the Son of the living God* (Matthew 16:16).

32. Furthermore, Jesus spoke of His death that was to come. He also prophesied that in ages to come God's unbiased judgment would be metered out upon all flesh. The sign of a Prophet is the fulfillment of his prophetical utterances. To date, the things Jesus prophesied concerning certain events, have come to pass. Without doubt, Spirit-filled believers know that those prophetical utterances Jesus spoke concerning future events will come to pass.

33. The Spirit-filled believer clings to the words of Jesus Christ regarding the future prophetical utterances that He spoke, and which have not yet happened. Not only do these believers see the event; they also see the purpose of the event. In virtually every instance, Jesus prophesied about the reconciling work He was sent to do: *I am come that they may have life, and that they might have it more abundantly* (John 10:10).

34. The very essence of His prophetical statements embraced the reconciling work He was sent to accomplish (John 16: 1-15). Jesus also said, *I go to prepare a place for you* (John 14:2 NKJV). Jesus spoke of the purpose of His coming into the world-to make a way for those who believed in Him long after His ascension into heaven and to reconcile them to the Father. Apostle Paul affirms this purpose when he says *that*

God was in Christ reconciling the world to Himself, not imputing their trespasses to them (2 Corinthians 5:19).

35. The Lord Jesus Christ's works incorporated His primary role as that of a Priest. Jesus served mankind. He asked for no accolade. He willingly became the sacrifice for them. Jesus proclaimed this when He said, *For even the Son of Man did not come to be served, but to serve, and to give His life a ransom for many* (Mark 10:45 NKJV); when He assured, *I have come that they may have life, and that they may have it more abundantly* (John 10:10 NKJV); and when He promised, *As the Father knows Me, even so I know the Father; and I lay down My life for the sheep* (John 10.15 NKJV).

36. Just as the office of prophet is evidenced throughout the Old and New Testaments, so is the God-ordained role of a Priest. Stephen D. Renn says, "An important redemptive-historical element underlies the ministry of priests throughout Scripture. Priests were one of three classes of people (along with prophets and kings) under the old covenant to receive a Spirit anointing from God as a guarantee of their legitimate ministry."

37. The Lord Jesus Christ was anointed by the Holy Spirit (Luke 4:18), a prerequisite for the office of Priest, and administered the office of Priest further than the Old Testament priests. While these Old Testament priests offered a sacrificial lamb on behalf of the people, Jesus Himself became the sacrificial Lamb for the people as Apostle John declares, *Behold! The Lamb of God who takes away the sin of the world!* (John 1:29 NKJV).

38. Furthermore, unlike the annual ritual performed by the priests of the old covenant, Jesus offered Himself once and for all time. Stephen D. Renn explains this distinction with deep insight as he says, "The supreme distinction, however, between the old covenant priesthood and that of Christ in the new, is its eternal unbroken effectiveness. Christ's death on the cross functions as an unrepeatable mediatorial sacrifice that guarantees the certainty of forgiveness of all who put their faith in that action."

39. Spirit-filled believers attest that Jesus was chosen by His Father to occupy this office, and in so doing He fulfilled all the requirements of the Priest. He took His Priesthood further than any earthly priest in that He became the sacrifice when He offered Himself as the ransom for mankind's sin. Christ, in essence, extended His duties as Priest by becoming the ultimate sacrifice Himself.

40. The result of this action was the pivotal event in the existence of the Levitical priesthood. Because Christ's sacrifice was sufficient for all sin, there is no need for another sacrifice. Thus, Christ spiritually met all the requirements the Father had in a sacrifice; and as such, He canceled the Levitical priesthood of the Old Testament. The curtain was rent in two; the entrance into the Father's presence was now no longer hidden and reserved for only a High Priest. At Jesus' resurrection, He exited the tomb not only as Priest but also as the Savior of the world. Apostle John makes this definitive statement about the resurrected Jesus Christ: *We have seen and testify that the Father has sent the Son as Savior of the world* (1 John 4:14 NKJV).

41. Once Jesus had completed all the duties of His Priesthood, it is only befitting that His Father promoted Him to the highest office in the priesthood, namely, the *great High Priest* (Hebrews 4:14). Spirit-filled believers are persuaded that the glorious Person of the risen Christ ascended to the right hand of the Father and that He is seated there for the express purpose of fulfilling His High Priestly role of making intercession on behalf of the righteous *holy priesthood* (Romans 8:34; 1 Peter 2:5).

42. The writer in the letter to the Hebrews explains the two offices the risen Lord Jesus Christ now holds while He waits for His Father's command to Him to return to the earth. Believers are encouraged to *consider the Apostle and High Priest of our profession, Christ Jesus* (Hebrews 3:1). First, is the office of *Apostle*, the One revealing the Father's deep truths through the Holy Spirit to the saints. Second, is the *High Priest* taking the message from the saints to the Father on their behalf.

43. There are no other words more worthy of a higher exaltation of Jesus than those recorded in Hebrews 7:24 (NKJV): *But because He continues forever,* [He] *has an unchangeable priesthood.*

44. In Jesus' offices of Prophet and Priest while he was on earth, He simultaneously held the office of King of the Jews. The question put to Him by the High Priest, Caiaphas, *Art thou the Christ, the Son of the Blessed?* (Mark 14:61), pertains to Christ's spiritual office. Someone had to ask Jesus this question; and it is only befitting that the highest office in the Jewish leadership, the ruling High Priest, asks Jesus to confirm His Sonship (Mark 14:62).

45. Since the Jews were primarily concerned with Jesus' confirmation that He was the Messiah, the Son of God, they paid little attention to His office of king. This office, on the other hand, was of more importance

to the procurator, Pontius Pilate. He does not concern himself with the Lord's role as the Christ, the Son of God, but focuses on His earthly rulership as King of the Jews (Mark 15:2).

46. Pilate was convinced that Jesus was the King of the Jews, to the extent that he personally wrote the words, *Jesus of Nazareth, the King of the Jews* (John 19:19 NKJV) on the plaque posted on the Cross. Even when confronted by the angry chief priests, Pilate refused to change his words and stated that he was personally responsible for the declaration of who he believed Jesus was. He declares, *What I have written, I have written* (John 19:22 NKJV), and no further argument prevailed.

47. As with the offices of Prophet and High Priest, Christ's Kingly office is eternally bestowed on Him. Apostle Paul gives a resounding accolade to the Christ, the Lord and the King as he says, *Now to the King eternal, immortal, invisible, to God who alone is wise, be honor and glory forever and ever* (1 Timothy 1:17 NKJV).

48. Spirit-filled believers understand that Jesus' kingship is a spiritual kingship. This is the highest office of rulership and authority that can be given to Him. In this instance, Christ's kingship is elevated to more than King of the Jews. After His resurrection, Jesus is declared the King of the Kingdom of God (1 Timothy 1:17). This is a spiritual Kingdom into which all born-again believers enter once they accept by faith Jesus Christ's finished work on Calvary, irrespective of their race, religion, or culture (Luke 1:33, John 3:1-7).

49. The Kingdom of God differs from the Kingdom of Heaven. While both kingdoms are from God, the Kingdom of Heaven is earthy and is the promised kingdom to the Jews (Isaiah 11:1-9). However, after Christ's resurrection, the spiritual Kingdom of God is now for the *whosoever* (John 3:16). This kingdom is not *eating and drinking, but righteousness and peace and joy in the Holy Spirit* (Romans 14:17 NKJV).

50. A king must have a kingdom, and a kingdom must be ruled by a king. A king rules his subjects who are submissive to him in all their ways. All believers become subjects in the Kingdom of God the moment they are born again.

51. From His resurrection, all things are now in subjection to Jesus Christ. He is the One endowed with *all authority* [that] *has been given to* [Him] *in heaven and earth* (Matthew 28:18 NKJV).

52. Herein is the annunciation of Christ's Kingship over all things. When Jesus was sent to the earth, He came as the King of the Jews. He was

rejected by them and, therefore, He had no subjects. This opened the door for His sacrificial offering to God the Father for the *whosoever* and not only for the Jews because *in every nation whoever fears Him and works righteousness is accepted by Him* (Acts 10:35). From His resurrection, Jesus was bestowed with a more inclusive Kingship that extended beyond the Jews and incorporated everyone who accepts His death and resurrection by faith (Romans 10:9-10).

53. Christ's kingship embraces more than Jesus' reply to Pilate, *My kingdom is not of this world* (John 18:36). From His resurrection, Jesus can rightfully declare that *all authority* is now granted to Him. He who created all things is endowed with the spiritual office of Ruler (King). From the moment He walked out of the tomb, Christ became the ultimate authority over all things. He was no longer subjected to His Father's will, but He was endowed with *all power* to rule as the Monarch over both heaven and earth *which* [the Father] *worked in Christ when He raised Him from the dead and seated Him at His right hand in the heavenly places, far above all principality and power and might and dominion, and every name that is named, not only in this age but also in that which is to come* (Ephesians 1:20-21). From that moment onward, Jesus commissioned the Holy Spirit to minister to the saved and convict the sinner (John 16:7-14).

54. Matthew's powerful record of Jesus' words must be carefully digested. This verse–*And Jesus came and spoke to them, saying, all authority has been given to Me in heaven and on earth.* (Matthew 28:18 NKJV)–is the proclamation of King Jesus Christ's all-encompassing credentials. With all His love for His devoted disciples, Christ graciously reveals to them exactly who He is, what power and authority He now has, and what their commission is thereafter.

55. Herein is the exquisite display of Jesus Christ's love and compassion for His disciples. Even though He is seen by all the disciples some still doubt that it is the Christ whom they see: *Some doubted* (Matthew 28:17). It is Jesus who *comes and speaks to them.* He does not hold anything against the doubters, but instead approaches them in love and compassion declaring His new status. It is the befitting action of one who shows compassion: Jesus approaches them. So often Jesus did this (Matthew 9:23, 17:7; Mark 6:34; Luke 14:15, 19:5; John 4:4; Acts 9:3-5).

56. Throughout His earthly ministry, Jesus demonstrated His power over every force that opposed Him and His disciples. He calmed the raging

sea, He cast out demons, His words withered the fig tree, He changed water into wine, and He healed and delivered all those who were sick and oppressed. And now He declares to the disciples, *All authority has been given to Me.* Until that moment, everything Jesus did was from the Father; and what the Father wanted him to do, He obediently did. Jesus now makes the declaration that He has been given all authority and power. He no longer needs to get instruction from His Father; He now has the power and authority to do all things.

57. Christ's authority was not taken or snatched from the hands of human kings on earth and passed to Him. He did not demand His rights and claim or proclaim His position as king. He did not assume the office; neither did He dethrone anyone so that He could occupy the office of king; it was *given to* [Him]. What Satan offered Jesus at the beginning of His ministry and which He refused, namely, all authority (Matthew 4:8-9), the Father freely gave and bestowed on Him (Matthew 28:18; Hebrews 1:13).

58. In his commentary, Matthew Henry gives clearer insight on this subject: "He did not assume it, or usurp it, but it was given Him, He was legally entitled to it, and invested in it, by a grant from Him who is the Fountain of all being, and consequently all power. God *set* [Him] *King* (Psalm 2:6) inaugurated and enthroned Him. He had power before, *power to forgive sins,* but now *all power* [authority] is given to Him."

59. It is worth pondering how unprepared the disciples were for their commission. They had been with Jesus for many years and relied entirely on His teaching and His instructions. When they hear Jesus telling them *go into all the world* (Mark 16:15) and to do this without Him. Jesus calms their doubts by announcing His full authority over all things both in heaven and on earth, and by explaining His authority comes from His Father.

60. This is the first step Jesus takes in showing them the tasks which He had in His heart for them to do. All things that are spiritual and that pertain to the spiritual Kingdom of God are from Jesus. His entire charter contained the spiritual endowment of the promise of eternal life in Him for everyone who believes. He commissions believers to *make disciples of all nations* (Matthew 28:19A). They are to teach the nations about the spiritual Kingdom of God and bring them to repentance of their sins, baptizing them *in the name of the Father and of the Son and of the Holy Spirit* (verse 19B). Their spiritual inauguration about Christ's Kingdom was launched as they accepted His commands.

61. The disciples were transitioning from seeing the physical and material miracles Jesus performed, actions which they would now undertake, to being introduced to the spiritual "signs and wonders" they would experience. They would witness the spiritual rebirth of people and the establishment of the spiritual body of Christ, which is His church.

62. Jesus' words are crisp and forthright as when He declares, *Go therefore,* the first royal command from the King of kings. The *going* is not filled with instructions that an earthly king would give his subjects. Jesus' disciples are not commanded to build huge cities with walls and staked boundaries. They are not told to build mighty armies capable of marching into battle, nor are they given the command to rule with a rod of iron over the enemy.

63. How beautiful are Jesus' instructions: *(1) make disciples of all nations, (2) baptize them in the name of the Father and of the Son and of the Holy Spirit, (3)* [teach] *them to observe all things that I have commanded you* (Matthew 28:19-20 NKJV). These are all spiritual directives.

64. As with all things from the Godhead, the disciples are not left on their own, comfortless, or powerless and without authority. Jesus leaves them with the most exhilarating promises, *You shall receive power when the Holy Spirit has come upon you; and you shall be witnesses to Me in Jerusalem, and in all Judea and Samaria, and to the end of the earth* (Acts 1:8 NKJV), and, *Lo, I am with you always, even to the end of the age* (Matthew 28:20 NKJV).

65. The highest office of authority, the most powerful Ruler over heaven and earth patiently waits for the Day of His return. At that soon-coming triumphant event that proceeds from heaven to earth, Jesus will return as *KING OF KINGS AND LORD OF LORDS* (Revelation 19:16).

Chapter 12

Jesus Died for Mankind

1. There has never been, and there will never be any human being that will fully grasp and understand the depth of the Heavenly Father's love for mankind that caused Him to send His only begotten Son to die for mankind. The pivotal verse in the entire Bible echoes through the caverns of the minds of countless millions who through the centuries have believed and quoted the Holy Writ that *God so loved the world that He gave His only begotten Son, that whoever believes in Him should not perish but have everlasting life* (John 3:16 NKJV).

2. Furthermore, it is probable that every man called by God into the ministry has preached the message contained in this verse. It has reached into countless millions' hearts that God's love for mankind caused Him to demonstrate that *in this is love, not that we loved God, but that He loved us and sent His Son to be the propitiation for our sins* (1 John 4:10 NKJV).

3. God chose His Son, Jesus Christ, to be the *Lamb slain from the foundation of the world* (Revelation 13:8 NKJV). The impelling cause for the Father to send His Son to that horrific death is embedded in His immeasurable love for mankind. God's unfathomable love was so compelling that He be reconciled to mankind and have fellowship with them that He made the greatest sacrifice possible and sent His only Son to die for mankind.

4. Chrysostom (A.D. 349-407) explains God's love towards mankind in this way; "'God so loved the world', shows such an intensity of love. For great indeed and infinite is the distance between the two. The immortal, the infinite majesty without beginning or end, loved those

who were but dust and ashes, who were loaded with ten thousand sins but remained ungrateful even as they constantly offended Him."

5. The incalculable depth of God's love never hinted at obliterating sinners; His desire was to save them from His wrath. He observed mankind's sin as the division and schism that severed the divine relationship, and God determined to reunite Himself with redeemed mankind. Chrysostom summarizes this explanation of God's love when he says, "This is He who loved. For God did not give a servant, or an angel or even an archangel but His *only begotten Son* and yet no one would show such anxiety even for his own child as God did for His ungrateful servants. He laid down His own life for us and poured forth His precious blood for our sakes–even though there is nothing good in us."

6. Too often believers ask questions as to why God did what He did for mankind. Perhaps the subject should be considered from this perspective: what was not in God that could have prevented Him from sending His Son to die for mankind?

7. First, God owed no man a debt. Mankind separated himself from God; it was not God who did anything to man that He owed him a reprieve. Second, God had no guilt in Him that made Him offer Jesus as the sacrifice (payment) for a guilty act God did. The responsible party was mankind who stands guilty before God for transgressing His holiness and righteousness. Third, God had no obligation that He had to meet to redeem mankind. This was man's transgression against God, not the other way making God obliged to remedy the problem.

8. Lastly, God knew no other way to redeem mankind than for Him to shed sinless blood as the sacrificial offering to redeem mankind from his sin and to reconcile man to Him again. Because *All have sinned, and come short of the glory of God* (Romans 3:23), according to God's standards for the atonement for sins, a sacrificial lamb without spot or blemish had to be offered. God used His only Son as that sacrificial Lamb because Jesus is the only One who had sin-free blood to meet all the requirements contained in God's standards for the remission of sins.

9. If God had used anyone else, or used any other method to redeem mankind, it would never have measured up to the fullest capacity of His love for mankind. God reached down into His very Being, namely who He is (*God is love*), and gave His uttermost for wretched mankind; He sent His only begotten Son, the ultimate and utmost of all He is.

10. The death of Jesus is so important that all four Gospels give exhaustive accounts of this. Furthermore, Apostle Paul states he could not occupy his mind with anything else *save Jesus Christ, and him crucified* (1 Corinthians 2:2).

11. Even the Old Testament prophet, Isaiah, speaks of Jesus' life on earth and declares that *He was wounded for our transgressions, He was led as a lamb to the slaughter* (Isaiah 53:1-12 NKJV).

12. While it is never the intention of Spirit-filled believers to ignore or take lightly the horrible, gruesome physical sacrifice of Jesus on the cross, they focus more fully on the spiritual implications; *for the message of the cross is foolishness to those who are perishing, but to us who are being saved, it is the* [spiritual] *power of God* (1 Corinthians 1:18 NKJV).

13. The magnitude of the spiritual message found in Jesus' death is never more eloquently expressed than when Apostle Paul writes under the anointing of the Holy Spirit, *But God has revealed them to us through His Spirit. For the Spirit searches all things, yes, the deep things of God. For what man knows the things of a man except the spirit of the man which is in him? Even so no one knows the things of God except the Spirit of God. Now we have received, not the spirit of the world, but the Spirit who is from God, that we might know the things that have been freely given to us by God. These things we also speak, not in words which man's wisdom teaches but which the Holy Spirit teaches, comparing spiritual things with spiritual. But the natural man does not receive the things of the Spirit of God, for they are foolishness to him; nor can he know them, because they are spiritually discerned* (1 Corinthians 2:10-14 NKJV).

14. Jesus' death was so all embracing that even the heavenly creatures acknowledged Christ's sacrificial death. Their accolade with the twenty-four elders pertaining to Jesus' death is pronounced as a worship anthem- *And they sang a new song, saying: "You are worthy to take the scroll, And to open its seals; For You were slain, and have redeemed us to God by Your blood out of every tribe and tongue and people and nation, and have made us kings and priests to our God; And we shall reign on the earth"* (Revelation 5:9-10 NKJV).

15. The first glimpse of spiritual insight into Christ's death is found when His human nature was put to the fullest test. First, it was the betrayal of one of His disciples, Judas, who unfaithfully kissed his Master on the cheek. Then, Jesus being *sorrowful unto death* (Mark 14:34) was abandoned by His three disciples in the Garden of Gethsemane; and

then, He faced the denial of one of His disciples, Peter. All this took place even before He began to suffer physically. How horrendous and cruel was the physical punishment He suffered and endured thereafter.

16. The Son of God suffered the worst experience of the Father's salvation plan; sin was thrust upon Him. Surely, it was "the worst kept for last." Sin, and all its consequences were rendered unto the Innocent One *and the LORD* [His own Father] *hath laid on Him the iniquity of us all* (Isaiah 53:6).

17. The birth of a person is with the purpose of living and then to die as Apostle Paul explains, *It is appointed unto men once to die* (Hebrews 9:27). However, the Lord Jesus Christ came into the world for the purpose of dying.

18. Jesus Christ's last utterance while on the cross, *it is finished,* seals the Old Covenant and its demand of a sacrificial offering of a one-year-old lamb. It points directly to the spiritual application of the New Covenant in His blood (Matthew 26:28) and fulfills an eternal prophecy about *the Lamb slain from the foundation of the world* (Revelation 13:8).

19. Jesus Christ, the Son of Man, died physically; and Jesus Christ, the Son of God, was spiritually banished into hell when mankind's sin was thrust onto Him. He drank of the cup (sponge) (John 19:29-30); and immediately, when He did that, God placed mankind's sin on Him; and Christ was *made to be sin for us* (2 Corinthians 5:21). The spiritual separation between the Father and the Son had to happen because the only way the Father could justify Christ in the Spirit was to place mankind's sin on Him on the Cross, banish Him into hell, and then release Him from hell, the abode of sinners' souls and spirits (Psalm 16:10; 1 Timothy 3:16).

20. Jesus' death annunciated by His shed precious blood was the required demand God instituted to remove His wrath from being poured out on mankind. God's spiritual punishment on man's sinful state (His wrath) was instated when Adam sinned. God had no choice but to vindicate His holiness that was violated by man's sin.

21. As gruesome as Christ's death was, so glorious was the result. Jesus took mankind's sin upon Himself and paid the price, conquered death and hell so that God could forgive the repentant hearts their sin. While sin is a mental conception and a physical action, it is also a spiritual schism that created a breach that was impossible for man to repair. God, who is Spirit, was the only One who could reconcile man to Himself.

22. The result was a spiritual victory Jesus achieved over hell, death, and the grave. He *destroyed the works of the devil.* He reconciled God and man through His shed blood that removed God's wrath against a repentant heart.

23. Jesus Christ's death opened the way for all mankind to enter the holy presence of the Father. The physical tearing of the veil that shrouded the Holy of Holies in the temple signified to the Jews that the shedding of Christ's blood opened the way for them spiritually to enter His presence. Sadly, they never acknowledged nor accepted His sacrifice for them.

24. Jesus lived a sinless life. He died for mankind to make the way for them to be reconciled to the Father. Jesus Christ achieved this spiritual victory. There is no assumption necessary; neither is there any doubt in Spirit-filled believers' minds and spirits that their Savior was victoriously raised from the dead and restored to the highest seat of honor. To bring it into reality, the following question needs to be answered: at what moment in time was the holy Son of God made sin for mankind?

The Cup

25. From the Passover meal until Christ's last breath, there is a spiritual message that pertains to the cup Jesus continually referenced regarding His becoming sin for mankind. Herein is the spiritual application and physical representation used by Jesus to demonstrate the spiritual process He applied to achieve total victory over sin and its penalty.

26. The significance of the cup referenced by Christ is first mentioned when two disciples' mother approached Him and asked that her sons be given the place of honor alongside Jesus in His kingdom (Matthew 20:20-21).

27. Turning to the two disciples, Jesus asked them, *Are you able to drink the cup that I am about to drink?* (Matthew 20:22). It is obvious that the two disciples were not fully aware of the contents of the question they were asked. They willingly answered that they would drink of the cup. They had little understanding of the physical punishment, mental anguish, and spiritual abandonment Jesus was referring to when He referenced the *cup.*

28. Old Testament prophets make mention of the cup of God's wrath and fury (Psalm 75:8; Isaiah 51:17; Jeremiah 25:15). This very same symbol

is used in a practical demonstration by Jesus when He was made sin for mankind.

29. When Jesus gathered the disciples around Him in the Upper Room and they had shared the Passover meal, He reached for the bread and told them that it was to be His body that would be broken for them: *Then He took the cup and gave thanks and gave it to them, saying, Drink from it all of you. For this is My blood of the new covenant, which is shed for many for the remission of sins* (Matthew 26: 27-28 NKJV). Here Jesus references a cup indicating that He will shed His precious blood for mankind.

30. This holy instruction is given to all believers to observe it as a reminder of the physical as well as the spiritual sacrifice of Jesus. His body was brutally mutilated, and His Spirit was also separated from the Father's presence.

31. Rising from the table, Jesus and the eleven disciples made their way to the Garden of Gethsemane. Jesus then *went a little farther* (Matthew 26:39) into the garden and started praying to the Father, *O My father, if it is possible, let this cup pass from Me; nevertheless, not as I will, but as you will.* The Son of God asked the Father three times if there was any way He could remove the *cup* for Him.

32. When Jesus referenced the *cup,* He revealed the magnitude of the purpose of the instrument (the cup) that would be used to demonstrate to the world the moment He became sin. Jesus did not ask the Father to remove the scourging, the false accusations; neither did He ask the Father to find a less punishing way than the crucifixion. He focused on the *cup* asking that this be taken from Him. Herein is the most haunting and worst aspect of Christ's sacrifice, His separation from His Father the moment He drank of the *cup.*

33. Once Jesus had settled in His heart that there was no other way than for Him to be made sin for man, He walked to the disciples, woke them up, and told them the hour had come. When Judas identified Jesus and the palace guards took hold of Jesus, Peter lunged forward with his sword and sliced off Malchus's ear. Jesus immediately performed a miracle and touched his ear and healed him (Luke 22:51).

34. Jesus then turned to Peter and said, *Shall I not drink the cup which My Father has given Me?* (John 18:11 NKJV). Jesus did not reference His crucifixion or His physical punishment that was soon to follow. He referenced the *cup* that He had to drink.

35. It was a usual practice for the Roman soldiers to offer the person who was about to be crucified, a drink of wine mingled with gall to lessen the physical pain they were about to inflict on the body. When they offered Jesus a drink, He refused it (Matthew 27:34). His refusal was not a sign of His bravery to endure pain; He refused to drink of that cup offered Him before He was nailed to the cross because it was not yet time for Him to demonstrate to the world that He would be made sin.

36. After Jesus had been on the cross for six hours, He made a profound statement, *I thirst* (John 19:29). To many who witnessed His last six hours, their focus was on His physical suffering. As brutal as it was, however, there was more happening than the physical suffering.

37. With all the agony and physical suffering Christ's body endured, the last thing on His mind would have been that He was thirsty. His face was bloated from the poisonous crown of thorns that pierced His brow. His torso was ripped to shreds from the scourging, the nails had torn His flesh, and His lungs were being filled with water due to His not being able to breathe. Yet He says, *I thirst*.

38. The time had come for Him to drink of the dreaded *cup*. The Lord Jesus Christ had but a few seconds left before He would give up His Spirit. A diligent Roman soldier heard the two words that proceeded from the Savior's lips. He reached for the closest available instrument he could find that he could use as a *cup*.

39. *Now a vessel full of sour wine was sitting there; and they filled a sponge with sour wine, put it on hyssop, and put it to His mouth. So when Jesus had* [drank of the cup] *received the sour wine* (John 19:30 NKJV), then it happened.

40. The moment Jesus sucked the sour wine from the sponge, God the Father thrust mankind's sin upon Jesus. The separation Jesus had begged the Father to take away took place the moment Jesus surrendered His spirit as He physically drank of the *cup*.

41. It was held back by the Father until the very last few seconds of Jesus' life. The holy Son of God was kept totally sinless until the last breath He breathed. He was made sin a few seconds before He gave up His Spirit. How precious was the Father's love for His Son that He held back mankind's evil sin until the very last moment when Jesus said, *"It is finished!"* and bowing His head, He gave up His Spirit. The Christ, the Son of the living God *who knew no sin, was made to be sin for us* (2 Corinthians 5:21 NKJV).

42. It must never be forgotten that Jesus was present as part of the Godhead when the first Adam sinned in the Garden of Eden. He witnessed the cataclysmic rending of the relationship and fellowship Adam had with the Father. The consequences of the sin were so daunting that Christ knew the repercussions that would ricochet throughout mankind's existence.

43. Then, the Lord Jesus Christ (the Last Adam) experienced this same horrific severing from the Father. This was what Jesus had seen as the most difficult part of the entire crucifixion because He pleads with His Father, *remove this cup from me* (Luke 22:42).

44. While paying attention to the instrument Jesus referenced, namely *the cup*, it is perhaps the one defining message that pertains to His precious blood. Christ's blood was incorruptible. It was, and still is, *precious*. The Father never allowed His Son's holy blood to see any corruption.

45. It was the most gracious, and yet divine command that Jesus' blood remain pure and without sin (the first Adam's blood lost its purity when he sinned).

46. Thus said, the Father had to wait until the very last breath His Son gave, and He had to wait until every last drop of Christ's *precious* blood had flowed and was drained from Jesus body before He made Jesus sin for mankind.

47. The very act of drinking from the sponge (the *cup*) signified the "emptiness" of Christ's life of His blood, and it was the declaration that Jesus had no more physical life in Him because every drop of His *precious blood* was no longer in His body.

48. The cup was the instrument the Father used to signify to the world that He had thrust upon His Son mankind's sin. The effect of drinking from this cup resulted in sin being placed upon Him and, ultimately, the separation from His Father.

Christ's Physical and Spiritual death

49. God's holy record, the Bible, gives details of the activities that took place after Jesus was arrested in the Garden of Gethsemane. His false trial before the Sanhedrin, the appearance before the *fox* (Luke 13:32) Herod, and the questions posed to Him by Pilate, together with the brutal scourging and platted crown of thorns, all resulted in the ultimate declaration that *they took Jesus and led Him away* (John 19:16 NKJV).

50. It was vital that every prophetic utterance concerning the Son of God's death had to be fulfilled. While the physical and mental experiences that Jesus endured are of utmost importance, Spirit-filled believers desire clarification on the spiritual implications of the purpose of everything that Jesus endured.

51. The Old Covenant demanded that the High Priest laid his hands on the "scapegoat" and it was taken into the "wilderness." He would take the sin-offering bullock and goat, *whose blood was brought to make atonement in the Holy Place, . . . outside the camp* (Leviticus 16:27 NKJV). So too, was Jesus led away *as a lamb to the slaughter* (Isaiah 53:7); and *therefore Jesus also, that He might sanctify the people with His own blood, suffered outside the gate* (Hebrews 13:12 NKJV).

52. The physical journey to outside the city walls spiritually sealed the fulfillment of God's holy demand that the sin-offering be removed from the presence of the people and *carried outside the gate.*

53. While the Son of God was being nailed to the cross, there was a long line of Jews carrying a lamb to be sacrificed on the altar in the temple. For the most part they were oblivious of the crucifixion. But more than that, they were totally unaware of the fact that, while they were fulfilling the physical offering of a lamb for the atonement of their sin, God was personally offering the Lamb of God for the spiritual redemption of their sin.

54. Every born-again believer needs to understand the spiritual implications of the physical sacrifice and shedding of Christ's precious blood. To merely analyze the events and understand every detail of the diabolical physical ordeal the Savior endured is only part of the divine message. It has deep spiritual implications that can be received only by revelation.

55. To begin, the relationship Adam severed between himself and God was a spiritual relationship. Therefore, the reconciliation of the spiritual relationship is the foremost purpose of Christ's sacrifice. Apostle Paul makes regular reference in his writings to *Jesus Christ and Him crucified* (1 Corinthians 2:2). He also states that *it came through the revelation of Jesus Christ* (Galatians 1:12 NKJV). The full import of the spiritual reason for Calvary is imparted by revelation to believers.

56. The most important point to be remembered is that it was God's offering His Son for mankind. This was not an angel or a good person He offered; it was God Himself who sent His only Son to die for mankind. The two parties involved in the severing of the relationship, man and

God, had to be involved in the reconciliation of that relationship. Man walked away from God and sinned; and in the sacrifice of His Son, God walked towards man to reunite the relationship.

57. The One who hung on Calvary's cross was none other than God's holy Son. And He suffered a spiritual death of being separated spiritually from His Father. Origen of Alexandria (AD 184-254) explains Christ's death as being real and not merely an appearance of death when he says, "It was not an appearance only that He died. It was a true death. The spirit did not expire since it was eternal and incorruptible. But there was One who had the spirit who indeed expired who, while expiring, commended the spirit to the Father. He is the One whom Joseph wrapped in the linen cloth and buried. He did not wrap up and bury a shadow but Him who was nailed to the tree."

58. This was not a sacrifice forced upon the Son of God, but rather Jesus Christ surrendered willingly to the act. His own words reveal this: *I lay down my life that I may take it again. No one takes it from Me, but I lay it down of Myself. I have power to lay it down, and I have power to take it again. This command I have received from My Father* (John 10:17-18 NKJV). Dionysius of Alexandria (A.D. 250) says, "He shows that His passion was a voluntary thing and besides that, He indicates that the life that is laid down and taken up again is one thing and the divinity that lays that down and takes it again is another."

59. The final three words Jesus uttered from the cross, *it is finished,* have such profound spiritual significance that it passes human comprehension. *Bowing His head, He gave up His Spirit* (John 19:30 NKJV). Here the divine Son of God signaled His surrender to His Father's will and had mankind's sin thrust upon Him. He knew His Father had just made Him sin for mankind, and He looked down, away from heaven. Now a sinner, he could not look the Father in the eye, and *He bowed His head.*

60. Arthur W. Pink in his book *Exposition of the Gospel of John* gives a serene and spiritual explanation of what happened when Jesus *bowed His head,* "This was not the despairing cry of a helpless martyr. It was not an expression of satisfaction that the end of His suffering was now reached. It was not the last gasp of a worn-out life. No, it was the declaration on the part of the Divine Redeemer that all for which He came from heaven to earth to do, was done."

61. It is fitting that the Eternal Son of God did not have His Spirit taken from Him. Scripture is clear the He *gave up His Spirit* (John 19:30 NKJV). When death befalls all of mankind, their spirits are taken from them. Not so with Jesus who gave up His Spirit. In this final act of surrender, Jesus hands over His soul and spirit into the fate of death's abode. Tertullian (A.D. 155-240) gives the rendering of the difference between mortal man's death and how Jesus died. "Nailed upon the Cross, He exhibited many notable signs by which His death was distinguished from all others. By His own free will, He dismissed from His spirit with a word, anticipating the executioner's work."

62. Apostle John clearly hears the word from the Savior's lips, *finished*. In the original tongue, Jesus uttered only one word for the English phrase used *it is finished*. This Greek word for "finished' is "teleo" and has a significant meaning. It announces that all the spiritual work Jesus came to do was concluded. There was nothing more He could do, nor was there anything else needed to be done to accomplish the victory over sin. He was the Lamb of God sacrificed; His precious blood was shed; His sinless, holy life was made sin; and His human body breathed its last breath.

63. Christ spiritually *made an end* (teleo) of all future sacrifices of the one-year-old lambs. His death canceled out the Levitical priesthood, broke down the middle wall of partition, and opened the door to the Father's heart for man's repentant heart to once again be reconciled to Him.

64. Arthur W. Pink says about Jesus' last three words, "This was the briefest and yet the fullest of His seven cross-utterances. Eternity will be needed to make manifest all that it contains. All things had been done which the Law of God had required; all things established which prophecy predicted; all things brought to pass which the types foreshadowed; all things accomplished which the Father had given Him to do; all things performed which were needed for our redemption."

65. Spirit-filled believers focus on the spiritual implications that followed Jesus' death. Apostle John gives a beautiful account of the laying to rest of both the Son of Man and the Son of God: *Then they took the body of Jesus* (John 19:40). This indicates the physical removal of Jesus' body, the Son of Man, from the cross. The human frame had died and was taken from the wretched cross. Apostle John is referencing Jesus's physical body born of a woman that lived for more than thirty years on earth which was now physically dead.

66. Explaining how they hurriedly prepared the *body* for burial in a tomb, Apostle John says, *there laid they Jesus* (John 19:42). This signifies the spiritual laying to rest of the Son of God. John does not say, "There they laid the body of Jesus." He is telling the reader that in His death, both the Son of Man and the Son of God died. The most precious word in any language throughout the world is "Jesus." The angel declares to Mary, *You shall call His name JESUS* (Luke 1:31 NKJV). In this passage, the original tongue emphasizes the name "Jesus" in all capital letters. He is the Son of God born of a woman. Yet, He is born of the Father, and also fully Man; and He died physically and spiritually.

67. The body was taken and laid in the tomb. Likewise, Jesus, the Son of God, was also laid in the tomb. Jesus died physically and was placed in a tomb separating Him from the living. Added to that, He was separated from the Father and *made sin*. Sin broke the relationship between God and man, and the sin-stained Christ was separated from His Father.

68. The spiritual significance of the gardens should never be forgotten. The most sublime place on earth was the Garden of Eden. There Adam sinned and was driven out of the garden from the presence of God. Jesus, the Son of God's dead body, was taken into a garden, and placed in a new tomb. Sin drove man out of the first garden (Eden), and Jesus' resurrection brought victory over sin from the garden tomb.

Chapter 13

The Precious Blood of Jesus

1. The Bible explains Christ's precious blood as the mightiest force because it means *that you were not redeemed with corruptible things, like silver or gold, from your aimless conduct received by tradition from your fathers, but with the precious blood of Christ, as of a lamb without blemish and without spot* (1 Peter 1:18-19 NKJV).

2. *For it pleased the Father that in Him all the fullness should dwell, and by Him to reconcile all things to Himself, by Him, whether things on earth or things in heaven, having made peace through the blood of His cross. And you, who once were alienated and enemies in your mind by wicked works, yet now He has reconciled in the body of His flesh through death, to present you holy, and blameless, and above reproach in His sight if indeed you continue in the faith, grounded and steadfast, and are not moved away from the hope of the gospel which you heard, which was preached to every creature under heaven* (Colossians 1:19-23 NKJV).

3. This subject is the central theme of the relationship between God and man. This is the ultimate expression of God's holy, divine love and reconciling work that reunites His relationship and fellowship once again with man. Andrew Murray in his book *The Blood of the Cross* gives a unique statement regarding the effect the shed blood of Jesus has: "The great event which moved heaven, earth, and hell; for which the world had to be prepared and for which it had to wait for four thousand years; the results of which will endure forever–the shedding of the blood of the Son of God on the cross–had an unspeakable great object– It was to bring about the destruction of sin itself, and of its consequences."

4. There is no other way mankind can ever be reconciled to God than through the shed, precious blood of Jesus Christ. No ritual, deed, vow, or sacrifice can ever save mankind from the inherent sin within them. There is no specially anointed person in any denomination, culture, or any other religion that has the power to forgive the inherent sin dwelling in every human being. It is only through the washing of the shed, precious blood of Jesus Christ that man can have his sin removed and be saved.

5. The very essence and power of God's forgiveness of sin is invested in the shed blood of Jesus Christ as the Holy Writ declares, *the blood of Jesus Christ cleanses us from all sin* (1 John 1:7-9 NKJV). Jesus Christ's shed blood is so important to the Godhead that the entire new covenant has its power, authority, and victory. It is so because the very life of the Son of God, His blood, was poured out on the Cross to appease the Father's wrath against sin.

6. W. A. C. Rowe says, "The precious blood of Christ is the vital heart and indispensable nourishment of the Gospel. As good, healthy, rich blood is to the physical frame, so the precious blood of the Lord and Savior Jesus Christ ministers to the eternal salvation of men. Every preacher and believer's testimony that deteriorates in the faith and proclamation of the essential truth concerning the blood of Christ proceeds surely to their death."

7. Throughout the Bible, God has always used blood as a means to atone, cover, and forgive man's sin. The Word says, *Without shedding of blood, there is no remission* (Hebrews 9:22 NKJV). It progresses and continues to the final blood sacrifice of Christ's own blood when the Father sent His only begotten Son to die and shed His blood for many, Christ Himself acclaiming, *For this is My blood of the new covenant, which is shed for many for the remission of sins* (Matthew 26:28 NKJV). Again, the Word proclaims, *In Him we have redemption through His blood, the forgiveness of sins, according to the riches of His grace* (Ephesians 1:7 NKJV).

8. God chose blood as the acceptable sacrificial offering for man's sins. God instructed man to use *the life of the flesh* (Leviticus 17:11) as the means to deal with sin. It was upon His instruction that Moses inaugurate the Day of Atonement and institute the offering of a sacrificial lamb's shed blood as a means to atone the person's sins.

9. This was not man's idea but entirely God's instruction, and it had God's approval as the means to appease His wrath against men's sins. Jesus

instituted the new covenant in His blood which believers accept by faith in His redeeming work on the Cross, namely His death and the shedding of His blood. The fulfillment of Christ's words, *This is the new covenant in My blood,* was the demand the Father made for the remission of sins.

10. There is a significant progression of the blood in the covenants God made with man to appease His wrath against sin. It is in the blood that the covenant had its foundation and power. R. A. Torrey references this progression when he says, "It is by the blood alone that God and man can be brought into a covenant fellowship with God. That which had been foreshadowed at the gate of Eden, on Mount Ararat, on Mount Moriah, and in Egypt was now confirmed at the foot of Mount Sinai in a most solemn manner. Without blood, there could be no access by sinful man to a holy God."

11. "There is, however, a significant difference between the methodologies of applying the blood in the former cases as compared with the latter. On Mount Moriah, the life was redeemed by the shedding of the blood. In Egypt, it was sprinkled on the doorposts of the houses; but at Sinai, it was sprinkled on the persons themselves. The contract was closer, the application more powerful (Exodus 24:8). When Israel had reached Sinai, God had given His law as the foundation of His covenant. That covenant now had to be established, but as it is expressly stated in Hebrews 9:7, *not without blood.*"

12. This crimson flow is evident throughout the Holy Writ. Nothing can dispense with the necessity of the blood. The covenant God made with Israel reflects the sacrifice and shedding of blood by the chosen delegates on behalf of the people, and then the precious blood of Jesus is shed for the total annihilation of the inherent sin in the repentant heart.

Atonement

13. The Old Covenant references "atonement" as the manner in which God dealt with man's sin. He required that a sacrifice be offered, and the blood of the sacrifice was to be poured out so that God could look favorably on those offering the sacrifice.

14. Before Jesus' blood was shed on Calvary, the blood of animals was the means whereby God "covered" the people's sins or atoned it.

15. The High Priest, with a priest, or a priest alone, received the offering of an animal from the people and made an atonement for their sins by sacrificing the offering on the altar in the Temple's Holy Place on behalf of the people. The High Priest took the blood with him into the Most Holy Place where God dwelt. He knew he had no access to God's holy presence if he went into it without the blood of the sacrificed animal. The blood was the representative offering the people made to God which was presented on their behalf by the High Priest on the mercy seat.

16. The sacrifice was made as an act of repentance; and if accepted by God, was sufficient to temporarily cover the sin of the one who brought the sacrifice. This was the "covering" of the sin through the atoning work in the sacrifice by the High Priest on behalf of himself and the people.

17. The sacrifice was not human blood, but that of an animal. Thus, the offering was an expression of the person's act of repentance. The ritual was designed to make the people do something that "cost them" something when they came to the altar. The atonement was the result of the ritual. However, it was the dogma (the belief in the meaning, tenets, and content of the ritual) within the performed ritual that achieved the atoning result.

18. The acceptance of the shed blood was the final step in the covering of the people's sins. Had the person offered himself as the sacrifice and shed his own blood, he would not have survived to live in the atonement for his sins. Thus, a substitute, an animal was sacrificed, and its blood was used on behalf of the person.

Redemption

19. In order that God restore the full relationship with mankind, He brought into mankind's presence the means and method to reunite Him to them. Proceeding from the sacrificial offering of blood for the atonement and covering of sin, God perfected the sacrifice and introduced *a better covenant* (Hebrews 8:6).

20. In the sacrifice of His only begotten Son, Jesus, and the shedding of His blood, God sent His own sacrifice and shed His own blood for mankind on the altar of the Cross. Apostle Paul affirms, *This is a faithful saying and worthy of all acceptance, that Christ Jesus came into the world to save sinners* (1 Timothy 1:15 NKJV).

21. To understand the redemptive work in the shed blood of Jesus, it is important to grasp what happens when a person in born again. Within every person there is the inherent sin in which everyone is born. This is the sinful (sin-filled) nature man inherits from Adam. The Bible says that *all have sinned and fall short of the glory of God* (Romans 3:23 NKJV). Everyone into whom God breathes the breath of life inherits the sinful nature.

22. From their earliest age, the Holy Spirit leads people to understand that they are born in sin and need to repent of their inherent sin so that they can again have a reconciled relationship with God. This is the new birth. Herein, the people who are *dead in* [their] *trespasses and sins* (Ephesians 2:1 NKJV) repent of the inherent sin they had when they were naturally born.

23. When individuals confess Jesus Christ as Lord and receive Him as Savior, they are washed in the shed blood of Jesus. This washing and cleansing flow in the blood of Jesus blots out their inherent sin (Isaiah 43:25) and removes it as far as the east is from the west (Psalm 103:12). From that moment, they are reconciled to the Father.

24. The immediate step that follows when the people confess Jesus Christ as Lord and they confess their sins, *He is faithful and just to forgive* [their] *sins and to cleanse* [them] *from all unrighteousness* (1 John 1:9 NKJV). The precious shed blood of Jesus immediately removes the sins they have committed while they were unsaved, forgiving them all their transgressions. This reconciles the born-again believers to the Father; both their inherent sin and their sins are washed clean in the shed blood.

25. Whereas in the old covenant, man brought a sacrifice to the altar, and it was the offering for the *atonement* of his *sins*, God brought Himself, His Son, as the sacrifice and shed His own blood for the *remission* of *sins* for many (Matthew 26:28; Ephesians 5:2).

26. *Atonement* was the acceptable response God performed as He annually covered the sins of the previous year when the High Priest entered the Holy of Holies and placed the blood on the altar. With Jesus Christ, the eternal High Priest, His one sacrifice, Himself, He bought eternal *redemption* of the inherent sin from Adam and the sins that mankind commits through His shed precious blood (Hebrews 9:23-28).

27. While atonement covered the sins of the person for a season, redemption remits man's sin (removes it as if it never existed), which

brings about reconciliation. Jesus Christ's shed precious blood is a "continuing remission of sin," "once for all", and *He will cast all our sins into the sea* (Micah 7:19). He does this because *He entered the Most Holy Place once for all, having obtained eternal redemption* (Hebrews 9:12 NKJV). Oswald Chambers says, "It is an injustice to say that Jesus Christ labored in redemption to make a person a saint. Jesus Christ labored in redemption to redeem the whole world and to place it perfectly whole and restored before the throne of God."

28. Christ's sacrifice did not focus only on the atonement of the people's physical sins of the flesh; rather, it is directed towards and includes redeeming the "conscience" of each person. This is the spiritual and soul redemption that is cleansed by His shed blood. The writer of Hebrews explicitly details that the efficacy of Christ's blood achieved this purging process of man's conscience: *It was symbolic for the present time in which both gifts and sacrifices are offered which cannot make him who performed the service perfect in regard to the conscience— concerned only with foods and drinks, various washings, and fleshly ordinances imposed until the time of reformation. But Christ came as High Priest of the good things to come, with the greater and more perfect tabernacle not made with hands, that is, not of this creation* (Hebrews 9:9-11 NKJV). That is why man *confesses with the mouth and believes in his heart* (Romans 10:9-10 NKJV) on the Lord Jesus Christ, whose shed precious blood cleanses him from all sin; and now, *how much more shall the blood of Christ, who through the eternal Spirit offered Himself without spot to God, cleanse your conscience from dead works to serve the living God?* (Hebrews 9:14 NKJV).

29. Jesus' incarnation was for the purpose of death. While humans are born to live, the Lord Jesus Christ was born to die. Jesus Christ's death was not a mere accident or incident of His human life; it was the supreme purpose of it. He became man in order that He might die as Man and for man. He died for a specific purpose, as *a ransom for many* (Matthew 20:28 NKJV).

30. The most glorious accolade that can be given comes from heaven's creatures who *sang a new song, saying: "You are worthy to take the scroll, and to open its seals; for You were slain, and have redeemed us to God by Your blood out of every tribe and tongue and people and nation, and have made us kings and priests to our God; and we shall reign on the earth.... saying with a loud voice: "Worthy is the Lamb who was slain*

to receive power and riches and wisdom, And strength and honor and glory and blessing!" (Revelation 5:9-12 NKJV).

31. The differences between the Old and the New Covenants are here summarized.

   The Old covered the people's sins while the New removes them (Romans 3:24-26).

   The Old needed a continual annual animal sacrifice while the New needs only One sacrifice (Hebrews 10:12).

   The Old required an animal sacrifice while the New requires God to sacrifice Himself (John 3:16).

   The Old needed an act of obedience while the New is an application of a believer's faith (Ephesians 2:8).

   The Old covered the people's physical sins while the New removes the physical and conscience sin upon repentance (Hebrews 9:9-14).

   The Old had numerous High Priests while the New has one High Priest who continues and is unchangeable (Hebrews 7:22-24).

   The Old needed a sacrifice from man, the sinner, towards God while the New needed God to sacrifice His Sinless Son for many (Matthew 26:28).

Intrinsic Qualities in Christ's blood

32. There are within the precious shed blood of Jesus Christ, intrinsic qualities that are unique to Him. Every quality is drenched in His love, holiness, pureness, divinity, and righteousness. The Lord Jesus Christ's obedience to the death on the Cross was with the express spiritual purpose that He shed His blood. The utmost that Jesus could give was His blood – His life. He could not give anymore; He had nothing more to give, and no one else could equal the offer that He gave–His matchless blood.

33. The Holy Writ is categorical when it says that Christ *gave Himself for our sins, that He might deliver us from this present evil age, according to the will of our God and Father* (Galatians 1:4). He also loves the

church so much that He *gave Himself for her* (Ephesians 5:25). Yet more intimately, Jesus looked passed His own self-worth and saw each person individually as Apostle Paul describes Jesus as the One, *who loved me and gave Himself for me* (Galatians 2:20). Jesus gave *Himself.* He gave His life, and His life was His precious blood.

34. The Lord Jesus could not give anymore because He had no more to give. Yet, the demand the Father made required that nothing less would suffice. W. A. C. Rowe says, "He was one offering of Himself, once offered as a full perfect and sufficient sacrifice and satisfaction for the sins of the whole world." Christ's blood is sufficient to save one repentant sinner, and all-sufficient to save the whole world of sinners if they would repent and receive Him.

35. Throughout the Old Testament numerous accounts attest to the value God attached to the blood. Just as oxygen is an integral part of water so is the blood an integral part of life (Leviticus 17:11). Even the shedding of a wicked person's blood, as well as the unnecessary shedding of an animal's blood, and even the drinking of blood, all are specifically addressed in the Bible. Then, to the eternal promise to the martyr whose life was slain, they rest eternally under the altar of God (Revelation 6:9-11). If the blood of animals and mankind is precious to God, how much more precious is His Son's blood – God's very own blood?

36. Andrew Murray in his book, *The Blood of Christ*, says, "The blood of Jesus is the greatest mystery of eternity, the deepest mystery of divine wisdom. Within this holy offering of His blood, there is a hidden value of the Spirit of self-sacrifice. The Son yielded up His Spirit and sacrificed Himself for mankind. When this revealed truth is witnessed by faith in the believer's heart, it works out in that heart a similar spirit of self-sacrifice."

Sinless

37. While the blood of fallen man is sin stained (Romans 3:23), the precious blood of Jesus, God's only begotten Son is *sinless*. The Bible's declaration that Jesus is conceived by the Holy Spirit is the evidence that the blood from Jesus' Father is God Himself. Therefore, it did not carry the same sin-stain that fallen man carries. This fact, in itself, is the most valuable

intrinsic quality that separates it from all of humanity's blood. Added to this, Christ's blood is not only sinless in its origin; it is also sinless in its existence. Jesus was tested and tried by the deceiver; but Jesus never succumbed to the devil's sinful devices when He *was in all points tempted as we are, yet without sin* (Hebrews 4:15).

38. The sinless state of Christ's blood separates it from all other blood ever to be produced in man on the earth. It has always been and will remain sinless. No trial by fire, torment through floods, or condemnation by mankind that Jesus' blood was artificial will ever change its sinless state. Through every test, from every quarter, and from any source whether good or evil, nothing can change the sinless state of Christ's blood.

Sin free

39. This intrinsic quality is inherent, and built into its source, namely God, the Father of our Lord Jesus Christ. Hence, it was from the sinless source and remained sinless throughout Christ's life on earth. Christ's blood needed no justification; it was *sin free*. His blood needed no cleansing; it remained sin free and was, therefore, acceptable to His Father.

40. Christ's sin-free blood was essential to the Father's purpose. Sin could not be offered for sin. The fundamental principle of the blood sacrifice was the offering of a sacrificial lamb without spot or blemish. Thus, the blood of *the Lamb of God who takes away the sin of the world* was wholly *sinless* and *sin-free* undefiled. It is *holy, harmless, undefiled, separate from sinners, and has become higher than the heavens* (Hebrews 7:26 NKJV).

41. Herein lies the most effective intrinsic value: Christ's blood was pure and free from sin and, therefore, is more powerful than anything man could offer as a self-sacrifice. His blood alone had the ingredients worthy of acceptance by the Father for the redemption of man.

42. One must consider the *wisdom of God* (1 Corinthians 2:7) that even as *the rulers of this age* reasoned that they knew enough to prosecute the Son of God and pronounce that He be crucified and thus shed His blood, they knew not that their demand was to no effect because His blood was sinless and sin free. Even though Jesus said that He was sent to save the lost and that He would die and be raised on the third day, the world refused to believe Him. It is fitting to quote the Bible that

says, *none of the rulers of this age knew; for had they known, they would not have crucified the Lord of glory* (1 Corinthians 2:8 NKJV).

Holy

43. Because Jesus Christ's blood was from the divine and sinless source, the Father, it had the intrinsic value of being *holy.* Not only did God offer through His Son a sinless, acceptable sacrifice when He shed His blood, but also the crimson river that flowed from Christ's life was *holy* blood. The essence of God's nature is His holiness, manifested in the quality of His blood; for *the life of the flesh is in the blood;* and God offered His Son's life, namely His shed blood. It was holy blood offered to redeem (buy back) the sin-stained blood of mankind (Hebrews 7:26).

44. It is biblically correct to state that the *life of the flesh is in the blood,* and to state that eternal life is in the shed blood of the Lamb of God. Christ's blood was from the eternal holy Father, and Jesus' life is in His blood which is eternal and holy.

45. This intrinsic value can only be applied to God, for He alone is holy (Revelation 15:4). All other comparisons, substitutes, and ritualistic ordinances pale in insignificance when considering the holiness of God.

Eternal Power

46. The indisputable quality in Jesus' blood is the power it has to remove sin from a repentant heart. This is possible because the repentant know as Apostle Peter explains, *knowing that you were not redeemed with corruptible things, like silver or gold, from your aimless conduct received by tradition from your fathers, but with the precious blood of Christ, as of a lamb without blemish and without spot* (1 Peter 1:18-19). There must be something in Christ's blood that gives it eternal power. So, what is in it that it possesses an intrinsic power unique and found in nothing else?

47. This is Christ's blood placed on the altar in the heavenly Holy of Holies for sin. Christ's blood placed on the holy altar of God in heaven possesses sufficient redemptive power. It has this because the life (soul) of the holy Son of God dwelt in that blood. The eternal life of the

Godhead was carried in that blood. The blood contains the eternal Spirit that gives life; and it is this power within Christ's blood that effectively removes man's sin even as the Word declares, *how much more shall the blood of Christ, who through the eternal Spirit offered Himself without spot to God, cleanse your conscience from dead works to serve the living God?* (Hebrews 9:14 NKJV).

48. It is therefore the eternal Spirit that is within the Savior's blood that gives it the power to redeem mankind from his rotten sinful state. The power of that blood in its many effects is nothing less than the eternal power of God because *the life of the flesh is in the blood* and because God had an everlasting covenant which He fulfilled when *the God of peace . . . brought up our Lord Jesus from the dead, that great Shepherd of the sheep, through the blood of the everlasting covenant* (Hebrews 13:20 NKJV). It has eternal power because its source is eternal and, in this power, the blood is sufficient to obtain eternal redemption for mankind; for the Bible says that *with His own blood He entered the Most Holy Place once for all, having obtained eternal redemption* (Hebrews 9:12 NKJV).

49. This eternal power can never, and will never, change because it is from the eternal Godhead. It has the unique ability to *redeem, reconcile, reunite, cleanse,* and give *eternal life* to the repentant heart.

Divine

50. Because the source of Christ's blood came from His Father, the eternal God who is divine, the blood (life) of Jesus is divine. This life is in His blood which makes His blood divine. It contains the purest and most holy, righteous, and eternal power that cannot be conquered. Christ's blood was not from His earthly father, Joseph. Jesus was conceived of the Holy Spirit. His blood is from His Father and His Father is divine.

51. A divine existence can only be used to describe God. No other creation, person or thing can have this attribute. God is divine because He is the only eternal One, and all His absolutes and attributes are eternal. As a divine Being, He has total power, total control, and total authority over all things. The eternal God has no need to justify His divine nature because it is who He is, eternal. Thus, God, who is eternal, exists as the divine life that has no beginning and end. This life Jesus had, has, and exists in the Godhead.

52. Jesus Christ's life on earth was infused with the eternal life blood of His Father, namely, the divine life that exists in the Godhead. This life is in the blood which is from the divine Father. This divine life with its power has, since the Resurrection of Jesus, been granted to everyone who believes in Him; and *His divine power has given to us all things that pertain to life and godliness, through the knowledge of Him who called us by glory and virtue* (2 Peter 1:3 NKJV).

53. Believers are washed in the divine shed blood of Jesus. They are immersed in the crimson flow from Calvary's Hill, justified and made righteous through the divine blood and *by which have been given to* [them] *exceedingly great and precious promises, that through these* [they] *may be partakers of the divine nature, having escaped the corruption that is in the world through lust* (2 Peter 1:4 NKJV).

54. Jesus said *I am the way, the truth, and the life. No one comes to the Father except through Me* (John 14:6), confirming that His absolutes and attributes are all *truth.* He is entirely truth and no falseness or crookedness exists in Him. This is the ultimate definition of being divine, namely that there is *no variation or shadow of turning* (James 1:17 NKJV); this all and absolute truth is the evidence of the divine life in Christ's shed precious blood.

Incorruptible

55. The Lord Jesus Christ was subjected to *all points of temptation* just as mankind is, yet He did not sin (Hebrews 4:15). As Son of Man, He could have relented and fallen into temptation just as Adam did. Because He did not fall, His blood remained uncorrupted. Having succeeded in remaining uncorrupted, Christ's blood remains incorruptible.

56. Therein is the eternal power source, the incorruptible blood that can never lose its power. This was the forgotten value the devil never thought of. Had the devil (*rulers of this age*) known that he could not conquer the incorruptible blood's power and that eternal life resided in Christ's blood, he never would have crucified Jesus.

57. This is the *hidden wisdom* which is in the power of God (1 Corinthians 2:1-8). This is the message within the incorruptible blood: For *the Lamb of God who takes away the sin of the world*, the means to redeem mankind is the slain Lamb's incorruptible blood.

58. What made Jesus' blood incorruptible is the question that demands an answer. It is from the Father who is eternal, and the eternal Spirit–Christ's life, is in His blood. This glorious truth resounds throughout heaven and earth: The blood of Jesus Christ, God's only begotten Son, *cleanses us from all sin* and is forever incorruptible.

59. Furthermore, it is in this never changing state because Jesus remained throughout His life on earth *holy, harmless, undefiled,* [and] *separate from sinners* (Hebrews 7:26 NKJV).

The Reason (Purpose)
Christ Shed His Blood

60. The almighty, eternal, and holy God looked on depraved man and stepped onto the platform of human life and sent His only begotten Son to die for man. His decision was direct and commanding. It was forthright and pitched to deal once and for all with the terrible sin that plagued mankind.

61. God's reasoning was all-encompassing, embracing every area that needed to be addressed. He gave His Son to be a sacrifice, and in so doing broke the power of sin and the works of the devil, shattering them into irreconcilable pieces. Christ's vicarious death accomplished eternal rewards that are freely given to everyone who believes in Him.

62. There are a number of reasons why Christ shed His blood for mankind. In each case, the promise of the Father was fulfilled, and man's eternal destiny was changed forever. Man's human comprehension of *Agape* (God is love) does not even reach the outer parameters of this love. There is no human reasoning or explanation for the shedding of Christ's blood except to say, *For God so loved the world that He gave His only begotten Son* (John 3:16).

Restoration

63. Flowing from His heart, His *agape* (love) for mankind, God made the immutable promise that He would right man's wrong (Genesis 3:15); and He made the way possible for this to happen.

64. Because Adam willfully transgressed God's command, he could not repair the wrong he did. The eternal damage on mankind that Adam caused when he reached for the fruit of the tree of knowledge of good and evil was the death knell for the entire human race. The separating force that unhinged the relationship and fellowship between God and man has ricocheted across the universe and echoed in the hearts of mankind across the millennia so that there existed a schism between man and his Creator. And man could not right the wrong.

65. This spiritual schism created by Adam's disobedience–sin against God, required a blood sacrifice to atone for mankind's sins before God. Man could not remove sin; only the One against whom sin was perpetrated had the ability to take care of the stain. In the normal course of life, the guilty makes amends to the offended one. However, in this eternal life, the Offended One paid the price for the wrong of the guilty party.

66. In this "price" it was God who paid. Before God could forgive man's eternal sin, there had to be something before forgiveness in order that it could be applied. That something was a sacrifice.

67. Only once the sacrifice was made could forgiveness flow towards a repentant heart. Thus, God sacrificed His Son and made Him shed His precious blood to right the wrong of sin against Him (1 Corinthians 6:20).

68. Even though the penalty of Adam's sin condemned mankind and separated him from God, the power in the precious shed blood of Jesus removes that sin stain and reunites mankind once again with God.

69. The overriding characteristic that resided in Adam's heart while he was in the garden was *peace* from God. There was no fear, doubt, or unbelief; never a day went by that Adam was not at peace with God and himself. Eden's abode was void of anxiety, nervous tension, and worry. God's peace permeated every area of the garden until sin entered it. From that moment on, fear ruled in the life of every human being. Then, God promised that He would take care of man's fall, and He did when He sent His Son to shed His precious blood and restore that peace *through the blood of His cross* (Colossians 1:20; Ephesians 2:11-18 NKJV). Now believers have peace even in the midst of their knowledge of good and evil (John 14:27).

Offering for Sin

70. The Lord Jesus Christ died as an explicit *offering for sin* (Hebrews 9:28); that is, He, a perfect, righteous One who deserved to live, died in the place of sinful men who deserved to die (1 Peter 3:18). *He bore our iniquities and was wounded for our transgression* (Isaiah 53:5; 1 Peter 2:24 NKJV). The substitutionary death of Jesus Christ was a specific sacrifice. It was on behalf of unjust ones who deserved to die. In His death, His blood was the sin-offering, the requirement of God for the remission of sin (Hebrews 9:22).

71. Jesus died as a *sin offering.* The Bible also says that *He who knew no sin was made (to be) sin for us* (2 Corinthians 5:21 NKJV). On the ground of Christ's death and His shed blood, and on this ground alone, is forgiveness of sin made possible for sinners.

72. An *offering for sin* (Hebrews 10:18) is a "guilt offering," which is the exact meaning of the Hebrew word translated as *an offering for sin.* Such an offering was a sacrificial death from which pardon was granted to sinners.

73. The Word of God declares that apart from the shedding of the blood of Jesus Christ there is absolutely no pardon for sin. There is absolutely no forgiveness outside the redeeming blood of Christ. Without Christ's *blood* being *shed for many* as the offering for sin, every member of humanity perishes forever.

A Ransom

74. Jesus died as a *ransom;* that is, His death was the price paid to redeem others from eternal separation from God (spiritual death). His shed blood was the price He paid to redeem mankind when *He gave Himself a ransom for all* (1 Timothy 2:6).

75. The redemption of mankind was dependent on the sacrifice that cost God His only Son. This price tag attached to mankind's redemption can never be measured in human terms, for there was no price that mankind could afford to pay. Mankind stood judged as guilty in the dock, and in no way could he argue or plead innocence. No means was available for mankind to escape the penalty of disobedience that led him to sin against God.

76. The ransom price was so exorbitant that it was outside mankind's ability to pay. God demanded a spotless Lamb's blood as the price of redemption. He knew He had the only qualifying One, His Son, who fulfilled the criteria. And to meet the ransom demand, God sent His Son who *became obedient to the point of death, even the death of the cross* (Philippians 2:8 NKJV).

77. Mankind owed a debt they could not pay, and Jesus paid a debt He did not owe. He was obedient to His Father's will and agreed to redeem mankind under the conditions (ransom) His Father demanded. Thus, Jesus *gave Himself a ransom for all* (1 Timothy 2:6 NKJV) and went to Calvary.

Propitiation

78. Jesus Christ died as the *propitiation* (redeeming sacrifice) for mankind's sins. God the Father gave Christ, His Son, to be the propitiation through His shed blood. Jesus Christ, through the shedding of His blood, is the sacrifice offered and accepted and by which God's holy wrath against sin is appeased (1 John 4:10; Romans 3:25-26).

79. Christ was a propitiation, an expiatory sacrifice, on behalf of mankind, and the means of appeasing God's holy wrath at sin. Or, in other words, Jesus, through the shedding of His blood, is the means by which the wrath of God against sinners is appeased.

80. God's holiness and consequent hatred of sin, like every other attribute of His character, is real and must manifest itself. His wrath at sin must strike somewhere, either on the sinner or upon a lawful substitute. It struck Jesus Christ, a lawful substitute, as God the Father *laid on Him the iniquity of us all* (Isaiah 53:6 NKJV). The death of Jesus Christ (and the shedding of His blood) fulfilled the demands of God's holiness.

Curse

81. Christ died to redeem humanity from *the curse* of the law by bearing that curse Himself (Galatians 3:13). His death by crucifixion redeemed mankind from the curse which they deserved when He took that curse upon Himself.

82. Jesus Christ did not sin. However, He took upon Himself the sin of the world thereby being made a curse according to the book of the law which states, *For as many as are of the works of the law are under the curse; for it is written, "Cursed is everyone who does not continue in all things which are written in the book of the law, to do them"* (Galatians 3:10 NKJV).

83. Jesus became cursed for mankind when He submitted to the law which He did not break. He humbled Himself, and the Father *made Him who knew no sin to be sin for us, that we might become the righteousness of God in Him* (2 Corinthians 5:21 NKJV).

Substitutionary Sacrifice

84. The Lord Jesus shed His blood as a substitutionary sacrifice. He did this in place of mankind shedding their own blood. Any sacrifice mankind made was stained in sin, and God required a Lamb without spot or blemish.

85. The only pure, holy, and worthy blood that has ever existed is His Son's blood. God willingly sent His Son to die. He willingly gave His Son as a sacrifice that shed His blood on behalf of mankind so that the relationship and fellowship that was severed in the Garden of Eden could once again be restored. Jesus said, *the Son of Man has come to seek and to save that which was lost* (Luke 19:10), "lost" meaning mankind had lost their relationship with God when Adam sinned in Eden.

86. What is more profound is that God loved sinful mankind so much that when He sent His Son to die for them, He was *pleased* (satisfied) with the sacrifice He offered. This sacrifice was the death on the Cross of Calvary when *it pleased the LORD to bruise Him* (Isaiah 53:10 NKJV). In this horrible death and because of God's love for mankind, the Father saw the *many* souls who would believe in the risen Christ.

87. In most cases, a person will offer a payment or action that will settle another's debt to the extent that it would not cost that person all he has. In this instance, God the Father gave His *only begotten Son* (all He had) to reconcile Himself to mankind. The Substitute paid the debt in full. The Substitute met every criterion needed to settle the account. The Substitute gained the full victory over Satan and sin when He *destroy(ed) the works of the devil* (1 John 3:8).

88. The perfect Substitute–the Son. The victorious Substitute–the Son. The only worthy Substitute–the Son. Christ's purpose of shedding His blood was for the redemption of mankind, for the Father needed a substitute who would meet all the demands of a perfect sacrifice. Jesus qualified in every respect to satisfy the Father's demands.

Remission

89. *Without the shedding of blood there is no remission* (Hebrews 9:22 NKJV). The only way God could ever consider pardoning man's sin was through a sacrifice and the shedding of blood. Jesus became that sacrifice. In His sinless, shed blood, there is *remission* (forgiveness) of sin. His blood had to be shed before any remission could occur. The reconciliation was made possible when mankind *was brought near by the blood of Christ* (Ephesians 2:13). He accomplished this when His shed blood was poured out on behalf of mankind. The remarkable fact is that no other blood was worthy enough to remit sin.

90. Christ's blood was, in itself, of infinite value because it carried His soul or life. Also, the remitting virtue of His blood was infinite because of the way it was shed. In holy obedience to the Father's will, He subjected Himself to the penalty of the broken law by pouring out His soul unto death, for He said, *My soul is exceedingly sorrowful, even to death* (Matthew 26:38 NKJV).

91. Because of the Person whose blood was shed and because of the sacrificial way in which it was shed, namely fulfilling the law of God and satisfying its just demands, the blood of Jesus has such vicarious power.

92. In all these explanations, it must never be forgotten that Jesus not only died in His flesh (Son of man), but He also experienced a spiritual death (Son of God). When he said, *Father, into Your hands I commit My Spirit* (Luke 23:46 NKJV), He was spiritually separated from God His Father and went into hell.

93. Even more profound is the fact that Jesus Christ did not have His Spirit taken from Him; He gave it up. This gives a deep insight into His fullest obedience even unto death, for He said, *Not My will but Yours be done* (Luke 22:42 NKJV). At this moment in His life, when the time came for fulfillment of the Word which says *behold the Lamb of God who takes*

away the sin of the world (John 1:29 NKJV), Jesus gave up His Spirit and became sin for mankind.

94. Remission is closely allied to the work of redemption. The purpose was, therefore, fulfilled that Jesus shed His blood for the redemption of mankind as the hymn writer says, "Redeemed by the blood of the Lamb." Because of Christ's redeeming sacrifice man has remission (forgiveness) of his sins (Matthew 26:28).

95. Jesus entered the heavenly Holy of Holies and presented His blood for Himself and for all who accept by faith the sacrifice of His blood for the remission of their sin. His presentation of His blood asks the Father to allow Him and repentant mankind entrance into the presence of the Holy One, according to His promise *that where I am, there you may be also* (John 14:3 NKJV).

96. Just as Christ's precious shed blood was sufficient to justify Him in the Spirit (1 Timothy 3:16), so it has the power to release repentant mankind from their sin. His blood has a supreme cleansing power to forgive those who repent of their sin as well as release them from the kingdom of darkness (1 John 1:7).

97. The word "redeemed" has a depth of meaning, particularly indicating deliverance from slavery by emancipation or purchase. The sinner is enslaved under the hostile power of Satan, the curse of the law, and sin. Christ's redeeming blood produces the remission of sin when a repentant heart confesses Jesus Christ as Lord, for it is proclaimed, *For You were slain and have redeemed us to God by Your blood* (Revelation 5:9). Christ's shed blood paid sin's debt and destroyed the power of Satan, the curse, and sin (1 John 3:8).

98. Redemption includes everything God does for a sinner, beginning with the pardon of sin and the removal of guilt and concluding with the deliverance of the body by its resurrection (Romans 8:23-24) which has no end *having obtained eternal redemption for us* (Hebrews 9:12 NKJV). In summarizing, redemption is the process of Christ's shedding His blood for sin; and remission is the promise God assures a repentant heart.

99. God's purpose and fullest intentions in offering His Son's life as a sacrifice were fully accomplished.

100. The most precious legacy of Christ's sacrifice, His shed precious blood, still resides in the presence of the Father on the mercy seat in the heavenly Holy of Holies. The victorious power of the shed precious blood in the presence of God will never lose its ability to redeem mankind.

Reconciliation

101. The crowning achievement of the shed precious blood is the *reconciliation* it brings. The result that flowed in that crimson stream from the Son of God has the power to blot out man's sin and remove it as far as the east is from the west. Based upon this premise, God *forgives* the repentant heart, bringing jubilation and rejoicing in the believer's heart. Because of the work of reconciliation, as Apostle Paul says, *much more then, having now been justified by His blood, we shall be saved from wrath through Him. For if when we were enemies we were reconciled to God through the death of His Son, much more, having been reconciled, we shall be saved by His life. And not only that, but we also rejoice in God through our Lord Jesus Christ, through whom we have now received the reconciliation* (Romans 5:9-11 NKJV).

102. The removal of man's inherent sin takes place when the repentant heart confesses by faith that the Lord Jesus Christ is the Son of God who died for him and was raised from the dead (Romans 10:9-10). The repentant heart receives by faith the promise that the shed precious blood of Jesus cleanses him from all sin. This purification from the blood of Christ breaks down the barrier that sin built, and the one who repents is immediately reconciled to God.

103. Sin is disobedience, contempt for the authority of God; it seeks to rob God of His honor as God and Lord. Sin is purposed and determined opposition to a holy God. It not only can but also must awaken His wrath.

104. Although the love of God toward man remains unchanged, sin made it impossible for God to allow man to have fellowship with Him. It compelled Him to, one day, pour out upon man His wrath and punishment. Yet, in this immense love that is beyond human comprehension, God sent His Son to die so that He could destroy sin's barrier, remove the schism it created, and breach the gap between Him and man. The shed precious blood was the instrument used, and the effect was redemption that resulted in the perfect reconciliation between God and a repentant man.

105. Because of the reconciling power in the shed blood of Jesus, mankind once more has a fully restored relationship and fellowship with the Father; and mankind now has access to the Father in the name of Jesus. More so, this relationship extends from the reconciled bond between

God and mankind to a unified *bond of peace* (Ephesians 4:3) between Spirit-filled believers.

106. This reconciliation unites every believer into *one mind, one mouth* (Romans 15:6) *and one body and Spirit* (Ephesians 4:4). Henceforth, the Scripture reveals, *Now all things are of God, who has reconciled us to Himself through Jesus Christ, and has given us the ministry of reconciliation, that is, that God was in Christ reconciling the world to Himself, not imputing their trespasses to them, and has committed to us the word of reconciliation* (2 Corinthians 5:18-19 NKJV).

107. Spirit-filled believers no longer walk in a disconnected and distanced relationship with the Father. They are not separated from Him through their sin-stained spirit. God in Jesus Christ has cleansed their heart/spirit and removed the schism, reuniting God and mankind through the shed blood of His Son as Scripture declares, *For he is our peace, who hath made both one, and hath broken down the middle wall of partition between us; having abolished in his flesh the enmity, even the law of commandments contained in ordinances; for to make in himself of twain one new man, so making peace; and that he might reconcile both unto God in one body by the cross, having slain the enmity thereby* (Ephesians 2: 14-16).

Forgiveness

108. When a repentant heart approaches the foot of the cross, confesses Jesus Christ as Lord, and pours out self, a gushing river of *forgiveness* flows into the heart/spirit. This is made possible because of the shed precious blood's power to remove the inherent sin. The disobedience dating back to Adam that permeates every living soul has no ability to stop the forgiveness that stems from God's heart, *He is faithful and just to forgive us* (1 John 1:9).

109. Nothing can stop that flow. No weapon the devil uses as a blockade to prevent God's forgiveness is powerful enough to stop the flow. The slain Lamb of God is raised from the dead; and the ultimate punishment of sin, death, is destroyed as Jesus openly triumphed over the devil, sin and evil, and *destroyed the works of the devil* (1 John 3:8).

110. Christ's shed precious blood removes the sin stain; and all that resides in sin is eradicated, is forgiven, and is removed as far as the *east is from the west* (Psalm 103:12).

111. God's forgiveness is apportioned to a repentant heart/spirit based purely on the heart's confession that Jesus Christ is Lord and heart-felt belief *that God has raised Him from the dead* (Romans 10:9 NKJV). There is no payment, ritual, or sacrifice needed to receive God's forgiveness.

112. This repentance and confession are done willingly and never forced upon anyone; it is the choice of the sinner to repent and receive Christ as Lord. Upon this confession, the sinner is forgiven and cleansed of all unrighteousness as it is written, *In Him we have redemption through His blood, the forgiveness of sins, according to the riches of His grace* (Ephesians 1:7, Colossians 1:14).

113. Sinners grope around in darkness seeking the way. They stumble and fall in their sin and are unable to make decisions that can save their souls. Then the light of the gospel shines in their hearts as a preacher declares the love God has for the lost souls who are walking in darkness. The response sinners make is the defining moment when they turn from their wicked ways and look into the light of the gospel and receive Jesus Christ as Lord. Therein salvation's door is swung wide open as it *open*(s) *their eyes, in order to turn them from darkness to light, and from the power of Satan to God, that they may receive forgiveness of sins and an inheritance among those who are sanctified by faith in Me* (Acts 26:18 NKJV).

Guilt Removed

114. Man is guilty before God. Guilt is debt. The sinner is guilty. God cannot disregard His own demand that sin must be punished; and His glory, which has been dishonored, must be upheld. If the debt is not discharged and the guilt removed, it is impossible for a holy God to allow the sinner to come into His presence.

115. Can the guilt of sin be removed? Can the effect of sin upon God in awakening His wrath be removed? Can sin be blotted out before God? The answer is undoubtedly, yes. This can be done, and the stronghold of sin shattered, releasing man from its bondage. Sin's guilty plague is removed when the repentant heart receives Jesus as Lord, and he is embraced in the reconciling arms of his heavenly Father.

116. God in His unprecedented mercy and grace forgives mankind his sin and removes their guilt. Mankind should have paid for their

transgressions that rendered them guilty before God, yet God forgives them and cleanses them of all guilt associated with their transgressions. Moses implored God to show grace and mercy towards the people, to which God replied, *The* LORD, *the* LORD *God,* [is] *merciful and gracious, longsuffering, and abounding in goodness and truth, keeping mercy for thousands, forgiving iniquity and transgression and sin, by no means clearing the guilty* (Exodus 34:6-7 NKJV).

117. This is what true reconciliation does. It removes the sin-producing guilt which plagues the human heart so that man can draw near to God in the blessed assurance that there is no longer the least guilt abiding in him to keep him away from God.

118. Holy Love was unwilling to let man go. Despite all mankind's sin, God could not give up mankind who had to be redeemed. Likewise, God's holy wrath could not surrender its demands. The law had been despised; God had been dishonored. God's holiness, rights, and demands had to be upheld. The guilt of sin had to be removed; otherwise, the sinner could not be delivered. It was Christ's shed blood that removed man's sin and the guilt with it, resulting in a reconcilable state accepted by God.

119. The love, mercy, and grace that was demonstrated on Calvary's Hill can never be fully comprehended. Someone had to take the sin and guilt to meet God's demands. Someone had to be judged guilty. Someone had to stand in the accused dock and be pronounced guilty of transgressing God's holiness.

120. How apt it was that Pilate *found no fault in Him* (John 19:4, 6; Luke 23:14-15). How reassuring to Jesus was the question Pilate asked, *What have You done* (John 18:35). Then, Judas Iscariot's confession solidified Jesus' innocence and guiltlessness when he said, *I have sinned by betraying innocent blood* (Matthew 27:4 NKJV).

121. Within the realm of guilt and innocence, the Father took the Innocent Man, *made Him who knew no sin to be sin for us* (2 Corinthians 5:21), thereby declaring Him guilty for the sins He did not commit, and condemned Him to death on the Cross.

122. The Father required the shedding of blood to remove the stain of sin and its guilt (Hebrews 9:22). Blood of a totally different character was necessary for an effective removal of guilt. Righteousness demanded it; Love offered it.

123. Redemption was the purpose, and the Son's shed blood was the instrument God used to achieve redemption. It was completely

achieved, and redemption in the shed precious blood of Jesus is continuously available to all who repent.

124. In our Lord's work of redemption, reconciliation is the ultimate and supreme result. It is the highest honor and sublime gift that welcomed the repentant heart as he applies the shed blood of Christ in his life. As he crosses the threshold of salvation, the reconciling effect releases him from his guilt, and he stands blameless before almighty God.

125. The divine, shed precious blood is poured out; guilt is removed; reconciliation is complete; and the message comes to everyone, *be ye reconciled to God* (2 Corinthians 5:20).

Cleansing

126. Embedded in God's immense love and mercy, the demonstration of His grace transcends human comprehension. God declares that *while we were yet sinners, Christ died for us* (Romans 5:8). There was, is, and will never be in variableness and change in the extent and value of God's love for mankind whether they be in sin or be forgiven. He loves mankind with an everlasting love that flows from the depths of eternity (love that has no beginning or end). It is worth meditating on the unfathomable mystery that this Love manifested itself before mankind was indued with the breath of life and extends itself beyond the grave.

127. It is this compelling eternal Love that propels God's forgiveness towards repentant hearts and provides the stream of cleansing of their sin as it gushes forth like a river of living water.

128. The union that is once again forged through reconciliation in the shed blood begins the effectual work promised by God. The first result that flows directly from His heart into man's spirit is the *cleansing* flow that the power in the shed blood brings, as Apostle John so demonstratively declares, *The blood of Jesus Christ His Son cleanses us from all sin* (1 John 1:7).

129. Sin's filth resulting from mankind's disobedience to God's holiness, has stained man's spirit since Eden. The Lord Jesus Christ's shed blood in the *better covenant* bursts the bonds of sin that shackled man's spirit and *cleanses* his heart with the power in the shed blood. Sin is removed, and the cleansing flow blots out the stain and replaces it with love.

Justification

130. The inconceivable result in human terms evolves from the cleansing flow when the repentant heart confesses Jesus Christ as Lord. Man's spirit and soul, freshly cleansed, receive permission to stand before God and the Lord Jesus Christ as *justified.*

131. Even more inconceivable is the fulfillment of the Word that a repentant heart can *be made the righteousness of God in him* (2 Corinthians 5:21).

132. The shed precious blood's cleansing flow breaks the bonds of sin, removes the guilt, reconciles God and man, justifies him to stand in the presence of God again, and allows the Holy Christ, *who became for us righteousness* (1 Corinthians 1:30), to take up residence in man's heart (Ephesians 3:17).

133. The obliteration of the devil's hold over man's spirit is forever removed when God forgives man of his sin. The sign on the door of man's heart heralds the message to the devil in a loud and invincible voice–*justified.*

134. Justification relates to the believer's standing while sanctification relates to his state. In lay terms, Justification is the verdict and the pronouncement of a judge who declares that he has found the accused person innocent of all guilty charges. In spiritual terms, justification is the judicial side of salvation. When Jesus Christ, the Son of God *was made to be sin for us that we might become the righteousness in Him* (2 Corinthians 5:21), God reviewed mankind's state and justified the repentant ones. How could it be possible for God to declare an unrighteous soul to be righteous while retaining His holiness, character, and integrity? That is the mystery; yet it has been perfectly done, producing infinite and eternal salvation.

135. The declaration of justification can be made because the justice of a holy God has been fully vindicated in the absolute righteousness and complete obedience of His only begotten and incarnate Son who shed His divine precious blood which *justified* (Him) *in the Spirit* (1 Timothy 3:16).

136. God's sentence of His judgment upon sin utterly spent and buried itself in the fullest measure in the slain *Lamb of God* (Revelation 5:6) so that divine justification might minister its vindication, release, and approval. Christ's righteousness is imputed fully and effectually to a

repentant heart; *righteousness is the gift of God* (Romans 5:17). The believer is justified by faith in the shed blood of Christ.

137. Justification originated in grace (Romans 3:24), was procured by the blood of Christ (Romans 5:9), was ratified by the power of the resurrection (Romans 4:25); and is appropriated by faith (Romans 5:1).

138. Being *justified* is the hallmark of a born-again soul. Justification through the blood of Christ is the wide-open golden gate of grace that leads into the bright and magnificent life of divine favor and fellowship. Everything, literally everything, depends upon the precious shed blood of Christ; but none of this can be man's unless by faith he lays hold personally of its reality and effectiveness.

Righteousness

139. The filthy, separating, and rotten sin that grinds away in a man's heart before he repents, is removed, and replaced with *righteousness* when the pure, holy, and divine righteous Christ who *is made unto us righteousness* (1 Corinthians 1:30) *that we might become the righteousness of God in Him* (2 Corinthians 5:21) resides in the believer.

140. This righteousness is not of man's doing; it is imparted to him through the forgiveness and cleansing flow in the shed precious blood; it is from God. Matthew Henry says, "The righteousness, which is of God by faith, ordained and appointed of God, *surely in the LORD I have righteousness and strength* (Isaiah 45:24 NKJV). The Lord Jesus Christ is the Lord of our righteousness (Philippians 3:9)."

141. The result that righteousness brings is the marvelous reconciliation man once again has with God. Sin is blotted out and righteousness opens the door to God's heart.

142. Matthew Henry gives the ultimate expression of Christ's righteousness when he says, "Had He not been God, He could not have been our righteousness; the transcendent excellence of the divine nature put such a value upon, and such a virtue into, His sufferings, that they became sufficient to satisfy for the sins of the world, and to bring in a righteousness which will be effectual to all that believe."

Fellowship re-united

143. It is God's ultimate desire that man fellowship with Him again as it was in the Garden of Eden. That relationship between God and Adam is what God purposed, and Adam severed it. Only God could heal the breach.

144. How exquisite is the fulfillment of God's promise that He would *put enmity between you and the woman, and between your seed and her Seed* (Genesis 3:15 NKJV). The separation of good and evil, truth and error were achieved when the *Seed* of the woman produced the Christ, the Son of the living God who destroyed the works of the devil (1 John 3:8).

145. This was unequivocally and vicariously achieved when Jesus Christ exited the tomb, presented His blood to the Father in the heavenly Holy of Holies, reconnecting the fellowship with the Father which Adam's sin had severed.

146. That *middle wall of separation* (Ephesians 2:14) had to come down, and only God could tear it down. God's holiness was violated, and His wrath had to be poured out to punish the perpetrators. The heavenly Father perfected the sacrificial offering. His holy Son would be the chosen One He would use to do it. The deepest gash in the Father's heart and the most painful agony the Father's soul experienced when He sent His Son to die were deemed by the Father as sufficient to appease His wrath against sinful man.

147. This divine sacrifice resulted in God opening wide His heart's door, inviting man to *enter in* and fellowship with Him. There is now no need for a veil; there is no need for a High Priest to enter on man's behalf. Neither is there any further sacrificial offering necessary or a pilgrimage to a holy city to stand in a temple made with human hands.

148. Once again, that intimate *fellowship* between Adam and God is restored to everyone who confesses Jesus Christ as Lord *for through Him we have access by one Spirit to the Father* (Ephesians 2:18).

149. Fellowship transcends the relationship between God and man and involves the fellowship believers have with each other. This occurs because the same Spirit dwells in them all and they identify with the relationship each one has in Christ. Thus, God's promise is evidenced in this fellowship as it states *God is faithful, by whom you were called*

into the fellowship of His Son, Jesus Christ our Lord (1 Corinthians 1:9 NKJV).

150. The forgiven, justified, and righteous believer *enters his closet and shuts the door* and has the privilege of *mounting up with wings like eagles* and *abides under the shadow of the Almighty,* as the *peace not as the world gives* floods his soul in the presence of Almighty God. This happens because of the shed precious blood of His Son and Savior, the Lord Jesus Christ; *now in Christ Jesus you who were once afar off have been brought near by the blood of Christ* (Ephesians 2:13).

Chapter 14

Jesus' Spirit and Soul Descended into the Place of the Dead

1. The divine Creator who fashioned everything by His almighty power and the holy testimony to His deity while He was on the earth, also spent three days in the abode of the dead.

2. Clarification of the place to where a dead man's soul and spirit descend is necessary before making a doctrinal statement on Christ's descent into it. The Bible speaks of this place as having "compartments" into which the righteous dead, the unrighteous/wicked dead, and the fallen angels went.

3. The Bible has names for the places of the dead. The Hebrew name for the entire abode of the dead is called *Sheol*. The Greek word that encompasses this word in Hebrew is *hades*. Scripture also speaks of the place of the dead as the *abyss* or *the deep* (Romans 10:7).

4. The Bible gives various words for the compartments. *Paradise* or *Abraham's Bosom* was the place of the righteous dead before Jesus was raised from the dead. *Hell*, or *Gehenna* in the Greek, is the place of the unrighteous/wicked dead. *Tatarus* is the place of the fallen angels (2 Peter 2:4).

5. When Jesus died, He descended into *hades* and went to the compartments of *paradise* and *Gehenna*. At His resurrection Jesus brought with Him the righteous dead out from *paradise* (Matthew 27:52-53).

6. *Paradise* was emptied when Jesus was raised from the dead, and it is now located in the third heaven (2 Corinthians 12:4). From that time, the righteous dead have their souls and spirits immediately taken from

them; and they are present with the Lord, *to be absent from the body and to be present with the Lord* (2 Corinthians 5:8).

7. Scripture confirms Spirit-filled believers' understanding that Jesus descended into *hades*. In the very first message ever preached from a church platform (on the Day of Pentecost, Acts 2:25-31), Apostle Peter quotes from Psalm 16 referencing Christ's descent in to *Sheol/hades*. David, the Psalmist, correctly uses the word *Sheol* because Jesus descended into both compartments of the underworld, hell, and paradise.

8. Apostle Peter makes a resounding statement that Jesus did not stay in *Gehenna/hell,* and that the Father had promised Him this victory from the dawn of time: *Behold the Lamb of God slain from the foundation of the world.* David declares in his Michtam, Psalm 16:10, *for You will not leave my soul in Sheol, nor will You allow Your Holy One to see corruption.* The apostle makes it clear that Jesus descended into *gehenna/hell,* and that the Father's promise was fulfilled when Jesus was raised from the dead (Acts 2:31-32).

9. Christ's purpose for descending into *hades* was two-fold. He had to go there because He was made sin, and the place of a sin-stained soul and spirit at death is *gehenna/hades* (hell). He also descended there because *for this reason the gospel was preached also to those who are dead* (1 Peter 4:6). Jesus appeared to the souls and spirits of the wicked dead and *preached* to them who had died from Adam to Noah's time (1 Peter 3:20). French L. Arrington in his book *Christian Doctrine a Pentecostal Perspective* says, "In the power of the Holy Spirit, Christ went into hades as a victor not as a victim. As a conqueror, He asserted His lordship and authority. Christ was triumphant even in the domain of the dead."

10. The Lord Jesus Christ went to both compartments in *hades*. His purpose for becoming Son of Man and Son of God was totally fulfilled as He ministered to the living and the dead. Apostle Paul states, *and without controversy great is the mystery of godliness; God was manifest in the flesh, justified in the Spirit* (1 Timothy 3:16 NKJV). The only way Jesus could be justified in the Spirit was if His Spirit that was made sin was condemned to the place of a sinful spirit, namely *gehenna,* and thereafter He presented His blood as the sacrifice for Himself and mankind (Hebrews 7:27, 9:7).

11. Jesus foreknew that the Father would not leave His soul in *hades*. Hence, He calls from the cross, moments before He dies, *Into Your hands I commit My Spirit* (Luke 23:46 NKJV). His call to the Father reaches past the protection of His Spirit. It is the reaffirming cry from the Savior to His Father that Jesus did not forget the promise made to Him that His Father would not leave His soul in *Gehenna/hell* (Psalm 16:10; Acts 2:31). This cry from the cross was not merely mouthed from the Son of Man; but it was the Son of God calling from His Spirit to His Father regarding the promise made to Him from the foundation of the world.

12. His purpose for going down into the realm of the dead can be summed up as follows: first, He descended into *gehenna/hell* and announced the wrath of God upon the disobedient unbelievers in Noah's time (1 Peter 3:19-20); and He declared to the rest of the unrighteous their state because they rejected the gospel (1 Peter 4:6). He also suffered as a sinner in *gehenna* (1 Peter 3:18). Second, on the dawn of the third day, and in fulfillment of the Father's promise that He would not leave Jesus in *sheol/hades,* as Christ took hold of the keys of *hades and death* (Revelation 1:18), He began His resurrection journey. This took Him through the upper compartment of hades, namely *paradise.* He visited *paradise* and emptied it taking with Him the righteous dead from *paradise* and the grave at His resurrection (Matthew 27:52).

Chapter 15

The Resurrection of Jesus Christ

1. The resurrection of Jesus Christ from the dead is the most powerful declaration the church makes. This undeniable event has drawn sinners to repentance, and it has induced eternal hope in the souls of countless millions. Conversely, the declaration that Jesus was raised from the dead has been shunned by countless millions.

2. As glorious as this fact is to every born-again believer, so distasteful is it to the unbeliever (Acts 17:31-32).

3. Spirit-filled believers are emphatic about the spiritual implications the resurrection brings to their salvation. The overwhelming victory and inestimable avenue of eternal life to everyone who believes can never be fully comprehended when this subject is contemplated.

4. At the outset, the resurrection demonstrates spiritual power that is unconquerable which Apostle Paul emphasizes as *the power of His resurrection* (Philippians 3:10). This *power* is a source that was applied to His being raised from the dead, and the reason for it was to introduce salvation's promise of everlasting life.

5. Apostle Paul's undoubting declaration that he believed in *Jesus Christ and Him crucified* encapsulated the totality of Christ's suffering, crucifixion, His being made to be sin for mankind, and the resurrection of Christ from the dead. The gospel he preached is proclaimed when he says, *Remember that Jesus Christ of the seed of David, was raised from the dead according to my gospel* (2 Timothy 2:8 NKJV).

6. Millard J. Erickson, in his book *Christian Theology* says, "The death of Jesus was the low point in His humiliation; the overcoming of death through the resurrection was the first step back in the process of His

exaltation. The resurrection is particularly significant, for inflicting death was the worst thing that sin and the powers of sin could do to Christ. Death's inability to hold Him symbolizes the totality of His victory."

7. To begin with, Spirit-filled believers attest to the fact that Christ's same body that was placed in the tomb was resurrected. It was not another body given to Jesus, but a body that had been glorified when the Holy Spirit entered the tomb and *raised Jesus from the dead by the glory of the Father* (Romans 6:4 NKJV).

8. After this fact, comes the consideration of what God did when He resurrected Jesus. As with all unexplainable events that relate to God and His miraculous ways, the Godhead is involved every time. *God raised Him from the dead* (Acts 13:30 NKJV) declares that God the Father, the Son, and the Holy Spirit were all involved in the resurrection. It was the Father's explicit promise to His Son that He would not let Him see corruption (Psalm 16:10), and the Holy Spirit *raised up Jesus from the dead* (Romans 8:11).

9. The Godhead reached into the deepest divine spiritual realm to bring back Jesus from the dead. When the Holy Spirit moved upon the dead body of Jesus, He used spiritual *power* to reunite Christ's soul and spirit with His body. Apostle Paul reflects on this event when he states that he hungers and thirsts for this exquisite and glorious power, explaining *that I may know him and in the power of his resurrection* (Philippians 3:10).

10. This resurrection power that stemmed from the highest and deepest recesses of the divine Godhead's source was transfused into Jesus' dead body, and the effectual working of that spiritual power birthed life into Jesus. He is, therefore, the *first born from the dead* (Colossians 1:18); and Jesus Christ was in essence "born-again."

11. Apostle Paul goes on to explain that Jesus was the *first born*. Herein he states that in the Kingdom of God and in the body of Christ, Jesus the Son of man is the "first" One that was raised to the newness of life. Rufinus of Aquileia (A.D. 340-410) gives this insight: "Inasmuch then as it is a spiritual body, and glorious, and incorruptible, it will be furnished and adorned with its own proper members, not with members taken from elsewhere, according to that glorious image of which Christ is set forth as the perpetual type. In reference to our hope of the resurrection, Christ is set forth all through as the archetype

since He is the firstborn of those who rise and since He is the head of every creature."

12. The Holy Writ further declares, *And what is the exceeding greatness of His power towards us who believe, according to the working of His mighty power which He worked in Christ when He raised Him from the dead and seated Him at His right hand in the heavenly places* (Ephesians 1:19-20 NKJV).

13. This magnificent power used to resurrect Jesus was the *glorious splendor of* [His] *majesty* (Psalm 145:5 NKJV) and the *excellence* of His *greatness* (Psalm 150:2) that are all found in His *Shekinah* glory. The Father was the Authority who empowered the glory, and the Holy Spirit was the channel that fused the *glory of the Father* (His *Shekinah* glory) into Jesus' body (Romans 6:4).

14. In human terms, the human mind cannot comprehend the awesomeness of His *Shekinah* glory. It is *spiritually discerned* (1 Corinthians 2:14). Apostle Paul yearned for this discernment (Philippians 3:10).

15. The Savior's first task as the glorified risen Son of God was to enter the heavenly Holy of Holies and present His shed precious blood on the mercy seat as the offering for both His and mankind's sin. *For Christ has not entered the holy places made with hands, which are copies of the true, but into heaven itself, now to appear in the presence of God for us* (Hebrews 9:24 NKJV). *For such a High Priest was fitting for us, who is holy, harmless, undefiled, separate from sinners, and has become higher than the heavens; who does not need daily, as those high priests, to offer up sacrifices, first for His own sins and then for the peoples, for this He did once for all when He offered up Himself* (Hebrews 7:26-27 NKJV).

16. The triumphant Christ now glorified was the victor over death (spiritual death), and the conqueror of sin's ultimate penalty, namely death. He *destroyed the works of the devil* (1 John 3:8) and the cataclysmic result of Adam's sin in the Garden of Eden. Namely the severing of the spiritual relationship with God was now annulled by the holy Son of God who reunited this spiritual relationship in His resurrection when He, spiritually, presented His incorruptible blood on the heavenly mercy seat.

17. It is not a boastful voice, nor is it a self-indulging declaration when Jesus says, *I am He who lives, and was dead, and behold, I am alive forever more. Amen. And I have the keys of hades and death* (Revelation 1:18 NKJV). It is from the overwhelming love that the Godhead has

for mankind, that Jesus achieved this glorious victory. The Lord Jesus Christ's words are His testimony of the spiritual reconciliation He achieved which was originally shattered by Adam.

18. This was achieved through His resurrection by the glory of the Father. The most holy and pure attribute of the Godhead, their *Shekinah* glory was the divine power the holy God used to achieve the resurrection. It broke the chains of death that had bound mankind from the time they were expelled from the Garden of Eden until Christ's resurrection from the Garden Tomb; from then on, *death is swallowed up in victory. O Death, where is your sting? O Hades, where is your victory* (1 Corinthians 15. 54-55 NKJV).

19. Christ's vicarious resurrection not only conquered death for mankind but also fulfilled His own words: *I am the resurrection and the life. He who believes in Me, though he may die, he shall live* (John 11:25 NKJV). All that Jesus achieved is now available to a repentant heart who by faith confesses Jesus Christ as Lord and believes in his heart that God raised Him from the dead (Romans 10:9). This is a continuous victorious walk in Christ; and should born-again believers sin, they have the ability to confess their sin to God and receive forgiveness; for *if we walk in the light as He is in the light, we have fellowship with one another, and the blood of Jesus Christ His Son cleanses us from all sin* (1 John 1:7 NKJV). *If we confess our sins, He is faithful and just to forgive us our sins and to cleanse us from all unrighteousness* (1 John 1:9 NKJV).

20. Jesus Christ's resurrection birthed the New Covenant. This holy event closed the Old Covenant and opened the New. It further postponed the arrival of the physical Kingdom of Heaven and birthed the spiritual Kingdom of God (Acts 1:1-6).

21. The emergence of the Kingdom of God reached further than the Jew and became the gospel that *whoever believes in Him should not perish but shall have everlasting life* (John 3:16 NKJV). It opened the relationship with God the Father to every human being. The exclusiveness of the Jew bound by the Old Covenant, and the relationship God had exclusively with the Jews was annulled as Jesus exited the tomb. Now the door to salvation because of the shed blood of Jesus was opened to *every kindred, and tongue, and people, and nation* (Revelation 5:9 NKJV).

22. The Kingdom of God is the message of the gospel of Jesus Christ to all mankind. An early church writer, Oecumenius, wrote that Jesus was "slain for us and who by [His] blood did acquire an inheritance from

the many nations under heaven, to grant this salvation to humanity. And with very good reason [Apostle John] said, 'from every tribe and tongue and people and nation'. For while [Jesus Christ] did not gain all nations, for many died in unbelief, yet He acquired from every nation those worthy of salvation."

23. The application of rituals, the obedience to physical duties and sacrifices, and the adherence to celebrations are all outside of the gospel and the Kingdom of God (Galatians 4:8-10). From Jesus' resurrection, the application of faith in the finished work of Jesus Christ at Calvary is sufficient for man to enter the presence of the Father. Henceforth, *there is One God and One Mediator between God and men, the Man Christ Jesus* (1 Timothy 2:5 NKJV).

24. *For the kingdom of God is not eating and drinking, but righteousness and peace and joy in the Holy Spirit* (Romans 14:17 NKJV). It is the application of faith that swings open the door to the Father's heart and initiates His mercy (2 Corinthians 4:1). Because of faith, God's mercy enables His grace that forgives the repentant sinner (Ephesians 2:8).

25. The Lord Jesus Christ's resurrection extends beyond His own physical rebirth. It sealed the future of everyone who believes in His finished work. At the appointed time of the Day of the Lord at the sound of the voice, the trumpet, the shout, and the righteous deads' bodies will be miraculously released from their graves and be reunited with their souls and spirits. Furthermore, almost simultaneously, the righteous ones living on earth at the time of the trumpet will be taken off the earth and will meet Jesus in the clouds (1 Thessalonians 4: 13-18).

26. While this physical resurrection of the bodies is important, it is more the spiritual application of the resurrection that is most important: *Behold, I shew you a mystery; We shall not all sleep, but we shall all be changed, In a moment, in the twinkling of an eye, at the last trump: for the trumpet shall sound, and the dead shall be raised incorruptible, and we shall be changed. For this corruptible must put on incorruption, and this mortal must put on immortality. So when this corruptible shall have put on incorruption, and this mortal shall have put on immortality, then shall be brought to pass the saying that is written, Death is swallowed up in victory* (1 Corinthians 15:50-58).

27. Jesus Christ's resurrection had three spiritual applications. First, He was raised from the dead when His Spirit and soul returned into His body. Second, He ascended into the heavenly Holy of Holies where He

presented His blood on the mercy seat. Only once He had done this was the resurrection complete. Without the acceptance of Christ's sacrifice placed on the heavenly mercy seat, the resurrection would have been spiritually to no avail.

28. Third, once Jesus had completed these two tasks, He could now appear to His disciples and those who believed in Him. Herein is the most profound spiritual application of the resurrection: Jesus' resurrection birthed the Kingdom of God for the *whoever.*

29. The rebirth of a human spirit is only effective when it by faith confesses Jesus Christ as Lord and *believes in* [its] *heart that God has raised Him from the dead* (Romans 10:9 NKJV). Without the confession that Jesus was resurrected, there can be no salvation for the human spirit. The only way the spirit can be born again is for it to have faith in the power of the resurrection. This is a spiritual rebirth and an entry into the spiritual Kingdom of God as Jesus said, *That which is born of the flesh is flesh, and that which is born of the Spirit is spirit* (John 3:6 NKJV).

30. Jesus foretold to Nicodemus that the resurrection would be complete once Jesus had ascended to heaven and presented His shed blood on the mercy seat, and Apostle John confirms; *No one has ascended to heaven but He who came down from heaven, that is, the Son of Man who is in heaven* (John 3:13 NKJV).

31. The Savior Jesus Christ's resurrection not only fulfilled every requirement of the salvation plan but also spiritually accomplished, as the ante-type, the final Passover act; for on the third day of the Passover celebration, God's people were instructed to bring the *firstfruits* of their harvest and present them in the temple (Numbers 28:26).

32. Apostle Paul gives the spiritual explanation of Jesus' ultimate purpose for rising from the dead; that is, that He is the *firstfruits of them that slept* (1 Corinthians 15:20). On the third day, the day the people presented their firstfruits in the temple, Jesus was the *first* to be raised from the dead. He declares that Christ's resurrection is the first One to be resurrected and thereafter *those who are Christ's at His coming* (verse 23).

33. Inasmuch as the people returned to their homes and harvested their fields, so Jesus ascended into heaven to reap the harvest of many righteous souls worthy to be presented to the Father.

34. Christ's resurrection extends beyond the present and incorporates all future events. He is the resurrected One who rules with all power

and authority in the Millennium Reign for one thousand years. His judgment at the Great White Throne is the final pronouncement of the penalty upon those who rejected His death and resurrection. He is the holy spiritual presence in the new earth and the New Jerusalem; and once this is accomplished, *then comes the end, when He delivers the kingdom to God the Father, when He puts an end to all rule and all authority and power. For He must reign till He has put all enemies under His feet. The last enemy that will be destroyed is death. For He has put all things under His feet. But when He says "all things are put under Him," it is evident that He who put all things under Him is excepted. Now when all things are made subject to Him, then the Son Himself will be subject to Him who put all things under Him, that God may be all in all* (1 Corinthians 15: 24-28 NKJV).

35. Therein is the full circle complete. Whereas Adam's disobedience inflicted sin upon the entire human race, Christ's obedience unto death and His resurrection have reconciled humanity to God; *For as in Adam all die, even so in Christ shall all be made alive* (1 Corinthians 15:22).

Chapter 16

Jesus Christ's Ascension and Present Work

1. Scripture says, *To* [His disciples] *He also presented Himself alive after His suffering by many infallible proofs, being seen by them during forty days* (Acts 1:3 NKJV). Jesus appeared to His disciples and followers over a period of forty days. During this time, He was *speaking of the things pertaining to the Kingdom of God.*

2. How precious is the thought that the Savior was present amongst the first group of believers who were now born again and in the Kingdom of God. Furthermore, how significant it is that He was physically present during the first forty days of the *new covenant* in the Kingdom of God. Amongst other teachings, Jesus' primary purpose was to lay the foundation of the spiritual Kingdom of God and His church, and prepare the born-again believers for the spiritual power that was to be imparted to them (Acts 1:2-3, 8).

3. Christ's divine presence was amongst the believers who not only recognized Him as the risen Christ but also witnessed that He was the same Jesus Whom they knew before His death. This testimony from those believers, who saw Him in the flesh, is sufficient for believers in this present day to accept by faith their witness that Christ is alive. Furthermore, it is the witness of the Holy Spirit in man's spirit that Christ is alive as it is recorded, *But if the Spirit of Him who raised Jesus from the dead dwells in you, He who raised Christ from the dead will also give life to your mortal bodies through His Spirit who dwells in you* (Romans 8:11 NKJV).

4. The ascension of Jesus Christ that followed after *many infallible proofs* that He was alive was witnessed by His followers who were also given the promise by two heavenly beings that *this same Jesus, which is taken up from you into heaven, shall so come in like manner as ye have seen him go into heaven* (Acts 1:11). The two men's message sealed the hope in the followers' hearts that they were about to start their journey of faith in Christ's finished work, and also that He would return again. The message of the Kingdom of God from the beginning to the ending encompasses Jesus Christ, the Savior of the world.

5. French L. Arrington says, "The ascension is the third stage in the exaltation of Christ. He was not only exalted by being raised from the dead, but He also ascended into heaven."

6. The divine and holy Savior, the Lord Jesus Christ stepped down from the throne room of heaven, and humbled Himself making *Himself of no reputation, taking on the form of a bondservant, and coming in the likeness of men. And being found in appearance as a man, He humbled Himself and became obedient to the point of death, even the death of the cross* (Philippians 2:7-8 NKJV).

7. Into the presence of sinful man, He came, carrying the love of God to everyone who encountered Him. His heavenly throne room was vacated for a period as He endured the humiliation of a false trial that was laced with lies and unprecedented hatred. He suffered at the hands of the Roman Procurator and was hoisted upon the Cross as they crucified Him amongst thieves. While hanging on the cross, He was bombarded by every demon force and sickness that saturated His being. He ultimately felt the heavy load of sin being thrust upon Him as He said, *It is finished.*

8. No one could have been more humiliated. No one could have been more cast down to the lowest level of humanity than Jesus Christ because He left the highest seat of power, laid aside His full authority, and was catapulted into hell to be a ransom for many.

9. Clinging to the promise of His Father, Jesus waited three days in hell to be resurrected. Thereafter, He spent forty days with His beloved followers teaching them the things pertaining to the Kingdom of God. How patiently He waited for the moment when His allotted time on earth would end. From the Mount of Olives, He was taken up in the cloud of God's *Shekinah* glory.

10. There is no biblical explanation as to what actually happened as Jesus set foot in heaven. What is told reveals the Father's magnificent exaltation of His only begotten Son: *God also hath highly exalted him, and given him a name which is above every name* (Philippians 2:9). Suffice it to say that it can be assumed that the angelic host welcomed Him with accolades similar to those expressed when He arrived in the manger in Bethlehem.

11. As Jesus Christ returns to the Father's side, He is elevated and honored to occupy the highest seat of authority as the Father proclaims, *Sit on my right hand, until I make thine enemies thy footstool* (Hebrews 1:13).

12. Christ's exaltation transcends human comprehension and can only be spiritually discerned as the Father proclaims, *Your throne O God, is forever and ever: a scepter of righteousness is the scepter of Your kingdom. You have loved righteousness and hated lawlessness; therefore, God, Your God, has anointed You with the oil of gladness more than Your companions* (Hebrews 1:8-9 NKJV).

13. It is a breathtaking accolade the Father makes as He annunciates the pre-existence, the present existence, and the future existence of His Son, Jesus Christ: *You, LORD, in the beginning laid the foundation of the earth, and the heavens are the work of Your hands. They will perish, but You remain; and they will all grow old like a garment; like a cloak You will fold them up, and they will be changed. But You are the same, and Your years will not fail* (Hebrews 1:10-12 NKJV).

14. The exaltation of Jesus is the proclamation that the Father's will is being accomplished in His Son. It is from this place that the Eternal Son is forthwith *the Apostle and High Priest of our profession* (Hebrews 3:1). Spirit-filled believers spiritually praise and worship Jesus in the spirit as the Holy Spirit gives them utterance. They acknowledge the offices of Apostle and High Priest that Jesus now fulfills. As Apostle, Jesus imparts the Father's will to Spirit-filled believers; as High Priest, Jesus makes intercession for the saints to the Father.

15. Furthermore, the Lord Jesus Christ baptizes the born-again believer in the baptism with the Holy Spirit (Luke 3:16). Henceforth, the Holy Spirit dwells in the believer's body (1 Corinthians 6:19). This indwelling power flows like a river from the mountain peak of Christ's heart and is directed by the Holy Spirit into the very existence of a born-again believer. It is then that *out of his belly shall flow rivers of living water* (John 7:38).

16. From the moment Jesus *sat down on the right hand of God* (Hebrews 10:12), and *even now,* and until the church is raptured off the earth, He occupies the most exquisite place and highest seat of honor and exaltation from the Most High God. Spirit-filled believers are drenched in the anointing of the Holy Spirit and join the heavenly host's chorus as they release their faith and *mount up on wings as eagles* with praise and worship, exalting their Savior, the Christ, the Resurrected and Ascended Son of the living God.

Christ's Present Work

17. *I will build My church* (Matthew 16:18). Immediately Jesus occupied His seat of authority at the right hand of the Father, and He began to fulfill His word that He would build *His* church. The Kingdom of God was already established; and from the born-again believers who are subjects to the King of the Kingdom, He baptizes them with the Holy Spirit. This baptism is the spiritual empowerment and is also the transfer of those who are baptized with the Holy Spirit into the body of Christ, which is His church (1 Corinthians 12:13).

18. Spirit-filled believers are convinced that the finished work of Christ includes the Father's exaltation of Him, and the continuous intercession of Christ who has all authority to do this because He said, *All authority has been given to Me in heaven and on earth* (Matthew 28:18 NKJV). The exalted Christ, who is seated at the right hand of almighty God holds the scepter of righteousness; and from that highest seat, He makes intercession for the believers.

19. He is no longer on earth separating Himself from His disciples, having gone *out into a mountain to pray, and continued all night in prayer to God* (Luke 6:12; Mark 1:35). He is now in heaven, no longer on earth, continuously in prayer making intercession for the saints (Romans 8:34; Hebrews 7:25).

20. The Lord Jesus Christ's authority, power, and office in heaven is the full expression of His entire ministry that includes, Prophet, Priest, and King. This is the fulfillment of the Old Testament fully achieving perfection of these offices in Him.

21. Jesus gave believers clear instructions on how to enter the presence of the Father. Now in heaven, the Savior occupies a supreme position

of *Mediator*. Apostle Paul referring to Jesus' position for mankind regarding their access to the Father in heaven, explains, *For there is one God, and one mediator between God and men, the man Christ Jesus* (1 Timothy 2:5).

22. Jesus taught the disciples how they must approach the Father when praying. He said, *I am the way, the truth, and the life. No man cometh unto the Father, but by me* (John 14:6). On three occasions in John's Gospel, Jesus tells the disciples, *Whatsoever ye shall ask the Father in my name, he will give it to you* (John 15:16, 16:23).

23. Spirit-filled believers enter the presence of the Father by reverently approaching Him in the name of Jesus as they begin their prayer with "Father, in the name of Jesus we come to you." It is this opening statement that they acknowledge the Father who exalted His Son to His right hand. Furthermore, believers know the only way they can enter the Father's holy presence is in the name of His Son, Jesus. Upon the mention of His name, Jesus, believers can make *supplications, prayers, intercessions, and giving of thanks* (1 Timothy 2:1).

24. Spirit-filled believers see the deep spiritual achievements of Christ's High Priestly office. His constant intercession for the church is done with the desire that the members of His body are endowed with the spiritual power, gifts, and abilities to accomplish the work the Father has for them.

25. As High Priest, Jesus has secured every need the believer has through His death and resurrection. Every earthly, temporal blessing and eternal spiritual blessing is achieved through His redemptive work. Christ can intercede in a manner that no human can comprehend. His mediatory role has such depth that the whispering between the Son and the Father on behalf of the saints and the church is uninterrupted communication.

26. The Son seeks the Father's attention for every need the believer has. They have such a close relationship that the Son continually lays the petitions before the Father. While the believers make their requests known unto the Father in *the name of Jesus,* the Son as High Priest has direct access to the Father on the believers' behalf.

27. Spirit-filled believers know and are assured that, when they enter the closet and call upon the name of the Lord, they are entering a Spirit-to-spirit communication and relationship with the Father. Their prayer is, therefore, not a demand for an earthly, physical need. It is not a request

to the Father to perform the impossible and bring about benefit to the one praying. Spirit-filled believers know that, when approaching the Father in the name of Jesus, they are doing so to secure the Godhead's spiritual endorsement of their petition.

28. They understand that the *High Priest of their confession* is aware of their petition, need, supplication, or intercession. What the believers are asking the Father to do is to give His spiritual direction and enforcement of the petition, as they assert, *Your will be done.*

29. Jesus, as High Priest, perfected the office. He fulfills all the duties ascribed to the office in the Old Testament. Peter C. Craigie in his commentary on the priesthood in *Baker, Encyclopedia of the Bible* says, "But his position (the High Priest) was more weighty than that of an administrator; just as all priests were servants and guardians of the covenant relationship, the High Priest was 'chief' servant and 'chief' guardian. In his hands rested spiritual responsibility for the entire people of God, and therein lay the true honor and gravity of His position." Craigie continues, "The High Priest entered the Holy of Holies, and standing before the 'mercy seat', he sought God's forgiveness and mercy for the whole nation of Israel (Leviticus 16: 1-9). The High Priest had the great honor and heavy burden of seeking God's mercy for all Israel."

30. Thus, the Savior of the world, the Lord Jesus Christ, abides in the presence of the Father as the saints' High Priest. The exalted Christ, who is the *Head of the church* (Ephesians 1:22-23; Colossians 1:18) is ultimately the "administrator" of the covenant as was the High Priest in the Old Testament. Christ is the presiding authority over everything that takes place in the church, The holy Writ declares that God *put all things under His feet, and gave him to be the head over all things to the church* (Ephesians 1:22). No human being, no matter how spiritual he may appear to be, can ever instruct the Lord Jesus Christ what to do in, and for, the church. It is His prerogative, and He said, *I will build my church; and the gates of hell shall not prevail against it* (Matthew 16:18). Henceforth, Jesus is Lord of the church and King of the Kingdom of God.

31. One of the worst calamities that has infiltrated the church is the interference of human hands in the divine sculpturing of the church.

32. As the office of a High Priest was in the Old Covenant, so Jesus is now fulfilling the "guardianship" role of the High Priest by ever making

intercession for the saints. He is the Supreme Protector of the New Covenant relationship. He orchestrates this by instructing the Holy Spirit to reveal, guide, and teach believers all truth (John 16:5-15).

33. In the Lord Jesus Christ's position as Savior, He holds and represents the "spiritual responsibility" of the New Covenant for the *whosoever*. He secured this when He entered the heavenly Holy of Holies; He placed his blood on the mercy seat, and He gained the Father's acceptance of His sacrifice as sufficient for the redemption of man's inherent sin.

34. Apostle Paul makes this beautiful statement about Jesus who is seated at the right hand of the Father, *Now unto the King eternal, immortal, invisible, the only wise God, be honor and glory forever and ever. Amen* (1 Timothy 1:17). Embedded in the kingship Christ holds while in heaven, royalty and kingship were likewise bestowed upon Him at birth, when the wise men attested when they arrived in Jerusalem and asked, *Where is He who has been born the King of the Jews* (Matthew 2:2 NKJV). Throughout His ministry, He held this office even though He was rejected, and how aptly Jesus answered in the affirmative to Pilate that He was the King of the Jews. Now in heaven, He still is and will forevermore reign as King.

35. As One who has all authority granted to Him, Jesus exercises power in upholding and controlling all things in the world. Furthermore, He rules as King of the Kingdom of God into which born-again believers enter as subjects when they accept by faith His finished work on Calvary. This sovereign rule as King of the Kingdom of God is immersed in His spiritual precepts of *righteousness, and peace, and joy in the Holy Ghost* (Romans 14:17).

36. It is in His full authority and power that Jesus allows Satan his time on earth. Christ tolerates the works of the devil. To everyone, God gives free will; and while as King, Jesus understands that not everyone will accept Him as Savior, He welcomes the decision of the *many who receive Him* (John 1:12).

37. While it is fitting to consider the work Christ the King is doing, it is as important to consider the lofty throne from which He rules. First, it is an eternal throne as Jesus is called, *the King eternal* (1 Timothy 1:17 NKJV). Second, it is a throne from which unlimited power flows.

38. Such is the office of King that the Savior now occupies. Filled with spiritual opulence and glory, Christ rules in this office according to His word. Yet that which awaits Him is even more marvelous.

39. The fulfillment of these three offices of Prophet, High Priest, and King is eclipsed by the role Jesus embraces as Lord of His church. In the organism of His body, the church, Christ as Lord and Savior gathers all believers as *members in particular* (1 Corinthians 12:27). No longer are those who are baptized with the Holy Spirit subjects of the King; they are now members of His body.

40. This is the One who lovingly encourages believers *whatsoever ye shall ask the Father in my name, he will give it to you* (John 16:23).

Summary

41. *The Word became flesh* (John 1:14). The holy, divine Jesus Christ *made Himself of no reputation, taking the form of a bond servant, and coming in the likeness of men. And being found in the appearance as a man, He humbled Himself and became obedient to the point of death, even the death of the cross. Therefore God has highly exalted Him and given Him the name which is above every name, that at the name of Jesus every knee should bow, of those in heaven, and of those on earth, and of those under the earth, and that every tongue should confess is Jesus Christ is Lord, to the glory of God the Father* (Philippians 2:7-11 NKJV).

42. His work on earth laid the foundation for the redeemed when He offered Himself as the sacrifice for mankind's sin. His continuing work as the exalted Christ now in heaven, solidifies His continuing presence as He promises, *I am with you always, even to the end of the age* (Matthew 28:20 NKJV).

43. The Lord Jesus Christ's ascension invoked the Father's highest honor, elevating Him *to be the head over all things to the church, which is his body, the fullness of him that filleth all in all* (Ephesians 1:22-23). This appointment of the Son of God incorporated His roles as *Apostle and High Priest* (Hebrews 3:1). He gave gifts unto men, *some, apostles; and some, prophets; and some, evangelists; and some, pastors and teachers* (Ephesians 4:11) for the fulfillment of His mission to *build* His *church* (Matthew 16:18).

44. Furthermore, Jesus is now the intercessor who *ever liveth to make intercession for them* (Hebrews 7:25). He is ever mindful of believers' plight as they *earnestly contend for the faith which was once delivered unto the saints* (Jude 3). Even though the believer stumbles during

his pilgrimage, the Lord Jesus appeals to the Father's mercy as He fulfills His role as Advocate on behalf of the believer (1 John 2:1). Confession and repentance in a believer's heart are secured and his sins are forgiven him because of the Advocate, Jesus, presenting the sincerity of the repentant heart to the Father.

Part 4

The Doctrine of the Holy Spirit

Chapter 17

Doctrine of the Holy Spirit

1. Spirit-filled believers are always seeking for more from God. They are aware that all they are taught, revealed, and led to believe is from the Holy Spirit. It was Jesus who said, *But the Helper, the Holy Spirit, whom the Father will send in My name, He will teach you all things, and bring to your remembrance all things that I said to you* (John 14:26 NKJV).

2. There can be no other source of teaching than the Holy Spirit. He is the only teacher, instructor, and guide believers need when seeking a deeper walk with God. The Holy Writ declares, *But the anointing which you have received from Him abides in you, and you do not need that anyone teach you; but as the same anointing teaches you concerning all things, and is true, and is not a lie, and just as it has taught you, you will abide in Him* (1 John 2:27 NKJV).

3. French L. Arrington launches his chapter on the Holy Spirit with these words, "The Holy Spirit in the One who applies the saving benefit of the cross to us. However, in the scriptures the work of the Holy Spirit is seen as manifold. Creation and new creation, the resurrection of the dead, eternal life, the Kingdom, and the final consummation of history are all the works of the Spirit. The story of Jesus Christ is an account of the works of the Holy Spirit. Christ's incarnation, mission, anointing, ministry, death, and resurrection were by the Holy Spirit as Apostle Paul clarifies, *for the law of the Spirit of life in Christ Jesus hath made me free from the law of sin and death* (Romans 8:2)."

4. Spirit-filled believers have an acute awareness that the Holy Spirit is not merely an agent of the Godhead; He is fully God. It is God, the Holy Spirit, that is active in their lives, and the operation of all they

do is God-invested and God-infested. He is not a whimsical fantasy that is only occasionally apparent. The Holy Spirit is omniscient, omnipresent, and omnipotent. He is there all the time, always present to guide, always fully operational in all His power, and all-knowing in every circumstance.

5. While the Holy Spirit is doing the bidding of Jesus Christ, He is not only a representative chosen by Jesus, but also is, in fact, an equal part of the Godhead fulfilling the operational procedures of the Godhead through believers. The combined unity of the Three-in-One is never more evident than when the Holy Spirit manifests Himself in the relationship with the Father and the Son by fulfilling their promises.

6. The biblical reference to the Holy Spirit's involvement in all that the Godhead does is inaugurated when in its first two verses the Holy Writ states, *The Spirit of God was hovering over the face of the waters* (Genesis 1:2 NKJV).

7. No subject is more difficult to fully comprehend than the Godhead, and in particular the evidence, existence, and work of the Holy Spirit. At best, it can be said of the Holy Spirit within the Godhead that He worked together with the Father and the Son to create the world mankind inhabits (Psalm 33:6); He is the creator of man (Job 33:4; Psalm 104:30); He adorned the heavens (Job 26:13); and He is the One who takes the eternal spirit from man (Isaiah 40:6-8). None of these statements can be reasoned in man's puny mind. They are spiritually discerned. Richard D. Paterson in his commentary on Job says, "Mankind catches a glimpse and a whisper of God's workings. Full knowledge is beyond human understanding" (Job 5:9, 11:7-8, 42:1-3).

8. As an opening salvo on this vast subject of the Doctrine of the Holy Spirit, Professor Charles Erdman's in his book *The Holy Spirit and Christian Experience* expounds, "The Spirit cannot be where Christ is denied as Redeemer, Life and Lord of all. Christ is 'The Truth' and the Spirit is 'The Spirit of Truth'; all is personal, not abstract, ideal, and the sum and substance of material wherewith the Spirit works in Christ.

9. "In brief, the Holy Spirit must be silent altogether in pulpits and churches where 'a different gospel which is not another gospel' is preached, and where unrebuked and unchecked prevail, although in a form of Godliness, 'the lust of the flesh, and the lust of the eyes, and the pride of life' and the things which are 'not of the Father, but of the world'; things which are not of the new nature and spirit in

which the Holy Spirit dwells and through which alone He can work and testify.

10. "We should be warned by the history of the apostolic churches, once so full of the Holy Spirit, but which perished from their places long ago. The same denial of Christ, the same worldliness is our danger today."

11. Spirit-filled believers concur with Professor Charles Erdman's statement and find it is heartbreaking that in today's church so many denominations shun the operation of the spiritual gifts, the ministries, and the acknowledgement of divine revelation; and in some cases, they condemn worship in *spiritual songs* (Ephesians 5:19) and regard the holy move of the Holy Spirit as evil and devilish. In the church's beginnings, every spiritual gift, fruit of the Spirit, and ministry was vibrant and penetrated every barrier (creed, race, gender, and nation), saving the lost and being used by the Holy Spirit *for the perfecting of the saints, for the work of the ministry, for the edifying of the body of Christ: till [they] all come in the unity of the faith, and of the knowledge of the Son of God, unto a perfect man, unto the measure of the stature of the fulness of Christ* (Ephesians 4:12-13).

12. It needs to be stated that the Holy Spirit never refuses to be included in the *perfecting of the saints.* He is never unavailable to teach and *edify the body of Christ* because He is preoccupied with something else. It is the rejection and denial by believers to allow the Holy Spirit to be operational in the church that has caused this vacuum and absence of spiritual power and the *effectual working in the measure of every part, maketh increase of the body unto the edifying of itself in love* (Ephesians 4:16).

13. In order that the operational procedures of the Holy Spirit be clearly understood, there needs to be an explanation of His working with believers and within Spirit-filled believers. The ever-presence of the Holy Spirit is constantly upon born-again believers while the Holy Spirit is constantly residing within the Spirit-filled believer's body (1 Corinthians 6:19).

14. Apostle Paul attests that the Holy Spirit lives in the Spirit-filled believer when he says, *Do you not know that you are the temple of God and that the Spirit of God dwells in you?* (1 Corinthians 2:16 NKJV). While it is the same Holy Spirit who resides upon born-again believers, He now takes up residence in the Spirit-filled believer's body. An ancient Syriac author said, "The body and heart in which our Lord dwells is in truth

a temple and an altar, seeing that [the Holy Spirit] our Lord resides there." It is no wonder Apostle Paul said, *If any man defile the temple of God, him shall God destroy; for the temple of God is holy, which temple ye are* (1 Corinthians 3:17).

15. When the Holy Spirit takes up residence in a believer's body (at the baptism with the Holy Spirit), the believer becomes the conduit the Holy Spirit uses to bring about the works He is instructed to do by Jesus Christ (John 16:7-15). Spirit-filled believers do not anticipate the Holy Spirit coming upon them; they live by the Holy Spirit that is within them.

16. The Holy Spirit is constantly at work with the born-again believer revealing to him the necessity of a spiritual relationship with the Godhead, namely spirit to Spirit. In the Spirit-filled believer's life, the Holy Spirit leads his spirit to accompany Him into the holy spiritual presence of the Godhead and reveals and guides the Spirit-filled believer into all Truth what things pertain to the effective working of the church (Ephesians 2:18-23, 3:1-21).

The Purpose of the Holy Spirit

17. Scripture is clear, and the eternal words of Jesus Christ personally proclaim the Holy Spirit's purpose in the world after Jesus ascended to heaven: *Nevertheless, I tell you the truth. It is to your advantage that I go away; for if I do not go away, the Helper will not come to you; but if I depart, I will send Him to you. And when He has come, He will convict the world of sin, and of righteousness, and of judgment: of sin because they do not believe in Me; of righteousness, because I go to My Father and you see Me no more; of judgment, because the ruler of this world is judged. I still have many things to say to you, but you cannot hear them now. However, when He the Spirit of truth has come, He will guide you into all truth; for He will not speak on His own authority, but whatever He hears He will speak; and He will tell you things to come. He will glorify Me, for He will take of what is mine and declare it to you. All things that the Father has are Mine. Therefore, I said that He will take of Mine and declare it to you* (John 16:7-14 NKJV).

18. Such a manifold task and application of these huge responsibilities Jesus speaks of, can only be entrusted into the hands of the Holy

Spirit who is the only One capable of accomplishing and fulfilling this enormous task.

19. Furthermore, it is only God the Holy Spirit who has the spiritual ability to achieve the Godhead's desired results. Ultimately, the desired result of the Godhead is the continuous revelation of the existence of God in the midst of mankind. God's eternal purpose is manifested through the Holy Spirit in every age and dispensation.

20. Prophets in the Old Testament received from the Holy Spirit that grace would come to everyone as well, for Jesus Christ would become the sacrificial Lamb of God; and Apostle Peter says, *To them it was revealed that, not to themselves, but to us they were ministering the things which now have been reported to you through those who have preached the gospel to you by the Holy Spirit sent from heaven—things which angels desire to look into* (1 Peter 1:12 NKJV).

21. Now in the Age of Grace that *which in other ages was not made known to the sons of men . . . has now been revealed by the Spirit to His holy apostles and prophets* (Ephesians 3:5 NKJV). The Holy Spirit is revealing to believers the truth for He is the *Spirit of truth* (John 16:13). Therefore, the purpose of the Holy Spirit in this dispensation and age is to reveal the will of God to all believers.

22. What Jesus Christ accomplished as Son of God and Son of Man is now continued through the Holy Spirit who testifies of Christ's glorious victory over death, and of the eternal presence of God to everyone who believes in Him, as Jesus promised, *But when the Helper comes, whom I shall send to you from the Father, the Spirit of truth who proceeds from the Father, He will testify of Me* (John 15:26 NKJV).

23. Dr. Norman Geisler in his book *Systematic Theology Volume Two* says, "The Father is the Planner, the Son is the Accomplisher, and the Holy Spirit is the Applier of salvation to believers. The Father is the Source, the Son is the Means, and the Holy Spirit is the Effector of salvation–it is He who convicts, convinces, and converts."

24. The Holy Spirit is fully capable and can achieve all that is required of Him because He is God, equal in power, attributes, and glory with the Father and the Son.

25. Spirit-filled believers stand fast on the foundation of the Word that declares what the Holy Spirit's purpose is in the church age. The Holy Spirit is the *power* source that empowers believers to walk victoriously. He is the Supplier of their ability to witness to a lost and dying world

even as Jesus said, *But ye shall receive power, after that the Holy Ghost is come upon you: and ye shall be witnesses unto me both in Jerusalem, and in all Judea, and in Samaria, and unto the uttermost part of the earth* (Acts 1:8).

26. In addition to the Holy Spirit being the power source for the Spirit-filled believer, He is the Member of the Godhead who reveals their purposes from God's throne in heaven to this church age on earth (1 Corinthians 2:10). This revealed truth is not a natural conviction; it is the total acceptance into man's spirit of God's uttered purpose (1 Corinthians 2:11-13).

27. Apostle Paul emphatically states that human comprehension cannot receive the things of God because they are revealed truths that can only be spiritually discerned. He said, *But the natural man receiveth not the things of the Spirit of God: for they are foolishness unto him: neither can he know them, because they are spiritually discerned* (1 Corinthians 2:14).

28. The Holy Spirit's spiritual purposes are numerous and untethered; He is the *plumb line* that exposes unrighteousness from righteousness; He is the "lighthouse" that beams the path of truth and life to all who seek it. He directs the believer towards Jesus Christ and what He accomplished for mankind. The Holy Spirit is the omnipresent One who constantly reminds believers of the omniscient presence of the holiness of God amid a perverse society. He is, in fact, the Person of the Godhead who *shall never leave thee nor forsake thee* (Hebrews 13:5).

The Works of the Holy Spirit

29. At the outset, The Holy Spirit's works, instructions, and duties do not come from man; they are conceived and agreed upon by the Godhead for man. As much as it is important to know the works of the Holy Spirit in the Old Testament, it is also vital for the church to know His current work.

30. In the Old Testament amongst His people the Jews, God directed them to the demands of the Law. He revealed the people's condition through the mouth of prophets and in the written word.

31. The Old Testament prophet Isaiah and the gospel of Luke record the foretelling of the Son of God who was sent by the Father and was in

the midst of His people to do the works of the Father: *The Spirit of the Lord is upon Me, because He has anointed Me to preach the gospel to the poor; He has sent Me to heal the broken hearted, to proclaim liberty to the captives and recovery of sight to the blind. To set at liberty those who are oppressed; to proclaim the acceptable year of the Lord* (Luke 4:18-19 NKJV). Jesus did all these marvelous works while He was on earth.

32. The Lord Jesus enlightens the disciples that there will be One after Him who will *guide* [them] *into all truth* (John 16:13). All that Jesus did while He was on earth was confined to the physical environment of Israel and its surrounding borders while the Holy Spirit's work is universal. Jesus' personal ministry was appropriated physically through word and voice to mankind and their senses while the Holy Spirit's ministry is Spirit to spirit reaching man's heart and will. Added to this are miraculous works of revealing the state of man's inherent sin; and the Holy Spirit also continues the work of Jesus Christ through believers who are, even today, saved, healed, delivered, and liberated from oppression.

33. A commentator in the *Pulpit Commentary on John* says, "While [Jesus Christ] remained with His disciples, they tenaciously clung to the idea of a temporal king and a temporal kingdom, and this idea would last as long as His personal presence; but His departure by death had a direct tendency to destroy this notion and blast this hope for ever, and prepare them for the advent of the Holy Spirit, who would, on the ruins of the temporal kingdom, establish a spiritual one, the *kingdom of God is within you* (Luke 17:21).

34. "The personal ministry of Jesus was essentially temporary; that of the Spirit is permanent. Jesus came only for a time, and under human conditions was subject to persecutions and death . . . but the Spirit came to remain with and in His people forever and was personally above any physical injury from the wicked world."

35. How magnificent is His work amplified in the age of grace, namely, the church age! Now He, the Member of the Godhead, proclaims Christ's finished work on Calvary to the entire world. From Jesus Christ's ascension, the Holy Spirit has been *sent* to proclaim the message of salvation.

36. It is appropriate to study this holy subject in three parts: The Holy Spirit's work in the world, the Holy Spirit's work in the believer's life, and the Holy Spirit's work in the church.

37. To expound on the words of Jesus regarding the work of the Holy Spirit, it is important to fully comprehend who it is that is referred to as the *Comforter/Helper* in John 16:7. Herein is the guidepost that illuminates the work of the Holy Spirit more clearly. The Greek word for *Comforter/Helper* is "parakletos". A more definite translation is *advocate* which expresses the effective working Jesus mentions the Holy Spirit will do.

38. W. A. C. Rowe says, "His first move in this direction is towards the World. He must begin here in order that they may be saved. In John 16:8 we see that *He will convict the world of sin, and of righteousness, and of judgement.* These are warning notes. They are decisive and sharp. This 'pointedness' was evident in the experience of Saul of Tarsus; *It is hard for thee to kick against the pricks* (Acts 9:5). This is the bible doctrine of conviction."

39. The work of the Holy Spirit in *the world* is how He reveals to mankind their state of sin and the consequences thereof. His work is a continuing work of the Lord Jesus Christ who came into *the world to save sinners* (1 Timothy 1:15).

40. It is into this *world* that the Holy Spirit continues to expose man's sinful state. Jesus *was in the world, and the world was by him, and the world knew him not* (John 1:10). This is nothing less than unbelief in Jesus Christ because they did not know or love Him. Arthur Pink says, "Unbelief is far more than an error of judgment, or nonconsent of the mind, it is aversion of heart" (1 Corinthians 2:8).

41. The tragic words of Jesus to His disciples echo throughout the world like a never-ending ringing in their ears. The Holy Spirit will convict the world *of sin because they believe not in me.* (John 16:8-9). Unbelief is the seed that germinates evil.

42. The presentation of the love of God to a lost and dying soul can only be presented by the Holy Spirit. Salvation deals with eternal life and the Author of this eternal life is God. Hence, the Holy Spirit's work in the sinner's life is divine in its origin and holy in its presentation. This is the Holy God (Holy Spirit) who is dealing with the eternal destiny of a human spirit.

43. He will of necessity present Christ's finished work of salvation with a sharp piercing effect that exposes the state of the sinner's evil nature who has a *hardness of heart* (Romans 2:5). This sharp pointedness reveals to sinners how far they have strayed from the truth. Every time

they reject the Holy Spirit's call to repentance, they, in essence, *kick against* the *sharp two-edged sword* (Hebrews 4:12).

44. The variance in presentation of God's eternal love for man by the Holy Spirit is also marked by the discernment within a man's heart and soul when he hungers for salvation. The Holy Spirit does at times, reach into the human spirit by gently exposing the divine love God has for him. This love reveals the purpose of God's sacrifice of His Son as He convicts the lost. Luke records the Holy Spirit's gentle wooing one *whose heart the Lord opened, that she* (Lydia) *attended unto the things which were spoken* (Acts 16:14).

45. In every method, the same message is presented, and the same conviction of sin is evidenced. This is the purpose of the Holy Spirit's work in the world: to convict the sinner. Rowe continues, "Warning or wooing, the purpose is the same; to snatch brands from the burning. He convicts, convinces and constrains."

46. Spirit-filled believers are aware that the convicting and reproving by the Holy Spirit of a sinner's spiritual condition and state are absolutely conclusive. When the Holy Spirit declares the truth, sinners have no argument, reason, or justification that can acquit them from the *wages of sin* (Romans 6:23).

47. The Holy Spirit, having convicted the sinner of his state, will expose the sinner to righteousness which the Lord Jesus Christ fulfilled to perfection in His life and His death. Christ *became for us righteousness* (1 Corinthians 1:30). Christ's righteousness is not done only for Himself (1 John 2:1-2) but for all mankind who believes in Him (2 Corinthians 5:21).

48. With the presentation that Jesus Christ is the Righteous One, the Holy Spirit then exposes the only remedy for the sinner's unrighteousness, the righteous Lord Jesus Christ. His work in the life of the sinner reveals the necessity of repentance of sin and the confession by faith in a risen Savior who is all righteousness and has achieved the victory over death and the grave, thus opening the way to forgiveness.

49. Arthur Pink continues this thought: "It is the Spirit's presence on earth which establishes Christ's righteousness, and the evidence is that He has gone to the Father . . . . The fact that the Father did exalt Him to His own right hand demonstrates that He was completely innocent of the charges laid against Him . . . The world was unrighteous in casting Him out; the Father righteous in glorifying Him, and this is what the Spirit's presence here established."

50. This striking contrast between righteousness and unrighteousness revealed by the Holy Spirit to sinners is the convincing element that enlightens the sinners' hearts to realize their guilty state. They discern that the work of Jesus Christ's death and resurrection confirmed Christ's righteousness which exalted Him to the right hand of the Father; and His presence is, by contrast, unavailable to sinners in their unrighteous, guilty state.

51. The Holy Spirit unashamedly declares that Christ's vicarious work has brought Satan's evil deception to naught *because the prince of this world is judged* (John 16:11). Let it be declared as vociferously as possible: *Christ has destroyed the works of the devil* (1 John 3:8), *He has conquered death and the grave* (1 Corinthians 15:54-55). The gavel has fallen on the judgment of Satan, he is judged and found guilty, hence his judgment is over because *the ruler of this world is judged* (John 16:11).

52. What is important for mankind is that in the heart of those who do not love Christ the Holy Spirit produces evidence, and the consequences of their refusal to love Him. The world is guilty of refusing to believe in Jesus Christ and His finished work at Calvary. They are condemned through the evidence of Christ's righteous exaltation to the right hand of the Father. Henceforth, God's wrath and judgment can be the only concluding action because *He who believes in the Son has everlasting life, and he who does not believe the Son shall not see life; but the wrath of God abides on him* (John 3:36 NKJV).

53. There is no refuting argument or defense that can be presented which will allow the unrepentant heart to escape God's judgment. Sin's conceiver, Satan, the devil, is judged; and sentence is passed on him. So, too, does the Holy Spirit reveal to the *world* the judgment that awaits them if they refuse to accept the Savior of the world.

Chapter 18

Doctrine of the Holy Spirit (continued)

1. *He shall glorify me: for he shall receive of mine, and shall shew it unto you* (John 16:14). Perhaps the most precious work the Holy Spirit does from the moment Jesus ascended into heaven is the *glorification* and exaltation of the Lord Jesus Christ. He directs the believers' attention to the Son and guides their focus towards Calvary's finished work. He removes the scales from believers' eyes and ushers in the most radiant vision they can receive as the glory of the resurrected Christ beams forth into their hearts like the brightness of the noonday sun.

2. Herein is the Godhead once again fully operational. The Father has *highly exalted* [Jesus] *and given Him a name which is above every other name* (Philippians 2:9 NKJV). Jesus has completed the work of salvation on earth; and into this *world,* the Holy Spirit exuberantly glorifies Jesus Christ as Lord and Savior.

3. The magnificence of the Holy Spirit's work has always been the same towards the exposition of Jesus. His miraculous work with the Son of God begins at Jesus' conception; He anoints the Son of God to *preach the gospel.* He raises Jesus from the dead by the glory of the Father, and now He invokes the glory as He *glorifies* [Jesus] on earth.

4. The spiritual work and mighty accomplishments the church achieved in the first century were so impactful that thousands of new converts turned from their wicked ways and walked in spiritual newness of life. In all their affairs, the early believers were *led by the Spirit* (Romans 8:14). They had no claim to any of their accomplishments, for those were wrought through the indwelling power of the Holy Spirit.

5. These men *preached Jesus Christ, and him crucified* (1 Corinthians 2:2); and they were anointed by the Holy Spirit to speak boldly to kings, the rich, and the poor. These members of the early church manifested the indwelling presence of the Holy Spirit by willingly sharing all they had with each other. As they testified and glorified Jesus Christ the spiritual fruit of the Spirit flowed like a river in their lives as they testified and glorified Jesus Christ.

6. Apostle John gives the all-embracing testimony of what the Spirit-filled believers of the early church witnessed and experienced as they started their journey on the newly paved gospel road: *That which was from the beginning, which we have heard, which we have seen with our eyes, which we have looked upon, and our hands have handled, concerning the Word of life— the life was manifested, and we have seen, and bear witness, and declare to you that eternal life which was with the Father and was manifested to us— that which we have seen and heard we declare to you, that you also may have fellowship with us; and truly our fellowship is with the Father and with His Son Jesus Christ. And these things we write to you that your joy may be full* (1 John 1:1-4 NKJV).

7. The Holy Spirit operated in the ministries as they heralded the gospel throughout the cities and across the hills. He manifested the gifts of the Spirit in their gatherings whether they met in a building or under the shade of olive trees. The Holy Spirit empowered apostles and prophets with revelation. In the divine organism of the church the Holy Spirit constantly diverted the believers' attention to Jesus Christ.

8. The divine harmony that existed within the Godhead functioned with precision and unity. The Holy Spirit was never jealous of Christ's accomplishments on earth. In fact, He exalted Jesus and glorified Him amongst believers. Neither did the Holy Spirit succumb to an attitude of second best because His work came after what Jesus did on earth. His work is a continuation and an extension of Christ's work on earth.

9. The explanation that the Holy Spirit glorifies Jesus Christ means that He is bringing believers into the presence of Jesus because, when the glory of the Lord is manifested, it includes His holy presence amongst the people. The desire within the hearts of the members was fueled by the Holy Spirit's presence that continually exalted Jesus. They desired to *know Him and the power of His resurrection, and the fellowship of His sufferings, being conformed to His death* (Philippians 3:10 NKJV).

God's glory is His presence amongst His people, a presence for which the early church hungered and thirsted.

10. God's love, mercy, and grace streamed into the believers' lives and it flowed with a dynamic force that powered the servants of God to boldly proclaim Jesus Christ as Lord. Their salvation was their life and became the reason for their dedication to present Jesus to the lost and dying world. Their witness that Jesus Christ is Lord was from the Holy Spirit's divine presence pulsating through them, making them declare, *whether it is right in the sight of God to listen to you more than to God, you judge. For we cannot but speak the things which we have seen and heard* (Acts 4:19-20 NKJV). Thus, the glorification of Jesus Christ was the fulfillment of Jesus' saying that the Holy Spirit will *glorify* [Him].

11. As the centuries continued from those early years when the church was birthed how tragic that the church has meandered from its roots of spiritual exaltation of Jesus Christ to an institution of profit and personal glorification instead of continuing in prophetical utterances and glorification of the Lord Jesus Christ. Clearly, this is the work of the adversary, the devil, to turn the church away from the power source that glorifies the risen Christ.

12. Thanks be to God, the Holy Spirit, for the return of those who seek the *deep things of God* (1 Corinthians 2:10), and now Spirit-filled believers are *led of the Spirit* (Romans 8:14) and are the channel through which the Holy Spirit once again glorifies Jesus in the church.

13. As the Lord Jesus Christ is seated in His exalted position at the right hand of the Father, now the body of Christ, the church, has a Divine Person continually with them, in them, and glorifying Christ through them. The Holy Spirit *quickens* (John 5:21; Romans 8:11), He *guides into all truth* (John 16:13), He confirms *the sonship bestowed* on believers (Romans 8:16), and He is the Helper who *helps their weaknesses* (Romans 8:26) and *has sealed* them *unto the day of redemption* (Ephesians 4:30). All this is done by the Holy Spirit to the glory of the Son of God, Jesus Christ.

14. While in the Upper Room during the night in which He was betrayed, Jesus said to His disciples, *Most assuredly, I say to you, he who believes in Me, the works that I do he will do also; and greater works than these he will do, because I go to My Father* (John 14:12 NKJV). This statement from Jesus to the disciples must have startled them. The three years with Him could never have been greater. Christ's ministry,

His teaching, and His holy walk overwhelmed them. Consequently, they could not perceive anything *greater*.

15. Jesus speaks of the unification of the Godhead, the Father, the Son, and the Holy Spirit and the oneness that exists among them: *I am in the Father, and the Father in Me. The words that I speak to you I do not speak on My own authority; but the Father who dwells in Me does the works. Believe Me that I am in the Father and the Father in Me, or else believe Me for the sake of the works themselves* (John 14:10-11 NKJV). This deep revelation Christ shares with His disciples caused them to ask Him for clarification regarding the indivisibility of the Godhead.

16. The unification of the Godhead is explained well by Augustine (A.D. 354-430) when he writes, "The activities of the divine three are inseparable, so that when an activity is attributed to the Father, He is not taken to engage in it without the Son and the Holy Spirit."

17. Regarding this unification, Apostle John records that Apostle Philip, lingering in the tradition and his attachment to the Law, asks that they be shown the Father. Jesus lovingly unfolds the explanation that He and the Father are one and the same. He says to Philip, *He who has seen Me has seen the Father* (John 14:9).

18. Gregory of Nyssa (A.D. 335-395) gives this explanation on the subject: "The Father does not have an overwhelming presence in the Son. The Son is not deficient in the Father. In all this there is no hint of any variation in glory or of essence or anything else between the Father and the Son." Arthur Pink's comment on Jesus' reply is, "The corporal representation of God, such as Philip desired, was unnecessary; unnecessary because a far more glorious revelation of Deity was right there before him."

19. Not only was there unity of thought and application in their words and works, but also their oneness is so intimate that all that the Godhead is and does is sublime and glorious. Spirit-filled believers immerse themselves in the anointing of the Holy Spirit who directs their attention to the Son of God who declares *at that day ye shall know that I am in My Father, and ye in me, and I in you* (John 14:20).

20. The Holy Spirit's constant reminder to Spirit-filled believers is, therefore, Jesus Christ's glorious work, vicarious death, and resurrection, thus conquering the devil's hold on mankind. Believers cannot, and must not, lose their vision of the ascended Christ, who is seated at the right hand of the Father, magnified and highly exalted. This exaltation and

revelation are given by the Holy Spirit into the believer's spirit. This continuous revelation has never varied in its capability and power since the first day of the church, and will continue until Jesus returns to the earth.

21. In the book *Pulpit Commentary on John*, a commentator states, "It is important to observe the order, so to say, of the Spirit's revelation concerning Christ. The great outstanding facts, of our Lord's manifestation to men are, His incarnation; His cross; His crown. It is around these that all the doctrines of faith are clustered.

22. "Out of these facts they are set to grow. From the very first–that is to say from Pentecost–the Holy Spirit bore a certain witness concerning them all. The words of Apostle Peter, *God hath made that same Jesus, whom ye have crucified, both Lord and Christ* (Acts 2:36). These words were the beginning of the ministry of the Holy Spirit. And then, as time went on, the full meaning of the cross was unfolded, and the Apostle Paul, who, above all things, preached *Jesus Christ and Him crucified.*"

23. The question asked is what the Holy Spirit does to glorify Jesus. Walter A. Elwell's exposition in *Baker's Encyclopedia of the Bible*, says, "The singular splendor of God and its consequences for mankind, (are) the glory of God (that) can be described as an attribute and a category referring to the historical manifestation of His presence. As an attribute God's glory refers primarily to His majestic beauty and splendor and the recognition of it by mankind. It is also an ethical concept and embraces His holiness, for to sin is to *fall short of the glory of God.*"

24. The Holy Spirit perpetuates this manifestation of God's glory by constantly glorifying Christ to the world, the believer, and the church. It is humanly impossible for the natural man to grasp the concept that a virgin woman could conceive a Son in her womb. It is beyond human comprehension that a man can be raised from the dead, ascend into heaven (a place unknown in human thinking), and will in the future return to this earth. However, the Holy Spirit achieves the spiritual revelation that opens mankind's eyes.

25. The Holy Spirit ministers to the sinner's spirit and soul and is able to reach past his unbelief and open the tomb that encases his spirit, thereby revealing to him the truth. The repentant heart confesses by faith all that he receives regarding Christ's glorious work and is thus born again. The work of the Holy Spirit does not direct the born-again believer to the revelation that He, the Holy Spirit, imparts to him, but

rather to the glorious work Christ wrought in His ministry on earth as Jesus said, *He will glorify Me.*

26. When Christ was born, He did not come in a *pillar of fire*; but after His ascension, the Holy Spirit was poured out as *tongues like as of fire* (Acts 2:3) as believers were baptized with the Holy Spirit. *The Spirit of truth* (John 16:13) reveals the majesty and splendor of Jesus Christ to the church by continuing Christ's ministry through the believers' lives. The glorification of Christ by the Father occurred when He was elevated and seated at the Father's right hand. Now on earth, Christ is continually glorified by the Holy Spirit through revelation *of the truth* to man.

27. Spirit-filled believers realize that the manifestation of the Godhead's presence and evidence of their works amongst men are all made known to them by the Holy Spirit. However, Spirit-filled believers immerse themselves in an even greater truth. The infinite, omniscient, and omnipresent eternal *God is a Spirit: and they that worship him must worship him in spirit and in truth* (John 4:24). This worship enables them to grasp the fact that all the deep truths hidden in the *secret place of the Most High* and all the hidden things of the divine Godhead's counsels are revealed in the truths the Holy Spirit reveals to the Spirit-filled believer.

28. The intimate fellowship that the Holy Spirit has with the Father and Jesus is never compromised by Him. He is in absolute harmony with the intent of the Godhead's spiritual motivation for mankind. In all this, the Holy Spirit indwells the Spirit-filled believer and glorifies Jesus Christ by exalting Him through the believer. The works that the Holy Spirit does, even to the extent that they exceed the works of Jesus (John 14:12), are never placed as a crown of glory upon the Holy Spirit; they are all done and achieved reverencing the ascended and exalted *Jesus Christ and Him crucified.*

29. Henceforth, Spirit-filled churches are intent on proclaiming *the Apostles Doctrine, fellowship, breaking of bread and prayers* (Acts 2:42). How exquisite is the fact that they never forget the *breaking of bread* which is the direct application of the Holy Spirit's constant reference to *Jesus Christ and Him crucified.* They cannot, and dare not to their peril, ever forget the Holy Spirit's counsel that glorifies Christ's death, resurrection, and ascension.

30. The Holy Spirit's dynamic task amongst believers focuses on the vital work of sanctification. W. A. C. Rowe says, "Regeneration gives place

to the further work of sanctification. Believers are the purpose of the Father (Galatians 1:15) and the purchase of the Son (1 Timothy 2:6). Sanctification is preparation: it is to make the believer separate, clean and beautiful (1 Corinthians 6:11).

31. "The sequence of the Holy Spirit's work and experience would seem to be (1) 'Sealed with (the) Spirit' (Ephesians 1:13); (2) 'Earnest of the Spirit' (2 Corinthians 1:22); (3) 'Filled with the (Spirit)' (Acts 2:4 and 2:38–39), which is the baptism with the (Holy) Spirit.

32. "The believer is the *temple of the Holy Ghost* (1 Corinthians 6:19). In possessing the believer, He controls the life for God. As in the Godhead so in the Body of Christ He is the communion between the member and the Head and member with member . . . *the communion of the Holy Ghost*" (2 Corinthians 13:14).

33. Then there is the work of the Holy Spirit in the church. Rowe continues, "He (the Holy Spirit) is the great Uniter. It is the spirit which gives life to a natural body. It is the spirit that holds the members together in vital union. When the spirit leaves the mortal body (in its death) it quickly passes into complete disintegration, returning to its original constituent element of dust. Thus, it would appear that it is the Baptism of the Holy Spirit (1 Corinthians 12:13) that is a decisive act in initiating and joining the members to the Body of Christ. The importance of a great act of the Holy Spirit in bringing together a body is seen in Ezekiel 37:1-10. It was the breath, the Spirit of God that brought the dry bones together as a new body and made them live.

34. "The Holy Spirit is the great Administrator in the Church of Jesus Christ (1 Corinthians 12:11). He presides and governs on behalf of the Ascended Head. This hallmark is seen in Acts 15:28, *It seemed good to the Holy Ghost, and to us.* His stamp or authority is clearly marked in Acts 20:28, *The Holy Ghost hath made you overseers (over) the Church of God.*"

35. This magnificent work of the Holy Spirit is evidenced when the members of the Body of Christ are unified in *one faith* and abide in the teachings of the Holy Spirit. It is not the teachings of man to man, but the holy, divine teaching from the divine, Holy Spirit to man. The tragedy in the modern-day church revolves around men whose gimmicks hook the members by offering them rewards for "sowing financial seeds" into their church's ministry while they omit the preaching of sin and the shedding of Christ's precious blood.

36. There is never any compromise when the Holy Spirit reaches deep into the heart of an ordained minister of Jesus Christ. W. A. C. Rowe continues about the work of the Holy Spirit in the church explaining, "He is the great Teacher. It is His work first of all to reveal the truth of God to the apostleship, so that, under His anointing, it can truly go forth as the 'Apostles' doctrine' (Acts 2:42).

37. "Moving in oneness with the Head, which is Christ, He breaks forth to the apostles and prophets with marked revelation (Ephesians 3:5). The Lord spoke of Him that *He shall teach you all things* (John 14:26), and that *He will show you things to come* (John 16:13). It is His divine business to do this through all the ministerial functions in the church. It is also His business to work inwardly in the hearts of believers that *the eyes of* [their] *understanding* [be] *enlightened* (Ephesians 1:18). To experience these two operations is to enjoy the privilege of real discipleship in the school of the Master."

38. To conclude the exposition of Jesus' words on the work of the Holy Spirit, it is prudent to look at John's gospel. A commentator in the *Pulpit Commentary* on John's gospel says, "His teaching is not self-originated, like that of Satan (John 8: 44). He shares in the intellectual fellowship of the Father and the Son, is initiated into the Divine scheme of salvation, and is thus enabled to make known the revelation which God gave to Jesus Christ (Revelation 1:1).

39. "His teaching lifts apostolic inspiration above the region of mere spiritual illumination enjoyed by all saints. It was an instruction as to things not yet disclosed or known on earth.

40. "His teaching lifts the veil of the future. (a) The things to come are the destiny of the Church till its final consummation. (b) The Holy Spirit thus declares beforehand the inspiration of the Epistles and the Apocalypse.

41. "The Lord has a full consciousness of the greatness of His Person and His truth, *All things that the Father hath are Mine: therefore, said I, He shall take of Mine, and shall show it unto you*" (John 16:15)"

42. There was, is, and will never be any doubt in the Father and the Son's heart about the effectiveness of the divine work of the Holy Spirit in the church and the world. He is the perfect One and the only One who is able to reveal Christ's majestic work that He accomplished on behalf of mankind. The Spirit is also able to reach into the spirit of a lost sinner as well as mature a believer's life.

43. The *fire* (Luke 3:16) promised to believers who are baptized with the Holy Spirit is still burning as brightly today as it did on the Day of Pentecost when the one hundred twenty were emblazoned with the *tongues of fire.* The power and effectiveness that are encased in the Godhead's love, mercy, and grace are still penetrating stony hearts, removing sin's stains, and blending believers into the harmony of the body of Christ, everyone being *members in particular* (1 Corinthians 12:27).

The Holy Spirit's Role in the Work of Sanctification

44. Once the repentant heart is washed in the blood of the Lamb, regeneration is instantaneously completed. Because his sin is blotted out, the forgiven man stands justified before God. Now the Holy Spirit begins the process of sanctification in the believer.

45. Sanctification is a divine process of cleansing and refining of the spirit and soul that the Holy Spirit undertakes when the believer surrenders his life to Jesus Christ, *for both He who sanctifies and those who are being sanctified are all of one, for which reason He is not ashamed to call them brethren* (Hebrews 2:11 NKJV). It is because of faith in the finished work of Christ on the Cross that believers can now acquiesce to the process the Holy Spirit begins in their lives, *for by one offering He has perfected forever those who are being sanctified* (Hebrews 10:14 NKJV).

46. Let it be clearly stated that this vital work in a believer's life involves the entire Godhead. The believer is *sanctified by God the Father* (Jude 1). The intrinsic holiness of the Father lays the foundation for the process to begin. Christ's glorious achievement at Calvary procures the guarantee of sanctification when He was *made unto us sanctification* (1 Corinthians 1:30); and ultimately, the Holy Spirit preens the believer's body, soul, and spirit unto cleanliness *through sanctification of the Spirit* (1 Peter 1:2).

47. It must be clearly understood that sinners are instantly forgiven, but the cleansing process of being sanctified is a progression in their lives. W. A. C. Rowe explains, "There is a twofold relationship in the

ministry of Christ to man: in reconciliation, His work was for us, but in sanctification His work is in us. Salvation makes us safe, whereas sanctification makes us sound. Regeneration is an instantaneous act, whereas sanctification comprehends the instantaneous act and a continual process."

48. It is again only right that the focus is on Jesus Christ and His plea to His Father, *Sanctify them by Your truth. Your word is truth. As You sent Me into the world, I also have sent them into the world. And for their sakes I sanctify Myself, that they also might be sanctified by the truth. I do not pray for these alone, but also for those who will believe in Me through their word* (John 17: 17-20 NKJV).

49. The Lord Jesus does not ask the Father to give them wisdom, power, or riches; He asks the Father to separate them, cleanse them, and make them worthy for the task ahead of them. Jesus asked His Father to separate them and seal them from all impurities in their spirit, soul, and body, namely, to *sanctify them.* Jesus' desire is that His disciples be holy, righteous vessels of honor (1 Thessalonians 5:23).

50. While it is observed in so many humanistic methods that apply force, dogmatic persuasion, and dictatorial demands compelling a person to become an instrument in the hands of others, how beautiful it is to follow the steps of the Godhead as they are involved with the sanctifying process of the believer. If the believer is desirous of a deeper walk in Christ, then there needs to be a progressive growth from the natural man (1 Corinthians 2:14) and then from the carnal man (1 Corinthians 3:1-4) and, finally, to the spiritual man (1 Corinthians 2:15).

51. Even more reassuring is the comfort and peace within a believer who knows that he is in the hands of the Master Surgeon, who operates with skilled precision and perfection. In order that the central focus is never lost, it is appropriate that reference is made again and again to Jesus Christ and His finished work on Calvary. In this divine sacrifice of the Son of God, sin was taken care of, as well as the sanctification process of every born-again believer because Christ was *made unto us sanctification* (1 Corinthians 1:30).

52. W. A. C. Rowe says, "Christ and the cross are the only and sufficient grounds for sanctification. The cross is the focal point of all divine dealings as it is the fixed place for sanctification, as it is for justification. Sanctification entails absolute oneness with the crucified, *He that*

sanctifieth and they that are sanctified are one (Hebrews 2:11). Calvary is a perfect sacrifice for justification and a perfecting sacrifice for sanctification. Calvary is the Savior's cross, the sinner's cross and the cross of the sanctified."

53. Sanctification is the biblical word for the "spiritual separation" and "anointing" and "spiritual cleansing" of the believer to do the bidding of God. The foundation principle of sanctification is to set apart for special divine ownership. The standard against which sanctification is measured is none other than the holiness (sanctified life) of the Lord Jesus Christ (Romans 8:29). It is the requirement a believer must adhere to in becoming Christ-like.

54. As previously stated, believers are subjected to the Master Surgeon's touch as they are sanctified. It is appropriate that consideration be given to the Godhead's involvement in this vital process. None of the sanctifying process is achieved by man's fleshy means or the bringing down of sin's stronghold; it is wrought by God. (John 17:19; Jude 1). God alone justifies believers' repentant hearts, and He sanctifies their unclean state; and they *are called, sanctified by God the Father, and preserved in Jesus Christ* (Jude:1 NKJV).

55. Believers are to *grow in grace, and in the knowledge of our Lord and Savior Jesus Christ* (2 Peter 3:18). They are transformed into the *same image from glory to glory* (2 Corinthians 3:18). Thus said, this implies a constant progressive growth, cleansing, and going *on unto perfection* (Hebrews 6:1), which is finally concluded on that great *Day of the Lord.*

56. Just as the Holy Spirit is constantly at work in believers' lives, so should believers adhere to the Holy Spirit's leading into a purer life. It is the Holy Spirit who leads, and the believers who turn from their uncleanness and impurities by the power and help of the Holy Spirit as the Bible declares, *The horse is prepared against the day of battle: but safety is of the Lord* (Proverbs 21:31).

57. Rowe continues, "It has the deep purpose of thorough cleansing. The Lord commanded the Levites to *Sanctify the house of the Lord God, carry forth the filthiness out of the holy place* (2 Chronicles 29:5). There must be a removal of iniquity to make possible an inflow of purity. As a divine habitation, we must be made meet for our royal guest in inward condition and outward action.

58. "Sanctification is a Person; it is absolutely, wholly and utterly the glorious Person of Christ. (*Ye in Christ Jesus who of God is made unto*

us ... sanctification... 1 Corinthians 1:30). Christ is as much the totality of our sanctification as He is of our justification. Just as salvation is not self-reformation, so sanctification is not self-culture. It is taking Christ as our life and making Him in very truth our *All-in all"* (Colossians 3:11).

59. The complete, finished work Christ accomplished for mankind as the crucified One and is now the exalted One at the right hand of the Father, Jesus Christ is the Object presented to the soul. Therefore, it is biblically correct to state that sanctification is not something, but Someone.

60. At the outset, there must be a purifying of the born-again believer's spirit which can only be cleansed (purified) by the Holy Spirit. Rowe states, "There is a vast amount of work to be done in the spirit of man between conversion and perfection, in the realms of sanctity, humility, love and deep desire for the life of fellowship with God. It is possible to be outwardly exemplary, but to have wrong things abiding in the spirit."

61. This sanctifying process is only possible when the believer obediently submits his spirit to the Holy Spirit's witness that He must purify the spirit within. The "crooked spirit" needs to be straightened, and the lingering impurities need to be purged so that man's born-again spirit can become a sanctified tabernacle for the Lord to inhabit. This work is a divine work purposed in God's heart for believers because He *gave Himself for us . . . and* [purified] *purify for Himself His own special people, zealous for good works* (Titus 2:14 NKJV).

62. The purifying of the spirit is a holy work, for *the Spirit itself beareth witness with our spirit, that we are the children of God* (Romans 8:16). The constant reassurance from the Holy Spirit to born-again believers is that their salvation is wrought through Jesus Christ, and all they now encounter on their journey through life is Spirit-led and taught. This is not found in textbooks, nor in the manifestation of good works; it is the Holy Spirit Himself, who *bears witness.*

63. The highest call and most important decision any person can make is the surrender of his life to Jesus Christ. The new birth is an awakening of the spirit within that comes from the heart of God to the heart (spirit) of man (John 3:5-7). Henceforth, the work of the Most High God is continued through the Holy Spirit's sanctifying process of purifying the born-again believer's spirit.

64. While the Holy Spirit purifies the spirit, He also purges man's soul. W. A. C. Rowe explains, "There is a work of sanctification for the soul which touches self and personal relationships. It involves deliverance from selfishness and is connected with soulish affections." Such affections are personal desires that can be contrary to God's will and, therefore, need to be purged and eradicated from the soul.

65. Again, as with man's spirit, the born-again believer must willingly submit in absolute obedience to the Holy Spirit's purging. The control that the devil has over many peoples' minds is one of the greatest hindrances man has in submitting to the perfect will of God. It is here that the battle is at its fiercest. Man must surrender his *carnal* thoughts and relinquish his control of every decision placing them into the hands of the Holy Spirit so that he can be led *into all truth*. There is a divine invitation from a holy God, saying, *Come let us reason together,* man with God the Holy Spirit, who can expose that which is contrary to God's will.

66. To continue, Rowe emphasizes the work the Holy Spirit undertakes with man in his body: "The body of the believer is an object of sanctifying ministry. The Lord Jesus, in becoming incarnate and taking a physical, human body, raised it to a place of reverence and made it a sanctified temple in which to dwell, an honored instrument through which He could express His life, *a body hast thou prepared me* (Hebrews 10:5).

67. "The Lord is the Savior of the body (Ephesians 5:23). The whole of creation is waiting for the redemption of the body (Romans 8:22-23). We are taught emphatically that the body is for the Lord (1 Corinthians 6:13) and that we must present it to God as a living sacrifice (Romans 12:1). *Let not sin reign is your mortal body* (Romans 6:12). Set the body apart for the Lord, yield it to the ministry of sanctification and, whatever happens, it must never be allowed to dominate life" (1 Corinthians 9:27).

68. The lust and works of the flesh are the result of the soul's intentions and decisions. To these, the *old man* must die, and the *new man* must *put on the Lord Jesus* and *grow in grace and knowledge of the Lord Jesus Christ.* This happens when the born-again believer totally surrenders and submits to the Master Sculptor, the Holy Spirit's sanctifying process.

69. The sanctification of believers is never more apparent than when they gather together as the church. It is a desire of Jesus that the believers be one and in one accord (John 17:17-21). In His prayerful request,

Jesus asks the Father to sanctify them, as He sanctified Himself for the church (John 17:19), for *Christ also loved the Church, and gave Himself for it; that He might sanctify and cleanse it* (Ephesians 5:25-26).

70. The sanctified state of believers is the blending of their spirits into one accord as they gather together as a body of believers, the church. Herein is the spiritual unity exercised and manifested when corporately, the members are fused through their sanctification and enter into unified praise, worship, and celebration of the Lord's Supper, and growing in the Word.

71. It is when the church gathers together in unity of Spirit and they are sanctified by the Holy Spirit, their righteousness is of Jesus Christ; and their expectations are in the promises of the Father. Then their fervent prayers and worship are as a united firebrand reaching the heart of the Father. This lofty height raises them above the world and its trappings, and they focus on the anticipated rapture of the saints.

Chapter 19

Doctrine of the Holy Spirit (continued)

The Baptism with the Holy Spirit

1. *He shall baptize you with the Holy Ghost and with fire* (Luke 3:16). John the Baptist declared that, while his baptism was an instruction from God, namely, man being used by God to bring the people to repentance, there was coming One after him, who would be *God manifest in the flesh* (1 Timothy 3:16), who would divinely baptize believers with the Holy Spirit. Thus, the Godhead is involved in this spiritual blessing made available to believers.

2. This is the experience born-again believers undergo that immerses them into the body of Christ (1 Corinthians 12:13), empowers them for a more Spirit-led witnessing of Jesus Christ (Acts 1:8), and endows them with spiritual gifts, which the Holy Spirit distributes to each one as He wills (1 Corinthians 12:11).

3. This beautiful, divine experience of which all believers can and should partake has enormous benefits for the one who is baptized with the Holy Spirit. These precious benefits need to be studied in detail to help everyone understand the promises spoken of in the Holy Writ.

4. To begin this all-important doctrine, it is worthy to note that the New Testament is translated from the original Greek, which never used prepositions, and include, prepositions to better clarify the Greek meaning. Hence, some translations state that the baptism is "in" the Holy Spirit while others state it is "of" the Holy Spirit. To ensure the

perfect will of God is fulfilled, it is only right that the correct emphasis is placed on the fact that Jesus baptizes believers "with" the Holy Spirit (Luke 3:16).

5. As with all doctrinal tenets, the baptism with the Holy Spirit involves the entire Godhead. It is the Father's will that the relationship between Him and man be fully restored and reconciled. It is the Lord Jesus Christ who unlocked the door and *through whom we have now received the reconciliation* (Romans 5:11 NKJV), and it is Jesus Himself who baptizes the believer with the Holy Spirit.

6. The Bible gives clear accounts of the fundamental doctrine that there are two experiences that are essential to fully equip and empower believers to be witnesses *unto the uttermost part of the earth* (Acts 1:8). The first experience is the new birth (born-again) for those who repent, and the second is the baptism with the Holy Spirit. These two experiences were the norm in the early church. They were an essential part of believers going *on unto perfection* (Hebrews 6:1), and it was never doubted by anyone who walked through redemption's holy entrance into the glorious light of the gospel.

7. The Lord Jesus Christ's accomplishment at Calvary tore down the middle partition of sin, made a complete provision for redemption that reached deep into the heart of the person lying in the miry clay, and gave him access to the holy presence of God. The pardon from sin was, and is, fully accomplished. Thereafter, the indwelling spiritual power to walk circumspectly in His presence is imparted to those who are baptized with the Holy Spirit. It is the glorious progression from Calvary to Pentecost, the provision of pardon to the promise of power.

8. The New Testament has various accounts of this experience believers had. These are found throughout the church's growth in the book of Acts and in the New Testament Epistles. To clarify any misgivings, when a person is born-again, he accepts Jesus Christ, and the Spirit of Christ dwells in his heart (Romans 8:9; Galatians 4:6). The Holy Spirit (the Spirit of Truth) reigns with Christ in the believer's heart.

9. What now follows, is the Holy Spirit's empowerment promised by Jesus (Acts 1:8). This divine process is none other than the baptism with the Holy Spirit at which moment the Holy Spirit takes up residence in the believer's body (1 Corinthians 6:19). An example of this process is found in Acts 19:1-8.

10. Apostle Paul is in Ephesus preaching and twelve men, disciples of Christ, approached him. These were men who had accepted Jesus Christ as their Savior, yet they had no knowledge of the Holy Spirit and the work He could do in their lives, and they had no affirmative answer to Apostle Paul's asking, *Have ye received the Holy Ghost since ye believed?* (Acts 19:2). This is a perfect example of a humble and obedient listener who hears the gospel and responds to the message of salvation but is not aware of the power Jesus promised which would follow them that believe (Mark 16:16). These twelve men believed and were saved. They needed to continue through the waters of baptism and the baptism with the Holy Spirit.

11. God's servant explains the fullness of being baptized by immersion in water, and they willingly accept his teaching, and they are baptized. He then lays hands on them to receive the baptism with the Holy Spirit, and they were baptized with the evidence of Holy Spirit taking up residence in their bodies when they spoke with tongues and prophesied (Acts 19:6).

12. In all the examples found in the book of Acts, the initial evidence of the baptism with the Holy Spirit is the speaking with tongues. This powerful witness that the Holy Spirit is in believers' bodies is the assurance that they have been endued *with power from on high* (Luke 24:49).

13. It is important to study in detail the spiritual experience of speaking in tongues simply because it is the great controversy that exists between Spirit-filled believers and believers. It must be remembered that the baptism with the Holy Spirit was the norm for the church. There was never any doubt about this divine endowment upon believers. It was the expected and anticipated blessing from God for them.

14. French L. Arrington in his book *Christian Doctrine A Pentecostal Perspective* says, "A local church that gives no vital place in its life and ministry to the exercise of spiritual gifts has departed from the biblical norm. The church can only become truly the church when the biblical practice of spiritual gifts has its place among God's people."

15. Scripture speaks of "tongues," "other tongues," "tongues of angels," and the "gift of different kinds of tongues." Apart from the "gift of different kinds of tongues," the initial sign that a believer is baptized with the Holy Spirit is expressed in one of these three ways. This is a divine and spiritual impartation into the believer.

16. On the Day of Pentecost, the disciples in the Upper Room spoke with "other tongues" (Acts 2:4). They were baptized with the Holy Spirit and spoke with other tongues (in languages) they had never learned at any time. This manifestation has occurred many times since the Day of Pentecost when believers who are baptized with the Holy Spirit speak in a language they have never learned, or perhaps even heard.

17. The same evidence also is witnessed in Acts 19:1-6 when Apostle Paul laid his hands upon them, and the men spoke with tongues. Here they did not speak in languages known to man, but *with tongues*. Scripture is silent on the origin of *tongues* other than to unequivocally state that it was from the indwelling Holy Spirit because it was done *as the Spirit* [gives] *them utterance* (Acts 2:4).

18. Apostle Paul speaks of "tongues of angels" (1 Corinthians 13:1). This heavenly language can be imparted to the believer who speaks in a language no human has ever heard. It is the language of the heavenly host who constantly praise God in heaven.

19. The Bible also declares that there are *different kinds of tongues* (1 Corinthians 12:10), thus confirming and emphasizing the explanation above. One of these three renderings of tongues will occur when a believer is baptized with the Holy Spirit. The evidence for the believer that he is baptized with the Holy Spirit takes place when he surrenders his spirit to the Holy Spirit and receives, by faith, the Holy Spirit into his very being.

20. The empowering of the believer is the result of his "surrendering" of his body, soul, and spirit to the Holy Spirit. There will be no baptism if the believer refuses to submit to the Holy Spirit. There will be no baptism if the believer does not exercise his faith in God. This baptism with the Holy Spirit is not a calculated, planned, and humanly designed step the believer must take. It is a God-ordained and God-imprinted impartation of the Holy Spirit who takes up residence in the believer's body because the believer exercises his faith and surrenders to the Holy Spirit's bidding.

21. This divine and holy spiritual experience, just as the born-again experience a believer undergoes, should never be tarnished by involving the human explanation for such a divine spiritual experience. This is God's holy business, and it is freely offered to God's children, believers.

22. The spiritual utterances, tongues, that flow from a Spirit-filled believer's heart as he speaks is the Holy Spirit's "language" that the Holy Spirit

uses through the person: The Holy Spirit within the person to *God who is Spirit* (John 4:24). This is the personal usage given to those who are baptized with the Holy Spirit. It is the private and individual interlude that is available to the person who submits his vocal cords and tongue to the Holy Spirit. Apostle Paul further explains this relationship, *Likewise the Spirit also helps in our weaknesses. For we do not know what we should pray for as we ought, but the Spirit Himself makes intercession for us with groanings which cannot be uttered* (Romans 8:26, Ephesians 6:18 NKJV).

23. This new language (tongues) is available to all who are baptized with the Holy Spirit and is also used when the individual praises and worships God in the Spirit. The hearers on the Day of Pentecost said, *We do hear them speak in our own tongues the wonderful works of God* (Acts 2:11).

24. Apostle Paul clarifies this when he says, *For he that speaketh in an unknown tongue speaketh not unto men, but unto God* (1 Corinthians 14:2). Thus, the person who worships God in the Spirit, is inspired by the Holy Spirit who brings him in direct communion with God.

25. Apostle Paul continues this clarification, *For if I pray in a tongue, my spirit prays, but my understanding is unfruitful. What is the conclusion then? I will pray with the spirit, and I will also pray with the understanding. I will sing with the spirit, and I will sing also with the understanding* (1 Corinthians 14: 14-15 NKJV).

26. When believers gather, and some are baptized with the Holy Spirit and some are not, tongues become the sign to believers who are not baptized with the Holy Spirit of the indwelling Holy Spirit in those who are baptized. Scriptures says, *With men of other tongues and with other lips I will speak to this people: and yet, for all that, they will not hear Me, says the Lord. Therefore tongues are for a sign, not to those who believe but to unbelievers* (1 Corinthians 14: 21-22 NKJV).

27. Spirit-filled believers are encouraged to constantly listen to the Holy Spirit, follow the Spirit of truth (John 16:13), and never quench the Spirit (1 Thessalonians 5:19). It is God-ordained that the church be empowered by the Holy Spirit and that He reveals and teaches members how to grow in grace and in the knowledge of Jesus Christ. Without the Holy Spirit's guidance, the members will not be edified, exhorted, and comforted (1 Corinthians 14:3).

The Gifts of the Holy Spirit

28. The glorious work of the Holy Spirit in Spirit-filled believers is manifested in many ways. At the outset, the fruit of the Spirit is the ultimate sign of the indwelling Holy Spirit in the life of believers as they *follow his steps* (1 Peter 2:21). The basis of everything believers and Spirit-filled believers are and do, is always rooted in the operation of faith. Thus, all glory and honor are bestowed upon the Godhead when any Spiritual fruit or gift is exhibited simply because the individual is not the author of the gift or fruit, but the channel through which the Holy Spirit operates. The Lord is sovereign in the realm of these gifts.

29. Rowe introduces this important doctrinal tenet by stating, "The Holy Spirit proceeding from the Father (John 14:26) and from the Son (John 16:7) is the glorious divine Agent. *There are diversities of gifts, but the same Spirit* (1 Corinthians 12:4). Every divine activity and particularly the nature and operation of the Gifts of the Spirit, are but manifestations of the blessed third Person, God, the Holy Spirit. Every true gift is of the actual nature of the Holy Spirit, and every anointed manifestation is His actual operation."

30. Rowe continues, "These Gifts are of Himself divine, supernatural, powerful, and consisting of the nature and ability of their individual designations. They are impartations by the Holy Spirit and of the Holy Spirit, and they are designed for a special channeling of the working of the divine attributes, from the glory of the Godhead, and concentrating them upon the needs in the region of the experience of men."

31. The gifts of the Holy Spirit are in their most exquisite operation when used amongst believers. Their operation brings enlightenment and comfort as they reveal the truth and beam light into the lives of the Spirit-filled believers who are gathered in one accord to worship God.

32. The Bible records nine Gifts of the Holy Spirit that are given to certain individuals in the body of Christ. These are given *individually as* [the Holy Spirit] *wills* (1 Corinthians 12:11 NKJV). Even more importantly, these diverse nine gifts are given *to each one for the profit of all* (1 Corinthians 12:7).

33. The nine gifts recorded in 1 Corinthians 12: 3-11 can be categorized into three dimensions: the revelation gifts, the power gifts, and the voice gifts. For greater clarity, it is appropriate that they be studied in each category.

34. *For to one is given the word of wisdom* (1 Corinthians 12:8). What the world needs in this modern age is not more knowledge, more gadgets, or more power; its greatest need is wisdom so that people may live in all their being with integrity and upright character. The lack of wisdom is often the demise of perfect application. Rowe states, "A person may have great knowledge and yet be crippled for a lack of wisdom to apply it. Wisdom is the instrument and handmaid of knowledge.

35. "The manifestation of the Gift of the Word of Wisdom is something extraordinary and intense. It is supernatural and brings a flood of light on the solution of a special problem or need, particularly in the services and affairs of the church."

36. This gift resides in those to whom the Holy Spirit chooses to impart it. They are not chosen because of their extensive education, wide-ranging worldly experience, or charismatic eloquence, but *as He* (the Holy Spirit) *wills.* The recipients of this gift have a humble heart, are submissive to the Holy Spirit's bidding, and often astound their hearers because the word of wisdom that flows from them far exceeds these gifted people's human understanding and comprehension.

37. Such is the example Jesus explains to His disciples. He is foretelling them about their forthcoming responsibilities and how they should respond when facing those of education and authority: *Therefore settle it in your hearts not to meditate beforehand on what you will answer; for I will give you a mouth and wisdom which all your adversaries will not be able to contradict or resist* (Luke 21:14-15 NKJV). Jesus reassures the humble men (fishermen) of Galilee that they need not concern themselves because they are unlearned (Acts 4:13). They will receive wisdom at the right time and answer their adversaries with astonishing wisdom.

38. This gift's use is for "the understanding and application of truth or principle; or in the right counsel and attitude for a truly divine course of action" (Rowe).

39. This "revelation" gift is not the result of human knowledge, but rather the disclosure of the Holy Spirit that explains the essence and necessary action required to fulfill a task. As with the *word of knowledge,* it should be noted that these two gifts do not consist of an entirety of wisdom and knowledge but will be used on occasions and for benefits to the members. The person endued with these gifts will not be universally wise or knowledgeable in all matters, but specifically for a subject that needs spiritual insight and explanation.

40. Of these nine gifts, *to another* [is given] *the word of knowledge through the same Spirit* (1 Corinthians 12:8). W. A. C. Rowe explains this gift as follows, "In the operation of this gift the blaze of illumination wrought by the Holy Spirit is a flash of knowledge which is not the product of reasoning, nor the reflection of the natural mind. It does not originate in the natural man. This knowledge is higher than the powers of self-education or attained through personal experience: it is even higher than knowledge ordinarily attained by a sanctified believer through devotional Bible study and Christian experience though that may be rich and good. Knowledge of this kind is completely divine in its origin and supernatural in its character. It is imparted and not acquired, revelation and not education."

41. The gift is extra-ordinary in that the one being used brings forth light onto a subject hitherto not known by anyone. It is used to direct, explain, or reprove error by exposing the true intent of a proposed action. In this world that is saturated with deceit and corruption, the truth needs to be presented, and this gift has often been used to throw light onto a path taken through lack of knowledge, and desperate for correction.

42. . . . *to another the* [the gift of] *discerning of spirits* (1 Corinthians 12:10). The ever-present spiritual satanic attack on believers, and the false anti-type of spiritual information, when Satan interrupts the life of a believer as he comes *as an angel of light* (2 Corinthians 11:14) and spreads confusion, must be checked and corrected every time. Furthermore, Spirit-filled believers are taught to *try the spirits whether they are of God* (1 John 4:1). The most exquisite demonstrating of God's presence occurs when the Holy Spirit is manifested through the gifts of the Spirit, yet how harmful and destructive the devil is when believers are led astray by a false spirit.

43. This gift of discerning of spirits is supernaturally in operation when it shines light into the lives of Spirit-filled believers enabling them to distinguish among the Spirit of God (Acts 14:9-10), the spirit of man (Acts 5:3-5) and things instigated by evil spirits (Acts 16:16-18). Rowe adds, "It is impossible for the natural man to do this for himself, because he cannot understand the mind and workings of God (1 Corinthians 2:14). Neither can he understand the strategies and activities of Satan and evil spirits, but the Holy Spirit reveals these (Acts 13:8-10)."

44. This gift's ultimate effect on the gathering of Spirit-filled believers is the confirmation that, at the time true spiritual revelation is presented to the believers, comfort and upliftment are assured because the use of this gift confirms the source of the revelation. It is the rudder that steadies the believer on his spiritual course, enabling him to stay away from false teaching and confusion.

45. ... *to another [the gift of] faith* (1 Corinthians 12:9). To understand the operation of this gift, it is paramount that the subject of faith be clearly understood. There is *the measure of faith* (Romans 12:3) that every person is given to receive Jesus Christ as his Savior. There is faith all has enabling them to walk believing *in the things hoped for* (Hebrews 11:1). Then there is the *gift of faith* which effectually brings about the exposition of spiritual and supernatural miracles.

46. The Holy Spirit will give this gift of faith to anyone He wills. Those so gifted are not the necessarily highly educated, most prominent, or influential members of the Body of Christ. They are the vessels the Holy Spirit chooses that are *full of the Holy Ghost and of faith* (Acts 11:24) and ready and able to be used in this potent measure. The evidence that the gift has been operational is the miraculous results that are witnessed. It is clearly the cause of supernatural faith that presents the result, for the result could never have been conceived in the natural mind.

47. The individual who receives this gift of faith is not the person who is physically strong or large in his body that gives the impression that he is confident enough to take on any size challenge. French L. Arrington says, "Such faith depends entirely on God and can accomplish far more than the greatest human efforts." Receiving this faith, therefore, is the person who has a life that is bathed in prayer. Arrington continues, "The power to accomplish the exceptional always resides in God and in the faith, He grants as a gift. Where the gift of faith is recognized and exercised, God does extraordinary things. God is glorified and His people receive a fuller ministry through the operation of the gift of faith."

48. ... *to another gifts of healings by the same Spirit* (1 Corinthians 12:9). The Bible clearly states that, when a member is sick, he calls for the elders to anoint the sick with oil and pray the prayer of faith (James 5:13-15). This is the duty elders perform in the course of their spiritual responsibilities. It is incumbent on them to visit the sick and pray for

them even if they do not have the gifts of healings. God's holy Word promises *the Lord shall raise him up* (James 5:15).

49. Rowe explains it the following way: "There are manifold modes of operation in obtaining healing: by prayer (John 15:16), by agreement of believers (Matthew 18:19), by the laying on of hands of believers (Mark 16:18), by the anointing of oil by Elders, together with the prayer of faith (James 5:14-15), by the application of the Word of God (Psalm 107:20), by inspired command (Acts 14:9-10)."

50. It is not a self-claimed gift a believer has; rather, it is the Holy Spirit who will impart to a believer this supernatural gift that is used in various ways. Rowe clarifies, "The gifts of healing compose that supernatural function through which the stream of healing virtue passes from the Holy Spirit to the person to whom it is to be applied."

51. It is the only gift the Holy Spirit imparts that is plural. There are many diseases, different types of bodily sicknesses, and needs that this gift covers. There are believers who receive the ability through the Holy Spirit to heal certain sicknesses while others are gifted to heal certain other sicknesses.

52. W. A. C. Rowe says, "The exercise of the Gifts of Healing is purely the power of God and the healing that results is exclusively divine healing. It is solely the work of the Holy Spirit and has no relationship in any way with the operation of so-called psychic powers, physical magnetism, mental exercises, auto-suggestion, or other attempts of mind-over-matter control."

53. *... to another the working of miracles* (1 Corinthians 12:10). A miracle is an exceptional event that has no human explanation and defies human comprehension and rational thinking. It is the fullest demonstration of the presence of God, the Holy Spirit, who brings about a result that benefits believers.

54. This gift is also a sign to the lost or those still seeking salvation of the promise of God's presence to everyone who believes. Sound preaching is required when such a demonstration is evident, so that the sinner desires the Giver of the gift and not merely the gift.

55. French Arrington, "The gift of miracles was never done by Jesus or by the apostles simply to display power, but to bring glory to God. Miracles are not to magnify those seeking to demonstrate their own greatness." The magnificence of the gift in operation is not used to impress the crowds or exercised to put on a show for people to be

entertained. It is used when members have compassion for those in need and the Holy Spirit works through the chosen vessel to impart the miracle, bringing glory to God.

56. . . . *to another prophecy* (1 Corinthians 12:10). This gift is the audible announcement of the Spirit's intentions to believers gathered together. Its entire reason for being used by the Holy Spirit is for the edification, exhortation, and comfort of believers (1 Corinthians 14:3-4).

57. It is different in its operation from the Spirit of Prophecy and the office of a Prophet. It is God revealing His deepest intentions to the heart of believers. The hearer is uplifted and encouraged as the Holy Spirit uses a human channel to impart words of comfort and edification. Furthermore, these who have this gift imparted to them by the Holy Spirit, never lose control of their human consciousness and enter into a trance or an unnatural spirit-world. The Holy Spirit does not sow confusion but requires that all things be done decently and in order (1 Corinthians 14:40).

58. Prophecy differs from a sermon a preacher delivers. Sermons are prepared messages a preacher has for the congregation, while the gift of prophecy is a Holy Spirit inspired revelation given through a chosen vessel in a spontaneous manner. The verification that the prophetic utterance is from God is none other than the eternal Word of God. The gift of prophecy like all the gifts of the Holy Spirit aligns itself with the Holy Writ.

59. . . . *to another different kinds of tongues* (1 Corinthians 12:10). The Holy Spirit is responsible for gifting some Spirit-filled believers with the *gift of different kinds of tongues* as well as gifting others with the *interpretation of tongues* (vs.10). These gifts are verbally expressed in a gathering of Spirit-filled believers and are exercised by the same Holy Spirit through them. It is the Holy Spirit who uses the gift through the Spirit-filled believer for the edification of those present (1 Corinthians 14:26).

60. While all Spirit-filled believers have the initial evidence of the baptism with the Holy Spirit, which is the spiritual utterance of other tongues, other tongues, or the tongues of angels, the *gift of tongues* is a unique gift imparted to only some and, therefore, differs from the initial manifestation believers have when they are baptized with the Holy Spirit.

61. The gift is used to edify those gathered in Jesus' name, and not for individuals in their private prayer time when they are alone with God. *He that speaketh in an unknown tongue edifieth himself* (1 Corinthians 14:4). The Holy Spirit, through Apostle Paul gives a detailed teaching on the use of the gift of tongues when he says, *For he who prophesies is greater than he who speaks with tongues, unless indeed he interprets, that the church may receive edification* (1 Corinthians 14:5 NKJV).

62. Apostle Paul declares, *Even so you, since you are zealous for spiritual gifts, let it be for the edification of the church that you seek to excel. Therefore, let him who speaks in a tongue pray that he may interpret. For if I pray in a tongue, my spirit prays, but my understanding is unfruitful. What is the conclusion then? I will pray with the spirit, and I will also pray with the understanding. I will sing with the spirit, and I will also sing with the understanding. Otherwise, if you bless with the spirit, how will he who occupies the place of the uninformed say "Amen" at your giving of thanks, since he does not understand what you say? For you indeed give thanks well, but the other is not edified. I thank my God I speak with tongues more than you all* (1 Corinthians 14:12-18 NKJV).

63. The Apostle goes further regarding the use of the gift of tongues: *How is it then, brethren? Whenever you come together, each of you has a psalm, has a teaching, has a tongue, has a revelation, has an interpretation. Let all things be done for edification. If anyone speaks in a tongue, let there be two or at the most three, each in turn, and let one interpret. But if there is no interpreter, let him keep silent in church, and let him speak to himself and to God* (1 Corinthians 14:26-28 NKJV). The gift of tongues is used to edify the believers and can only do so if there is someone who can interpret the tongue. This is either done by someone else in the meeting or by the person who uses the gift of tongues.

64. *. . . to another the interpretation of tongues* (1 Corinthians 12:10). This gift is imparted by the Holy Spirit to those of His choosing, and it can never be assumed by a person that he has the gift. Each of these is a spiritual gift and, as such, spiritually endowed. It is never applied from the person's intellect; rather it is the Holy Spirit who enables the interpretation to be uttered from the person's spirit.

65. Clarification regarding this gift is needed. It is the "interpretation" of tongues and not the "translation" of tongues. Translation necessitates the verbal conversion of the words spoken in tongues while interpretation allows the gifted believer to interpret the message

of the tongue. Hence, the believer who brings forth the utterance of the gift of tongues might have a short message, and the interpreter could have a longer explanation of the interpretation.

66. The application of the gift of tongues and the interpretation of the tongues often are not used in accordance with the word of God. Consequently, definite parameters exist for the use of these gifts.

67. At the outset, there should never be less than two utterances or more than three utterances of the gift of tongues in a meeting. These two or at the most three utterances can be delivered by one person or more than one person; however, there should be only one interpreter (1 Corinthians 14:27).

68. Furthermore, the gifts are used in a specific order. The person who is led by the Holy Spirit to be used in bringing the first utterance of the gift of tongues will speak while the assembly remains silent. Thereafter, the interpreter will interpret the gift. Once the message is interpreted, the next use of the gift of tongues is brought forth. Thereafter, the same interpreter who interpreted the first gift of tongues will continue with the interpretation. The gift of tongues could be used a third time with the same person interpreting the message.

69. It is tragic to learn that many denominations emphatically decree that the gifts of tongues and interpretation are literally banned in their meetings while the Bible declares, *wherefore, brethren, covet to prophesy, and forbid not to speak with tongues* (1 Corinthians 14:39).

Chapter 20

The Fruit of the Spirit

1. The demonstration of the fruit of the Spirit is the most definitive explanation of the extent of a believer's *knowledge of our Lord and Savior Jesus Christ* (2 Peter 3:18). When the fruit of the Spirit is manifested in the believer's life, it speaks volumes of his relationship with Jesus Christ.

2. Nothing should ever precede his relationship with Jesus Christ. All that a born-again believer is and will be is surrounded by his knowledge and intimate commitment to his Savior. The ever-present desire within propels him towards being in the likeness of Christ (Romans 6:5). The perfect demonstration of Christ's indwelling presence in a believer is never more apt than when the fruit of the Spirit radiates from the believer.

3. Apostle John recalls these words of Jesus: *I am the* [true] *vine, you are the branches. He who abides in Me, and I in him, bears much fruit; for without Me you can do nothing* (John 15:5 NKJV). The pure, holy, and divine clusters of fruit that are produced from the holy Source and meticulously dressed by the *vinedresser* are freely available to all who *diligently seek Him* (Hebrews 11:6).

4. The *True Vine* is perfect; the *Vinedresser* is perfect; and believers can freely partake of the fruit and fully become Christlike. It is the responsibility of the believers to *build up their most holy faith* (Jude 1:20), *stand fast in the liberty wherewith Christ has made* [them] *free* (Galatians 5:1), and *launch out into the deep* (Luke 5:4), as he *draws nigh unto God* (James 4:8).

5. The fruit of the Spirit should be evidenced in every word and action believers say and do. The level of their spiritual maturity and their

knowledge of the Lord Jesus Christ are assessed by the quality of the fruit they produce. Their words and actions, if they are enriched by the lush fruit of the Spirit, will mirror Jesus' words and actions. However, when there is a distant relationship with the Savior, and the believer is *unskilful in the word of righteousness he is a babe* (Hebrews 5:13), and there is little evidence that he truly knows the Lord (Acts 4:13; Philippians 3:10).

6. When the fruit of the Spirit beams forth from radiant hearts, believers immediately detect that the indwelling Holy Spirit's intentions are far more important than the works of the flesh. This is the purpose of the Holy Spirit's purging and sanctifying process in believers' lives. They are to be brought into a new and productive life that can be used by God for His glory. Warren W. Wiersbe in his book *The Bible Exposition Commentary* says, "The old nature cannot produce fruit; only the new nature can do that."

7. As mentioned above, the *true vine* and the *vinedresser* are the handiwork of holy God. Therefore, the fruit is entirely God's work and not man's. It is God who producers the fruit, and man who shows it forth to the world. Wiersbe continues, "The characteristics that God wants in our lives are seen in the ninefold fruit of the Spirit."

8. The fruit of the Spirit is one fruit with nine parts or aspects. The vine's produce glistens in the sun as the skin shines absorbing the nourishment of the heat; the flesh of the grape is enriched by the chemicals in the soil; the seeds feed the whole fruit as it takes shape around them; and the brightness of the radiant color of the grape draws the onlooker to partake of it. All these attributes make up the fruit. So, too, the fruit of the Spirit possesses all the qualities that enable a believer to become fully Christlike. Again, Warren Wiersbe well explains this matters, "It is possible for the old nature to counterfeit some of the fruit of the Spirit, but the flesh can never produce the fruit of the Spirit. One difference is this: when the Spirit produces fruit, God gets the glory and the Christian is not conscious of his spirituality; but when the flesh is at work, the person is inwardly proud of himself and is pleased when others compliment him."

9. Bringing the explanation into a clearer view, Evan Hopkins dissects the biblical passage on the fruit of the Spirit into three parts: "Condition that embraces *love, joy,* and *peace* which explain the condition of the spirit and soul. Conduct, which includes *long-suffering, gentleness,* and

goodness which demonstrate the external evidence of the indwelling Spirit. Character, which includes *faith, meekness,* and *temperance* that produce personal results in the believer's life."

10. *Love.* This aspect is the distinctive quality that attracts the observer to the believer. It exceeds charity, caring, and helpfulness. This *agape* is from the root Source that encases the entire fruit.

11. Love is the light that shines from the believer into the sinner's dark world, displaying the sincere, righteous Holy Spirit that resides in the believer. Furthermore, it is the identification of the Christlikeness that believers discern in each other when they gather together. It is the quality that resides in the believer's heart which embraces every deed. The believer is filled with unprecedented appreciation for his salvation, which is expressed in his love for God.

12. The extent and depth of love in a believer's heart is the testimony of his relationship with Jesus Christ, who mandates, *You shall love the LORD your God with all your heart, with all your soul, with all your strength, and with all your mind, and your neighbor as yourself* (Luke 10:27 NKJV). These words of Jesus encompass the whole fruit. It is the believer's love for God that radiates in him and is expressed towards his neighbor as the remainder of the fruit's joy, peace, and goodness flow from his love-filled heart towards others.

13. Jesus' teaching goes further than loving the loveable. He says, *But I say to you, love your enemies, bless those who curse you, do good to those who hate you, and pray for those who spitefully use you and persecute you* (Matthew 5:44 NKJV). The *enemies* of the gospel of Jesus Christ have their *heart pricked* when believers demonstrate the overriding characteristic of love in the Spirit's fruit towards them. Their love shines as a beacon into the darkened heart and draws the sinner towards the truth.

14. *Joy.* W.A.C. Rowe says, "Joy, as the fruit of the Spirit, is an enlarged capacity for the impression and expression of this experienced quality of the divine life." It echoes the Psalmist's praise, *in thy presence is fullness of joy; at thy right hand there are pleasures for evermore* (Psalm 16:11).

15. The joy that flows through the Spirit-filled believer's heart comes from the *river of life* that has its source in the heart of almighty God. The rejoicing spirit is elated because the witness of the Holy Spirit within constantly testifies about abundant life. The knowledge that God

whom the believer serves is the Way, the Truth, and the Life (John 14:6) assures him that God cannot lie and will always be truthful. Mankind can never be fully trustworthy, but God is beyond any doubt that He is faithful and true. This is more than sufficient for believers to rejoice and be glad knowing the Lord *will never leave* [them] *nor forsake* [them] (Hebrews 13:5 NKJV).

16. At times, spiritual joy at His right hand brings vociferous praise to God as it expresses the intentions of a rejoicing heart. Then, there is the quiet calming satisfaction of a Spirit-filled heart that is amazed at the work the Holy Spirit has done in his life. This joy provides the believer with contentment knowing that God's word is *yea and amen.*

17. The spiritual fruit of joy is not dependent on any achievement or deed; it is out of a grateful heart that grasps the fullest assurance of God's forgiveness. It does not bring emotional exuberance to the soul, but rather an inner joy in the spirit that is Spirit led and Spirit filled. It is an overflowing expression of spiritual things that brings joy to the believer.

18. *Peace.* The first emotional exhibition Adam and Eve experienced in the Garden of Eden, after they sinned, was the evaporation of the peace of God they had enjoyed. Fear replaced peace. This evil emotion, fear, has dwelt with mankind since that day. However, into the heart of the believer, the Holy Spirit imparts again spiritual peace which the devil had robbed mankind of when they originally succumbed to his deceit.

19. This divine impartation is not only present in times of refreshing and comfort but also present in times of discomfort and trouble. Apostle Paul declares that the church is to continue in *the bond of peace* (Ephesians 4:3). This spiritual peace flows like a river from the Source, and is, first, a reconciling peace with God; second, peace in God; and third, the bountiful supply of peace from God that overthrows fear. About this peace, Jesus assures believers, *My peace I give to you; not as the world gives do I give to you. Let not your heart be troubled, neither let it be afraid* (John 14:27 NKJV).

20. How magnificent is the precious characteristic of peace Jesus leaves for believers. In this world of turmoil and strife, Christ, who is our peace, tells His followers that He will leave His *peace* to all who walk in His light. Believers echo the Psalmist who says, *God is our refuge and strength, a very present help in trouble. Therefore we will not fear* (Psalm 46:1-2).

21. Spiritual peace flows throughout man's body, soul, and spirit. It is an abiding protector that conquers carnage, serenely settles a disturbed soul, and calms the troubled emotions as Apostle Paul says, *The peace of God, which surpasses all understanding, will guard your hearts and minds through Christ Jesus* (Philippians 4:7 NKJV).

22. W. A. C. Rowe elucidates that the peace of God "is the whole redeemed nature of man in perfect harmony within itself, as well as the complete harmony of the whole man with his Maker and Redeemer."

23. *Longsuffering.* How appropriate the translation in this instance is regarding the Greek word *makrothymia*. It is correctly translated as "longsuffering" and not as "peace" which in Greek is *eirene*. Mankind must exercise patience with things over which he has no control. He cannot hasten the hours in a day; he cannot speed up the orbit of planet earth; he has no control over the events of nature and must, therefore, exercise patience as he waits for them to take their course. On the other hand, he has influence over mankind. He can encourage, force, or compel another person to act more hastily. Conversely, he can wait, or exercise longsuffering, with the person. Mankind suffers mankind; he is to be longsuffering with his counterpart while he must be patient with things in life over which he has no control.

24. This characteristic flows constantly from God's heart towards mankind as Apostle Paul says that believers abide in *the riches of His longsuffering* (Romans 2:4). Jesus shows this fruit with the lost (1 Timothy 1:16). God's longsuffering is best expressed by Apostle Peter when he says, *The Lord is not slack concerning His promise, as some count slackness, but is longsuffering toward us, not willing that any should perish but that all should come to repentance* (2 Peter 3:9 NKJV).

25. As the Source expresses the quality of the characteristic of longsuffering, so ought His children abundantly yield and exercise the fruit towards each other (Ephesians 4:2). It is only the Holy Spirit that can manifest such a characteristic in mankind; and longsuffering has the unquenchable and conquering power to overcome any devilish influence such as hatred, bitterness, and strife.

26. Believers are to bear the fruit of the Spirit in both good and evil circumstances. Longsuffering allows the believer to go beyond attacking the enemy, showing hatred when hatred is shown towards him, expressing frustration towards another, and being critical of

another's incompetence. Longsuffering calms the emotional intentions of a frustrated reaction and responds with temperate endurance.

27. If Spirit-filled believers are to walk *circumspectly in Him* (Ephesians 5:15), then they are to resist the emotional discharge of taking offense, rendering evil for evil, and leveraging due recompense towards a carnal infraction against them. This is God's fruit from the Holy Spirit. It is only right that Spirit-filled believers earnestly seek to be more Christlike, and with disciplinary accord, express longsuffering towards his followman.

28. *Kindness.* This characteristic is the quality that demonstrates the way believers treat others. Their meekness is a quality that brings others to a closer understanding of the Christ within them. This quality is evidenced because the Source of the fruit is from a gracious heart that loves others with all kindness and meekness (Matthew 11:29).

29. Kindness is never abrasive or filled with harmful intent but shows grace and charity. It is a moral discipline that links self-control in every word and deed. This is particularly the case when dealing with those who are intolerant and unforgiving. The way believers express their *love for the enemy* is manifested when they *bless them that curse* [them], *do good to them that hate* [them] (Matthew 5:44), actions chiefly expressed as believers show kindness to those less fortunate than they are.

30. When kindness is shown to others, it never seeks a reward. It is done unselfishly and with the single purpose of drawing a person closer to Jesus Christ. How enlightening is the fact that those showing kindness (or meekness) towards others are highly blessed of God and *inherit the earth* (Matthew 5:5).

31. *Goodness.* The aptitude with which every activity must be approached is with the desire to be regarded by God as "well-being." Most assuredly, the motive must always be with "well-doing"; but it is of little emphasis if the heart is inflicted with wrong intentions. A well-being believer is driven by the desire to constantly fill others with God's goodness. It is a generous heart that produces goodness (Ephesians 5:9).

32. The manifestation of the active grace of goodness depends upon the rightness of heart. Evan H. Hopkins says, "Character and conduct; creed and deed; word and work should always be united."

33. This characteristic is the antibiotic the world so desperately needs to heal its disease of hatefulness. The indwelling Holy Spirit's goodness is the only means that can heal the crooked and perverse world's rampant

hatred. For centuries mankind has praised God and said, *How great is thy goodness* (Psalm 31:19). It contains a power to defuse a hateful approach *and fulfil all the good pleasure of his goodness, and the work of faith with power* (2 Thessalonians 1:11).

34. Every attribute of God's nature is good; He alone is *good* (Matthew 19:17). It manifests the fullness of the Holy Spirit residing in believers, and it draws them ever closer to God as they *grow in the grace, and in the knowledge of* [their] *Lord and Savior Jesus Christ* (2 Peter 3:18).

35. *Faithfulness.* The ultimate purpose of the fruit of the Spirit is the outpouring of the indwelling Holy Spirit that flows like a river from the believer towards the world. This characteristic demonstrates the faithfulness of a believer. First, it is the commitment in the believer's heart to be faithful to His Redeemer. Second, he is faithful to his fellow believers; and third, it is to the lost in the world where there is no trust.

36. The unwavering obedience Jesus showed towards His Father is rewarded by the Father when He crowns His Son with the title: *Faithful and True* (Revelation 19:11 NKJV). Hasten the day when believers are elevated to this gracious position to *be like Him* (1 John 3:2).

37. Believers are called to *finish the race* (2 Timothy 4:7), remain faithful to God in all their ways. This race need not be seen as who crosses the finish line first as who has run the race faithfully to the end. Life is not only about winning; it is about faithfully contending throughout the entire journey. Rowe says, "God allows circumstances in our life, even of darkness and disappointment, in order to nurture and develop faith or faithfulness."

38. It is the Word that seals this reward for those who are faithful, for Jesus promises, *Be thou faithful unto death, and I will give thee a crown of life* (Revelation 2:10).

39. *Gentleness.* This is the characteristic that displays the divine all-powerful God ministering every moment of the day as He handles the repentant heart. The analogy of the lioness in the wilderness is a perfect example: This ferocious beast attacks its prey, and with her powerful jaws snaps the neck of a large catch. It deals swiftly and decisively as the jaws inflict a deathly grip. However, these same jaws can pick up her cubs and with gentleness carry them from one place to the next without so much as a scar on the young cubs' necks. How apt, the *lion of Judah* (Revelation 5:5) inclines His ear to the need of a believer and with gentleness carries them through their ordeal.

40. Gentleness is power; greatness depends upon gentleness and not upon mightiness! Worldly axioms have it that knowledge is power; money is power. The Scriptures say gentleness is power.
41. True followers of the "gentle Jesus, meek and mild," must exhibit the excellent quality of gentleness if others are to be won as they hear these followers speak about the kindness and love of God, the Savior.
42. This is in total contrast to the natural or carnal man's thinking. However, when the Holy Spirit is in residence, the majestic fruit of gentleness transforms the Spirit-filled believer into someone who is understanding, caring, and compassionate for the wayward one.
43. The Savior, Jesus Christ, is the most exquisite pattern of gentleness to follow. This gentleness is the tender and experienced touch of the loving Shepherd in dealing with His flock, and Christ has been set before the church as the *good Shepherd of the sheep* (John 10:11; Psalm 79:13). It is within the framework of a gentle spirit that believers approach their everyday activities and conversations wherein guidance by force creates a reaction, but guidance from a gentle spirit creates a response.
44. *Self-control.* A writer has said, "Self-control (temperance) is the right handling of one's soul." W. A. C. Rowe says, self-control (temperance) "is the throne of man's will, under the sweet influences and direction of the Holy Spirit, bringing every power and possibility into its fullest and best harmony and use."
45. It is the ultimate exhibition of the born-again spirit that is no longer freewheeling along life's broad way but is carefully harnessed by the loving Spirit of Christ that guides them along the *straight* and the *narrow way* (Matthew 7:13-14).
46. The Holy Spirit imparts this characteristic that strengthens the believer's moral code of conduct, enabling him to bring into subjection every action (1 Corinthians 9:27).
47. Furthermore, there is no variance in believers' conduct regarding similar tasks or teaching they are required to share. There is an even keel that keeps them always the same throughout every word or deed. They do not *stray* (1 Timothy 1:6 NKJV) or sway like a reed in the wind, but they are stable and able to be entreated with respect because of the temperate spirit they manifest.
48. The word is filled with beautiful examples of how Jesus remained temperate and demonstrated self-control throughout His many difficult encounters with those who misunderstood Him. When the

self-righteous and indignant Jewish leaders brought the woman caught in the act of adultery, Jesus stunned them with His words, and brought their high-mindedness down to self-examination: *He that is without sin among you, let him first cast a stone at her* (John 8:7).

49. In conclusion, this divine characteristic within the fruit of the Holy Spirit is the purest evidence of the indwelling Christ residing in the believers' hearts. Love is the ultimate motivator for the remaining eight fruit to be engaged in all that believers do and speak.

50. Spirit-filled believers strive to uphold the perfect will of God (Romans 12:2). If there are any deficiencies and poor application of the nine fruit of the Spirit, then Spirit-filled believers' lives are not perfect. They can be likened to musical instruments that are hindered by missing parts; the harmony and function will be marred. Spirit-filled believers' conduct is tarnished by a lack of, or weak display, of any of these divine qualities. Hence, they are encouraged to *earnestly contend for the faith which was once delivered unto the saints* (Jude 3).

Bibliography

Arrington, French L. – *Christian Doctrine a Pentecostal Perspective.* Pathway Publishers, Cleveland, Tennessee

Bergen, Robert D. Study Note contributor on Genesis. - *Holman Study Bible NKJV Edition.* Holman Bible Publishers, Nashville, Tennessee

Berkhof, Louis – *Systematic Theology.* Wm. B. Eerdmans Publishing Co. Grand Rapids, Michigan

Bettenson, Henry – *Documents of the Christian Church.* Oxford University Press, London U.K.

Bishop, Jim – *The Day Christ Died.* Harper Collins Publishers, New York, New York

Black, Jonathan – *Apostolic Theology.* Published by The Apostolic Church Administrative office, Luton, United Kingdom

Bromiley, Geoffrey W. General editor and Associate editors – *The International Standard Bible Encyclopedia.* Wm. B. Eerdmans Publishing Co. Grand Rapids, Michigan

Buswell Jr. James, Oliver – *A Systematic Theology of the Christian Religion.* Zondervan Publishing House, Grand Rapids, Michigan

Chafer, Lewis Sperry – *Systematic Theology.* Kregel Publications, Grand Rapids, Michigan

Chambers, Oswald – *The Complete Works of Oswald Chambers.* Discovery House Publishers, Grand Rapids, Michigan

Dake, Finis J. – *Revelation Expounded*. Dake Bible Sales, Inc. Lawrence, Georgia

Dick, John – *Lectures on Theology*. Applegate and Co., Cincinnati, Ohio

Elwell, Walter A. – Commentary in the *Encyclopedia of the Bible*. Baker Books; a division of Baker Book House Co., Grand Rapids, Michigan

Erickson, Millard J. – *Christian Theology*. Baker Academic, Grand Rapids, Michigan

Gaebelein, Frank E. General editor - *The Expositor's Bible Commentary*. Zondervan Publishing House, Grand Rapids, Michigan

Geisler, Norman – *Systematic Theology*. Bethany House, Minneapolis, Minnesota

Grudem, Wayne – *Systematic Theology*. Zondervan Publishers, Grand Rapids, Michigan

Henry, Matthew – *Matthew Henry's Commentary*. Hendrickson Publishers Inc., Peabody, Massachusetts

Hopkins Evan – *The Law of Liberty in the Spiritual Life*. Andesite Press, Warsaw, Poland

Klug, Eugene F.A – Commentary in the *Encyclopedia of the Bible*. Baker Books; a division of Baker Book House Co., Grand Rapids, Michigan

Larkin, Clarence – *The Greatest Book on Dispensational Truth in the World*. Rev. Clarence Larkin Est. Glenside, Pennsylvania

Lockyer, Herbert – *All about the Holy Spirit*. Zondervan Publishing House, Grand Rapids, Michigan

Lockyer, Herbert – *All the Doctrines of the Bible*. Zondervan Publishing House, Grand Rapids, Michigan

Lockyer, Herbert – *All the Angels in the Bible*. Zondervan Publishing House, Grand Rapids, Michigan

Menzies, William W. and Horton, Stanley M. – *Bible Doctrines a Pentecostal Perspective*. Logion Press, Springfield, Missouri

Montgomery, G.E – *Commentary on the Bible.* Wm. B. Eerdmans Publishing Company, Grand Rapids, Michigan

Murray, Andrew – *The Blood of the Cross.* Martino Publishing, Connecticut

Murray, Andrew – *The Power of the Blood of Christ.* Whitaker House, New Kensington, Pennsylvania

Nee, Watchman – *The Spiritual Man.* Christian Fellowship Publishers Inc. New York

Orr, James – *The Virgin Birth of Christ.* Hodder-Stoughton Publisher, London

Patterson, Richard D - *The Expositor's Bible Commentary.* Zondervan Publishing House, Grand Rapids, Michigan

Pearlman, Myer – *Knowing the Doctrines of the Bible.* Gospel Publishing House, Springfield, Missouri

Pink, Arthur W. – *An Exposition of Hebrews.* Baker Book House, Grand Rapids, Michigan

Pink, Arthur W. – *An Exposition of the Gospel of John.* Zondervan Publishing House, Grand Rapids, Michigan

Piper, John – *God's Passion for His Glory.* Crossway Publishers, Wheaton, Illinois

Renn, Stephen D. – *Expository Dictionary of Bible Words.* Hendrickson Publishers Inc., Peabody, Massachusetts

Rowe, W.A.C. – *One Lord, One Faith.* Puritan Press LTD, Bradford, Yorkshire, England

Schaff, Philip – *History of the Christian Church.* Hendrickson Publishers, Inc. Peabody Massachusetts

Scofield, C.I. – *The Scofield Reference Bible.* Oxford University Press, New York

Scott, Martin J – *The Virgin Birth.* P.J. Kennedy First Edition (1925), United States

Smith, James and Lee, Robert – *Handfuls on Purpose for Christian Workers and Bible Students*. Wm. B. Eerdmans Publishing company Grand Rapids, Michigan

Smith, Malcolm – *The Power of the Blood Covenant*. Harrison House Publishers, Tulsa, Oklahoma

Spence, H.D.M. and Exell, Joseph S. and various contributors to the volumes – *The Pulpit Commentary*. Hendrickson Publishers Inc., Peabody, Massachusetts

Strauch, Alexander – *Biblical Eldership*. Lewis and Wroth Publishers, Littleton, Colorado

Strong, A.H. – *Popular Lectures on the Books of the New Testament*. Griffith and Rowland Publishers, Philadelphia

Strong, A.H. – *Systematic Theology*. Wentworth Press, New York

Thiessen, Henry Clarence - *Lectures in Systematic Theology*. Wm. B. Eerdmans Publishing Company, Grand Rapids, Michigan

Torrey, Reuben A. – *The Fundamental Doctrines of the Christian Faith*. George, H. Doran Company, New York

Torrey, Reuben A. – *What the Bible Teachers – Updated edition*. Whitaker House, New Kensington, Pennsylvania

Wiersbe, Warren W. – *The Bible Exposition Commentary*. David C. Cook, 4050 Lee Vance Drive, Colorado Springs

Williams, D.P. – Various Manuscripts and Articles from D.P. Williams' teachings available from the Apostolic Church of Great Britain, Luton, Great Britain

Wilson, Cyril D. – Article on *Jesus Christ Son of God, Son of Man* distributed by the Christian Fellowship, Durban, South Africa

Printed in the United States
by Baker & Taylor Publisher Services